FIELD GUIDE TO
Invasive Plants and Animals
in Britain

FIELD GUIDE TO
Invasive Plants and Animals in Britain

Olaf Booy

Max Wade

Helen Roy

BLOOMSBURY

LONDON · NEW DELHI · NEW YORK · SYDNEY

Bloomsbury Natural History
An imprint of Bloomsbury Publishing Plc

50 Bedford Square
London
WC1B 3DP
UK

1385 Broadway
New York
NY 10018
USA

www.bloomsbury.com

BLOOMSBURY and the Diana logo are trademarks of Bloomsbury Publishing Plc

First published 2015
© Olaf Booy, Max Wade and Helen Roy, 2015

Olaf Booy, Max Wade and Helen Roy have asserted their right under the
Copyright, Designs and Patents Act, 1988, to be identified as Authors of this work.

British Library Cataloguing-in-Publication Data
A catalogue record for this book is available from the British Library.

ISBN: PB: 978-1408-1-2318-8
ePDF: 978-1472-9-1154-4
ePub: 978-1472-9-1153-7

10 9 8 7 6 5 4 3 2 1

Designed by Fluke Art
Printed in China

To find out more about our authors and books visit www.bloomsbury.com. Here you will find extracts,
author interviews, details of forthcoming events and the option to sign up for our newsletters.

Contents

Introduction

Invasive non-native species represent one of the greatest threats to biodiversity worldwide. However, despite increasing awareness of environmental issues, people remain largely unaware of these plants and animals and their potentially devastating impacts. Although most biological introductions fail, those species that successfully establish in a new region can have far-reaching and in some cases disastrous impacts on native fauna and flora, economic interests and can even affect human health and society.

This field guide will assist in the identification of a range of invasive non-native species found in Great Britain, as well as a number that are not yet present or considered invasive but could soon become so (known as horizon-scanning species). Although these species are of particular concern to conservationists, this guide should also be of interest to the amateur naturalist and an important tool for ecologists and land managers attempting to tackle the problems posed by invasive non-native species.

Invasive non-native species impact on rare native species in Britain. In this case Himalayan Balsam *Impatiens glandulifera* is out-competing the native Tansy plant *Tanacetum vulgare*, which supports the last population of the endangered Tansy Beetle *Chrysolina graminis* in Britain.

A non-native species is one that has been transported from its native range to a new region with the assistance of humans. The introduction of non-native species has led to dramatic changes in the composition of Britain's flora and fauna. There are now almost as many non-native plant species established in Britain as there are native, and significant proportions of established non-native mammal, reptile, amphibian and fish species. The proportion is much lower for birds and invertebrates. The majority of non-native species are found in terrestrial habitats, with smaller numbers in freshwater and marine habitats.

Non-native species – a species that has been transported from its native range to a new region with the assistance of humans.

The majority of established non-native species in the wild in Britain are benign, having no or negligible impact. However, a significant minority cause harm – it is these that are termed invasive non-native species.

Invasive non-native species – a non-native species that has a negative environmental, economic or societal impact.

About 10–15% of the established non-native species in Britain have a negative impact, although this proportion varies between different groups of species. For example, about 8% of established non-native plants become invasive, while the same figure for animals is much higher, about 40%. Certain habitats are more vulnerable to invasion than others. Small islands are particularly vulnerable, as are freshwaters where about 40% of all established non-native species have a negative impact.

Invasive non-native species can have particularly severe impacts on islands, for example this American Mink *Neovison vison* attacking the chick of a Gannet *Morus bassanus*, classified as a vulnerable species by the IUCN.

The consequences of invasive non-native species becoming established can be as severe as wholescale ecosystem change, the loss of ecosystem function and the decline of native species, including rare and protected species. Such consequences have been likened to a form of 'biological pollution', but worse than chemical pollution as they rapidly spread beyond the initial point of introduction and persist well after the source of the introduction has been removed.

The invasive non-native Water Fern *Azolla filiculoides* smothering a water body.

Grey Squirrels *Sciurus carolinensis* have displaced native Red Squirrels *Sciurus vulgaris* throughout most of their range in England and Wales. This Red Squirrel is suffering from squirrel pox, a disease introduced with and spread by the Grey Squirrel.

American Skunk-cabbage *Lysichiton americanus* in the New Forest, smothering important wet woodland habitat and displacing important native species.

In addition to environmental damage, invasive non-native species have a wide range of other effects. They cost the British economy at least £1.7 billion per annum in damage and control. Other impacts experienced frequently include human health impacts, increased risk of flooding, reduced value of recreational land, and nuisance and damage to construction and infrastructure.

Japanese Knotweed *Fallopia japonica* growing up through tarmac – this is just one of the invasive non-native species that causes significant economic impacts, estimated to cost £165 million each year in damage and control costs.

Asian Hornet (*Vespa velutina*) 'hawking' outside a honey bee colony. Asian Hornets invaded France in 2004 and now cause approximately 1 death per year as a result of anaphylaxis following stings; while not yet present in Britain they are likely to arrive soon.

The introduction and establishment of non-native species is not a new phenomenon, but it has been increasing rapidly as trade, transport and travel continue to increase. In the past 200 years Britain has seen a seven-fold increase in the number of non-native species established, from 260 in 1800 to almost 2,000 at the time of publication. Introductions have reached unprecedented levels, with on average ten new non-native species establishing in Britain every year, and this trend is set to increase.

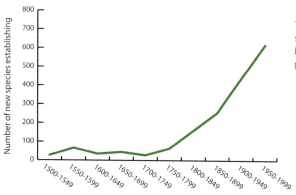

The number of new non-native species establishing in Britain has been rapidly increasing over the past 200 years (Roy *et al.* 2012).

How can we reduce the impact of invasive non-native species? Once established and widespread, invasive non-native species are difficult and costly to manage. For example, it has been estimated that to eradicate Japanese Knotweed in Britain would cost over £1 billion and so implementing such an eradication attempt is impractical and unfeasible.

The agreed strategy (Defra 2008) is therefore to:

- Prevent invasive non-native species from becoming established in the first place – 'prevention is better than cure'.

- Rapidly detect those species that do establish and, if they pose a significant threat, eradicate them where feasible.

- If the species does become well established and widespread, seek opportunities to reduce and mitigate its impacts.

Users of this guide can support this approach by recording and reporting non-native species that they encounter in the wild in Britain. In particular those species marked with the '!' symbol should be reported as soon as possible if found in the wild. Page 14 provides more guidance on how and where to report records.

Scope

The geographical coverage of this guide is Britain: that is England, Scotland and Wales. Invasive non-native species found in terrestrial and freshwater habitats are included, but not marine species. We have included, with certain exceptions, the majority of established invasive non-native species from these environments, as well as a number that are not yet established but could become invasive in the future, so called horizon-scanning species. In determining which species to include, the authors consulted various existing lists (see References, page 286) as well as a range of experts in the field.

For practical reasons, we have not been able to include:

- most agricultural and horticultural pests and diseases (although some insects are included where they may have wider environmental impacts)
- animals and plants for which reliable identification requires a microscope, e.g. planktonic crustaceans and blue-green algae
- plants and animals native in one part of Britain which have been introduced to other parts
- non-native plants that were introduced and established in Britain in 'ancient' times, usually regarded as prior to 1500 AD.
- While the impact of some species is clear and well-studied, the impact of other species is less clear (if there is an impact at all). Although we have made every effort to include as many relevant species in this guide as possible, it should not be considered a definitive list of invasive non-native species in Britain.

How to use this field guide

General

The first half of this guide deals with plants, which are ordered according to growth habit, for example: trees, shrubs, climbers and creepers, herbs, grasses and bamboos, mosses and liverworts and aquatic plants. The second half deals with animals, which are ordered according to their major taxonomic grouping: mammals, birds, amphibians, reptiles, fish, freshwater invertebrates and terrestrial invertebrates. Introductory pages for each section help to provide background information and identification guidance for the group of species that follows.

A glossary is provided to help clarify technical words (page 282). A large range of references has been used to help compile the information in this guide. It was not practical to cite these directly in the text, but a full list of references is provided (page 286).

Species accounts

An account for a single species is usually given using the following structure:

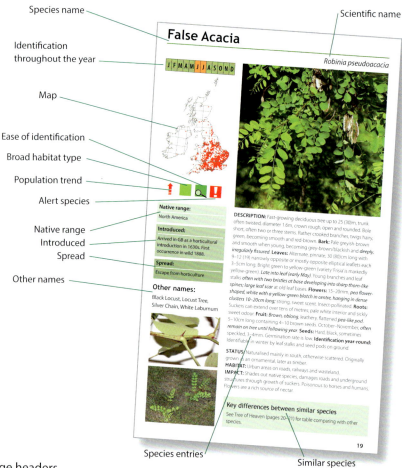

Species name → False Acacia

Scientific name → *Robinia pseudoacacia*

Identification throughout the year

Map

Ease of identification

Broad habitat type

Population trend

Alert species

Native range → Native range: North America

Introduced → Introduced: Arrived in GB as a horticultural introduction in 1630s. First occurrence in wild 1888.

Spread → Spread: Escape from horticulture

Other names → Other names: Black Locust, Locust Tree, Silver Chain, White Laburnum

DESCRIPTION: Fast-growing deciduous tree up to 25 (30)m, trunk often twisted, diameter 1.6m, crown rough, open and rounded. Bole short, often two or three stems. Rather crooked branches, twigs hairy, green, becoming smooth and red-brown. **Bark:** Pale greyish-brown and smooth when young, becoming grey-brown/blackish and *deeply, irregularly fissured.* **Leaves:** Alternate, pinnate, 30 (80)cm long with 9–12 (19) narrowly opposite or mostly opposite elliptical leaflets each 3–5cm long. Bright green to yellow-green (variety 'Frisia' is markedly yellow-green). *Late into leaf (early May).* Young branches and leaf stalks *often with two bristles at base developing into sharp thorn-like spines; large leaf scar* at old leaf bases. **Flowers:** 15–20mm, pea flower-shaped, white with a yellow-green blotch in centre, *hanging in dense clusters 10–20cm long;* strong, sweet scent. Insect-pollinated. **Roots:** Suckers can extend over tens of metres, pale white interior and sickly sweet odour. **Fruit:** *Brown, oblong,* leathery, flattened *pea-like pod,* 5–10cm long containing 4–10 brown seeds. October–November, *often remain on tree until following year.* **Seeds:** Hard, black, sometimes speckled, 3–4mm. Germination rate is low. **Identification year-round:** Identifiable in winter by leaf stalks and seed pods on ground.

STATUS: Naturalised mainly in south, otherwise scattered. Originally grown as an ornamental, later as timber.
HABITAT: Urban areas on roads, railways and wasteland.
IMPACT: Shades out native species, damages roads and underground structures through growth of suckers. Poisonous to horses and humans. Flowers are a rich source of nectar.

Key differences between similar species
See Tree of Heaven (pages 20–21) for table comparing with other species.

19

Species entries

Similar species

Page headers

The recognised English or common name.
The recognised scientific name.

Identification throughout the year

For plants green = plant is able to be identified; orange = plant is in flower; blank = identification difficult or impossible. For animals orange = optimal time to identify the species; green = suboptimal time for identification; blank = identification difficult or impossible.

Maps

A distribution map for the species. Maps comprise: solid red dots = species recorded; open dots = species recorded, but no longer present; X = species recorded in this location, but subsequently eradicated. For mammals red = main areas of establishment and grey dots = species may be present (the remaining symbols are the same as for other species). Where a species has not been recorded in Britain this is stated in words across the map. How thorough the recording has been will vary from both species to species and from one region to another.

Population trend

↓ population decreasing

≡ population neither increasing nor decreasing

↑ population increasing

↑↑ population increasing rapidly

X population eradicated

NP no population present

Broad habitat type

Indicating whether the species is:

🟩 terrestrial

🟩 partly terrestrial and partly aquatic

🟦 aquatic

Ease of identification

An estimation of how difficult the species is to identify and distinguish from similar species likely to be encountered.

🔍 easy

🔍 moderately difficult

🔍 difficult

Alert species

❗ It is particularly important to be on the look-out for, and to report, some species. We have indicated these species with a '!' symbol.

Native range

Indicates where the species is native.

Introduced

Indicates the year and in some cases the method of introduction to Britain. For plants the year of first arrival and year first found in the wild is usually given. For animals, the year of establishment in the wild is given unless otherwise stated.

Spread

Indicates how the species is currently spread by humans. Note that methods of natural spread are not included here but may be covered in the text.

Other names

Gives names that might be used for the species, both common and scientific names.

Species entries

Entries are provided for each species based on the species as it is found in the wild in Britain and follow the format of: description (incorporating different elements for different plants and animals); status, habitat and impact. Where information is used for species in cultivation or captivity or from another country, this is specified.

The most important identification features of the species are emphasised in ***bold italic***. The most common measurements of the species are provided, with the maximum and/or minimum size recorded in brackets, e.g. 5–9 (12)cm long.

Similar species

If species of similar appearance might be encountered in Britain, guidance is provided on how to distinguish them from each other. Similar species may be native or non-native and sometimes other invasive non-native species (in which case cross reference with other relevant pages in the guide is provided). Where relevant, further advice on identifying a given species or group of species is provided. These can be found in the reference(s) (page 286) to which attention is drawn.

Recording invasive non-native species

Useful biological records can be provided by anyone, from amateur naturalists and environmental professionals to members of the general public.

As a minimum you should always record:

• Your name and contact details (if submitting the record to a database)

• The name of the species

• The date of the record

• The location of the record (usually a six-figure grid reference or GPS location)

• A photograph or voucher specimen if possible

When you submit a record, it is useful to check whether the scheme or system you are reporting through shares your data with the National Biodiversity Network (NBN) Gateway. This way you can be confident that your record will contribute to mapping the national distribution of the species as well as supporting action where required.

There are a number of different ways to submit biological records:

• **Online**. Where possible online records should be submitted through the iRecord website. This has been developed by the national Biological Records Centre as a tool for all biological data to be simply and quickly entered into the NBN Gateway.

• **Using a dedicated phone application** (app). There are a growing number of mobile phone apps dedicated to recording invasive species. These have the advantage of automatically recording your location and quickly allowing you to upload a photo. Again, make sure the app you use submits its data to the NBN Gateway, this should be made clear in the information that comes with the app.

• **By email or post**. Although less immediate and less reliable, you can email or send paper records to the Biological Records Centre at: Biological Records Centre, CEH Wallingford, Maclean Building, Crowmarsh Gifford, Wallingford, Oxfordshire OX10 8BB, England, or to your local records centre, details for which can be found by searching the internet for "county name" and "environmental records centre".

• More information about recording and links to relevant websites and phone applications can be found here: www.nonnativespecies.org/recording.

Biosecurity

Many invasive non-native species are easily spread as seeds, larvae and eggs, for example in mud, water or vegetation attached to boots, clothing and equipment. It is important to use good biosecurity practice when in the field to reduce the risk that you might accidentally spread something.

Biosecurity is usually common sense. Points to remember include:

- When walking, stay on footpaths, be aware of signage that may be alerting you to particular risks and clean your footwear and clothing before moving between sites. It is often easier to keep a clean spare pair of boots in the car to change into if you are moving onto another site.

- Keep a stiff brush and some water in your car to clean your boots with at the end of the day or between trips.

- Aquatic invasive species and diseases are particularly easy to transmit. If you are accessing water make sure to check, clean and dry your boots, clothing and equipment before using it elsewhere (ideally washing in hot water and then keeping equipment dry for 48 hours which will help to sterilise it).

- Disinfectants are often used to reduce the risk of spreading diseases, particularly those of fish, livestock, amphibians and trees. Make sure to follow any disinfection instructions provided by the landowner.

Invasive non-native species and the law

The law relating to invasive non-native species is different in England, Scotland and Wales. We do not provide detail here, but in general the various laws relate to:

- Importing, transporting, keeping and selling certain species

- Releasing or allowing the escape of non-native species

- Managing and disposing of non-native species

Those simply observing non-native species in the wild are unlikely to have any specific legal duties. However, you should remember never to introduce or spread invasive non-native species, either accidentally or deliberately. Some surveys could result in the capture of live non-native animals, in which case it may be an offence to subsequently release them. If in doubt you should check with the relevant authorities before undertaking such work.

It is possible to confuse some invasive non-native species with legally protected native species, for example the protected native White-clawed Crayfish with the invasive non-native Signal Crayfish. Some survey techniques could also damage or disturb native habitats and species. You should always be mindful of the potential impact on native species and habitats and if in doubt consult the relevant authorities.

This limited account of non-native legislation is not a replacement for assessing your own legal responsibilities, which you should always check. The legal framework for non-native species is regularly updated. Up-to-date information can be found at the Non-Native Species Secretariat website (www.nonnativespecies.org).

Plants introduction

There are more than 1,400 non-native species established in Britain, such that there are almost as many established non-native species as there are native. However only a small proportion of these non-native species have gone on to become invasive.

The invasive non-native plant species found in Britain come from across the plant kingdom: including mosses, liverworts, ferns, grasses, herbs and trees. The proportions however vary, for example, there are many grasses in Britain but only a few are non-native and invasive whereas almost all the balsam species are invasive and non-native. Invasive non-native plants can be encountered in all habitats from woodlands and coastal habitats to rivers, lakes and ponds. Not surprisingly many invasive non-native plant species are found in urban habitats. In contrast, these plants are noticeably infrequent in some other habitats such as grasslands.

Many of the plant species described in this field guide are characteristic and especially when in leaf and in flower are easy to see and relatively easy to identify. In some cases, there are similar species, usually in the same genus, and/or hybrids which make identification more difficult. The field guide draws attention to these other species, both native and non-native, and provides guidance on how to distinguish between them. In some cases there are similar species and hybrids that have either been seen in the wild only on a few occasions, typically escapes from cultivation, or might be expected to spread outside of cultivation. Whilst some such plants have been included in the field guide, space has limited their inclusion.

Most of the plants described in this field guide originated in gardens as ornamental species from where they have moved into other habitats, mostly with human assistance though sometimes naturally, for example spread by the wind or birds. These origins mean that the plants can be variable in their characteristics and can be known by a number of names. The descriptions of the plants which follow come from a range of sources, all of which are listed in the References section at the end of the book (page 286).

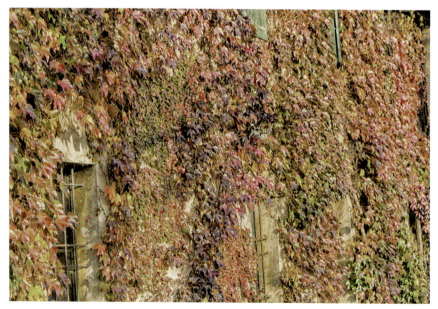

Swathes of Virginia Creeper *Parthenocissus quinquifolia*, festooning an old house are very characterful, but these plants can quickly overwhelm native trees and bushes if allowed to get out of control.

Red Valerian *Centranthus ruber* is able to colonise a wide range of habitats including old walls and bridges. It can displace native species and reduce nesting opportunities for birds in coastal dunes, shingle and on limestone pavements.

The majority of entries in the field guide are for specific species, for example Tree of Heaven or Water Fern. In some cases it is more efficient to deal with a group of species (or genus) such as the Honeysuckle shrubs and the cotoneasters. In these instances, the photograph(s), distribution map and other information in the left hand margin refer to a particular named species from the genus.

The Description section follows a similar pattern for all the species (or group of species), providing key aspects of the plant's habit (size, perennial, biennial etc.) and nature of plant (tree, shrub, creeper etc.) followed by an account of the leaves, flowers including how pollinated, fruits and in some cases seeds, roots and rhizomes. For trees and shrubs the bark is described. A guide is given to identification year-round and the remainder of the entry follows the format: Status (including how the plant spreads), Habitat and Impact.

Trees

A large number of non-native tree species have been planted in Great Britain in gardens and parks, for example as part of landscaping schemes and as forestry crops. A minority of these tree species have become established outside the area in which they were planted and some have become invasive. This field guide describes 11 such non-native tree species (pages 19–33) which are causing problems in some habitats. Reference is made to other species, similar to those described in detail, a number of which are also non-native.

Trees have a number of useful characteristics to help in their identification. These include the shape of the tree itself, and parts of the tree including material shed from the tree such as flowers, leaves and fruits. With practice it is possible to identify trees at any time of the year, even after they have shed their leaves.

Leaves The shape can range from simple, a single leaf as in a needle (Lodgepole Pine) or in Grey Alder, to a compound leaf where a single leaf is made up of several leaflets which can be arranged along a central axis (pinnate, as in False Acacia) or radiate from a single point (palmate, as in Horse Chestnut). Leaves on a stem can be opposite (Tree of Heaven), alternate (Evergreen Oak) or appear to spiral around the end of the stem. Leaves can be untoothed with a straight edge, have serrated edges (cherries) or distinctive lobes (most oaks). For deciduous trees, there are other identification features during the winter on, e.g. twigs and leaf scars, and beneath the tree, e.g. leaf stalks and fruits.

Height Tree height in this field guide is the maximum height normally attained. Many will be smaller due to age and/or growth conditions, for example exposure or soils.

Crown, trunk and branching pattern Trees can have straight column-like trunks, be taller than wide, or broader with a shorter trunk. Branches can be relatively straight as in Turkey Oak, or twisted like Pedunculate/English Oak.

Bark Colour and texture of bark can be useful though texture usually becomes rougher and tends to crack and fissure with age. Note whether the bark strips or flakes to reveal brighter layers beneath.

Flowers The Tree of Heaven and False Acacia have showy and obvious flowers but many trees have insignificant flowers that are green-yellow in colour and not easy to see but still useful for identification.

Fruits Valuable later in the season, especially once the leaves of deciduous species fall. Fruits can vary from berries and pods to acorns and cones. Remember that the fruit is only borne on trees with hermaphrodite flowers or female flowers. In the latter case, the males of the species will not bear fruit.

Tree of Heaven *Ailanthus altissima* can quickly form thickets in a range of urban habitats and tolerates both pollution and poor soil. The roots can cause damage to buildings and others structures including pavements and drains.

False Acacia

Robinia pseudoacacia

| J | F | M | A | M | J | J | A | S | O | N | D |

Native range:
North America

Introduced:
Arrived in GB as a horticultural introduction in 1630s. First occurrence in wild 1888.

Spread:
Escape from horticulture

Other names:
Black Locust, Locust Tree, Silver Chain, White Laburnum

DESCRIPTION: Fast-growing deciduous tree up to 25 (30)m, trunk often twisted, diameter 1.6m, crown rough, open and rounded. Bole short, often two or three stems. Rather crooked branches, twigs hairy, green, becoming smooth and red-brown. **Bark:** Pale greyish-brown and smooth when young, becoming grey-brown/blackish and *deeply, irregularly fissured.* **Leaves:** Alternate, pinnate, 30 (80)cm long with 9–12 (19) narrowly opposite or mostly opposite elliptical leaflets each 3–5cm long. Bright green to yellow-green (variety 'Frisia' is markedly yellow-green). *Late into leaf (early May).* Young branches and leaf stalks *often with two bristles at base developing into sharp thorn-like spines; large leaf scar* at old leaf bases. **Flowers:** 15–20mm, *pea flower-shaped, white with a yellow-green blotch in centre, hanging in dense clusters 10–20cm long;* strong, sweet scent. Insect-pollinated. **Roots:** Suckers can extend over tens of metres; pale white interior and sickly sweet odour. **Fruit:** *Brown, oblong,* leathery, flattened *pea-like pod,* 5–10cm long containing 4–10 brown seeds. October–November, *often remain on tree until following year.* **Seeds:** Hard, black, sometimes speckled, 3–4mm. Germination rate is low. **Identification year-round:** Identifiable in winter by leaf stalks and seed pods on ground.

STATUS: Naturalised mainly in south, otherwise scattered. Originally grown as an ornamental, later as timber.
HABITAT: Urban areas on roads, railways and wasteland.
IMPACT: Shades out native species, damages roads and underground structures through growth of suckers. Poisonous to horses and humans. Flowers are a rich source of nectar.

Key differences between similar species
See Tree of Heaven (pages 20–21) for table comparing with other species.

Tree of Heaven

Ailanthus altissima

| J | F | M | A | M | J | J | A | S | O | N | D |

Native range:

East Asia

Introduced:

Arrival in GB as a horticultural introduction in 1751. First occurrence in wild 1935.

Spread:

Escape from horticulture

Other names:

Chinese Tree of Heaven, Stinking Sumac

DESCRIPTION: Rapidly growing small to medium-sized deciduous tree, 20 (25)m tall, with stout twisting wide-spreading branches from a short straight trunk, diameter 0.9m. Crown typically a straight cylindrical bole, then stout, strongly ascending branches bearing a tall, irregular dome. Twigs coarse, hairy, yellow-green becoming smooth, reddish-brown. **Bark:** Smooth, grey-brown, sometimes *chequered* with *pale vertical stripes* as it matures, becoming broken into diamond-shaped spaces. Bitter if tasted. **Leaves:** *Alternate, pinnate*, 30–60 (80 or more on new growth)cm long with 5–12 pairs leaflets, 10–17cm long, opposite or mostly opposite, unpleasant smell. Glossy, underside lightly downy at first. *1 to 6 large teeth* towards the base of each leaflet. **Flowers:** Small, 7–8mm *in cream or green-white plumes up to 25cm long*. Male and female flowers on different trees. *Sometimes unpleasant and acrid scent*, worse in male flowers. Insect-pollinated. **Roots:** Horizontal, becoming substantial. **Fruit:** One-seeded, 3–4cm long and 1cm wide, densely clustered in bunches of 1–5, like ash 'keys', each seed centrally located within a papery wing; given warm weather, ripening to bright orange or scarlet in late summer fading to reddish-brown becoming pale brown. **Seeds:** Round, 1cm diameter, compressed. Can be more than 300,000 seeds per tree. **Identification year-round:** Identifiable in winter by distinctive bark, large leaf scars on its twigs, and remains of leaf stalks and papery-winged fruits on ground or on tree.

STATUS: South-east England, especially in Greater London and East Anglia. Ornamental, grows rapidly, suckering freely, sometimes establishing by seeds. Suckers extensive, reaching up to 15m from parent tree. Resprouts vigorously from cut stumps and root fragments. **HABITAT:** Mainly restricted to the urban environment where planted widely and tolerant of pollution, aridity and poor soil. **IMPACT:** Forms thickets inhibiting ground flora both by shading and through production of a toxic chemical that suppresses germination and growth of other plant species. Roots and suckers can disrupt structures, pavements, drains and buildings.

Key differences between similar species

Possible to be confused with other deciduous trees that have pinnate leaves. For False Acacia see page 19.

	Leaf			Flower		Fruit/pod shape	Bark
	Leaflets	Serrated edges	Alternate	Shape	Colour		
Tree of Heaven *Ailanthus altissima* (non-native)	Pinnate, 5–12 pairs opposite or mostly opposite leaflets	Partially (teeth at base of leaflet)	Yes	Plume-like cluster of very small flowers	Cream	Winged fruit with central seed	Smooth, grey-brown, sometimes with vertical stripes
False Acacia *Robinia pseudoacacia* (non-native)	Pinnate, 9–12 pairs opposite or mostly opposite leaflets	No	Yes	Pea-like flower	White	Pea-like seedpod	Pale greyish-brown becoming fissured
European Ash *Fraxinus excelsior* (native)	Pinnate, 4–6 pairs opposite leaflets	Yes	No	Dense cluster of tiny flowers	Purple	Winged fruit in 'keys'	Smooth, grey
Elder *Sambucus nigra* (native)	Pinnate, 2–7 pairs opposite leaflets	Yes	No	Umbel of small flowers	Creamy-white	Cluster of black berries	Fissured, creamy-brown
Stag's-horn Sumach *Rhus typhina* (non-native)	Pinnate, 5–7 pairs opposite leaflets	Yes	Yes	Dense furry 'cone'	Crimson	Dense furry fruiting 'cone'	Grey-brown
Walnut *Juglans regia* (non-native)	Pinnate, 2–4 pairs of large opposite leaflets	No	Yes	Catkins	Yellow-green	Large round green fruit	Pale grey, smooth at first becoming fissured
Rowan *Sorbus aucuparia* (native)	Pinnate, 5–7 pairs opposite leaflets	Yes	Yes	Cluster of small flowers	White	Cluster of red berries	Smooth, grey
Laburnum *Laburnum anagyroides* (non-native)	Three leaflets	No	Yes	Pea-like flower	Yellow	Pea-like seedpod	Smooth pale greenish-brown

Tree of Heaven
Ailanthus altissima

False Acacia
Robinia pseudoacacia

European Ash
Fraxinus excelsior

Elder
Sambucus nigra

Stag's-horn Sumach
Rhus typhina

Walnut
Juglans regia

Rowan
Sorbus aucuparia

Laburnum
Laburnum anagyroides

Italian Alder

Alnus cordata

J F M A M J J A S O N D

Native range:

S Italy, Corsica and Albania

Introduced:

1935 (1820)

Spread:

Escape from horticulture

Other names:

Speckled Alder

DESCRIPTION: Vigorously growing deciduous tree up to 28m, diameter 3m with *conical-pyramidal relatively dense crown* up to 7m wide.
Bark: Pale *grey-brown* aging to grey, *smooth with blisters* and few vertical, shallow, wide fissures. Twigs dark brown, angled when young with grey bloom. Buds pale green, speckled red-brown. **Leaves:** *Dark glossy, pear-like*, paler beneath; hairless except for *large tufts of pale orange hairs under vein joints* (use hand lens); with a very long season in leaf, (April to November), falling grey-green. *Heart-shaped, regularly crenate toothed* with 40–55 teeth either side, (4)5–8(12)cm long, 5–7cm wide, leaves flutter on long leaf stalks, 2–3cm long. Rolled when young, new leaves in summer often tinged orange. **Flowers and fruit:** Male and female catkins found on the same plant. Male flowers 0.5cm long grouped in fawn-yellow, showy pendulous *catkins of up to 10cm*. Reddish female flowers, 1cm long, grouped in 1-3 short erect catkins developing into 1–2(3) *relatively large* green 'cones' maturing in the autumn to a dark-reddish brown, 1.5–3cm long and remaining on the tree for about 2 years. Wind pollinated. **Seeds:** Numerous, small and winged. Wind dispersed. **Roots:** Deep rooted, developing nitrogen fixing nodules. **Identification year-round:** Distinctive crown and bark and large cones enable identification throughout year.

STATUS: Found over much of Britain but less so in Scotland.
HABITAT: Increasingly planted as an ornamental tree in parks and along streets and in shelter belts. Unlike other alders, thrives on poor, dry soils, including over chalk.
IMPACT: Unknown.

Key differences between similar species

Can be confused with other alder species.

	Italian Alder *Alnus cordata* (non-native) CS&T	Grey Alder *Alnus incana* (non-native)	Alder *Alnus glutinosa* (native)	Red Alder *Alnus rubra* (non-native)
Leaf shape	*Heart-shaped at base, regularly crenate-toothed, rolled when young. Tufts of orange hairs on veins on underside (use hand lens)*	*Small lobes, subacuminate to subacute at tip, coarsely toothed; not sticky when young, wedge-shaped to rounded at base; edges of leaves flat (not rolled), distinctly paler on underside; 9–12 pairs of lateral veins*	*Broadly obtuse with shallow blunt notch at tip, wedge-shaped at base; sticky when young; not or scarcely pale on underside, 4–8 pairs of lateral veins*	*Pronounced small lobes, subacuminate to subacute at tip, not sticky when young; distinctly paler on underside; 7–15 pairs of lateral veins. Edges of leaves narrowly but strongly rolled under*
Female catkins	*In clusters of 1–3, with short stalk on a common stalk. Much larger than Alder*	In clusters of 3–8, *stalkless* or with short stalk *on a common stalk*	In clusters of 3–8, *with short stalk on a common stalk*	*In clusters of 3–6, stalked*
Twigs	Dark brown, angled when young	*Ends of last year's twigs with short hairs, weakly angled when young*	Smooth and ridged when young	*Often conspicuously reddish, ends of last year's twigs smooth*

Alder
Alnus glutinosa

Red Alder
Alnus rubra

Grey Alder
Alnus incana

Rum Cherry

Prunus serotina

| J | F | M | A | M | J | J | A | S | O | N | D |

Native range:

Eastern North America

Introduced:

Arrived in GB as a horticultural introduction in 1629. First occurrence in wild 1853.

Spread:

Escape from horticulture

Other names:

Black Cherry, Wild or Mountain Black Cherry, American Cherry, Whisky Cherry

DESCRIPTION: A small or medium-sized deciduous tree, 15–23 (30)m, stout trunk, diameter 0.7–1.2m, with little tapering, often slightly bent with few lower branches, upper branches spreading with open round crown. Scratching a young twig produces a foetid almond-like scent. **Bark:** Dark reddish-brown to black, initially thin and striped with horizontal lines, with age (>10 years) developing *large conspicuous peeling strips* (like burnt potato crisps), green inner bark tastes bitter and smells aromatic. **Leaves:** Simple, lance-shaped, alternate, 5–15cm long, 2.5–4.5cm wide, shiny dark green above and paler and slightly downy below; resembling a bird's beak; fine-toothed margin with forward-projecting teeth, *row of fine brown hairs along underneath of midrib.* Leaf stalk 0.7–2.5cm long with glands near to leaf blade. **Flowers:** Creamy-white flowers up to 1cm wide, usually 10 or more in elongated closely packed clusters, 10–15cm long on relatively rigid hairless or sparsely hairy stalk 0.3–1.2cm long. *Petals 3–5mm long* with small teeth at margins. **Fruit:** Green-red cherry, spherical but slightly flattened, becoming purplish-black on ripening, 0.6–1cm wide, borne in clusters. Sepals remain until fruit is ripe. Edible but bitter. **Seeds:** A spherical stone, smooth. **Identification year-round:** Leaves turn yellow in autumn. Bark characteristic in older trees.

STATUS: Found in southern England although known from further north and in Wales. Spreading steadily. Berries readily eaten by birds (no suckering).
HABITAT: Commonly planted in gardens. Naturalised in woodland, hedgerows, roadside verges, riversides and heaths.
IMPACT: Dense patches can displace native species.

Key differences between similar species

Bird Cherry *Prunus padus*

Native (non-native in some parts of Britain). Shiny bark. Heavily scented blooms, spike-like in elongated, closely packed, drooping clusters of 10–40 flowers. Large petals (6–9mm) and sepals fall off before the fruit is ripe. Leaves smooth or with white hairs in tufts along lower side of midrib, turning a rich red in autumn. Stones pointed, oval, 6mm long, 4mm wide with a rough wrinkled surface.

Rum Cherry and Bird Cherry are distinguished from other cherries by their flowers in groups of more than ten on elongate spikes, and young twigs which have strongly odorous inner bark when scratched (Rum Cherry smells foetid) and the absence of suckering. See also Cherry Laurel (page 50) and Portuguese Laurel (page 51): both evergreen with tough and leathery leaves.

Rum Cherry
Prunus serotina

Bird Cherry
Prunus padus

Turkey Oak

Quercus cerris

| J | F | M | A | M | J | J | A | S | O | N | D |

Native range:

South central Europe to south-eastern Asia

Introduced:

1905 (1735)

Spread:

Escape from horticulture

Other names:

Wainscot Oak, Mossy-cup Oak

DESCRIPTION: Deciduous tree up to 35 (40)m tall, diameter 2.6m. Straight trunk, crown open, slender and conical in young trees becoming broadly domed; usually tall with long, ascending branches swollen at base. **Bark:** Pale mauve-grey to dark grey-brown, thick, rough (rougher than Pedunculate Oak (native)), with wedge shaped fissures deep within which are streaks of bright tangerine orange. **Leaves:** (6) 9–12cm long, dark green, alternate, leathery, slender and variable often with 4–9 simple pointed/rounded lobes sometimes cut to midrib on each side of leaf. Leaf stalk up to 2cm. Rough on both surfaces, often felt-like and somewhat sticky beneath. *Thread-like stipules remain until following season. Leaf buds with distinctive whiskers.* **Flowers:** Male and female flowers borne separately on same tree. Males in axils of new leaves, obovoid 5mm, crimson before opening, brownish-golden yellow, drooping catkins (3) 5–6 (7)cm in long dense bunches, often hanging dead for months. 1–3 inconspicuous female flowers, dark red stigmas surrounded by pale yellow-pink slender scales. Wind-pollinated. **Roots:** Shallowly rooted. **Fruit and seeds:** Small stalkless or short stalked acorns, 15–20 (30)mm long in clusters of 1–4. Acorn cup covered in long slender scales or whiskers and enclosing up to half of the acorn. **Identification year-round:** Can be identified year round by thread-like stipules and acorn cups in winter and in young trees brown faded leaves retained on branches through winter until spring. Acorns ripen in autumn of second year.

STATUS: Frequent in southern England and increasingly so in central and northern England and Wales. Dramatic increase since early 1960s. Self-seeds freely. Grey Squirrel (non-native) implicated in the dispersal of acorns.

HABITAT: Often naturalised on free-draining acid sandy soils. Planted in urban parks, estates, large gardens, and by roadsides spreading to woodland fringes, woodlands, dry grassland and heathland, railway embankments and waste ground.

IMPACT: Encroaches onto open grassland and heathland and displaces native species. Its associated Knopper Gall Wasp (*Andricus quercus-calicis*) affects the acorns of the native Pedunculate Oak (native) which may be more of a threat than the tree itself.

Red Oak

Quercus rubra

Native range:

Eastern North America

Introduced:

1942 (1724)

Spread:

Escape from horticulture

Other names:

Quercus borealis, Quercus maxima

DESCRIPTION: Fast growing large deciduous tree up to 20 (30)m, diameter 1.8m, *straight trunk and straight branches*; crown conical becoming broader and rounder with age. Twigs shining, stout, at first green becoming reddish and finally dark brown. **Bark:** Silver-grey and smooth, forming furrows with age. **Leaves:** *Large* up to 20 (25)cm long, thin, sharply angled, ovate to obovate, alternate leaves, matt dark green and smooth above, paler below, orange to scarlet in autumn; *variable often with 4–6 slender irregularly toothed lobes* on each side dividing the leaf about halfway to the midrib, each with 1–3 large whisker-tipped teeth ending in a bristle-like point; wedge shaped or rounded at base. Leaf stalk 2–5cm long. Leaf buds with slightly hairy tips. **Flowers:** Male and female flowers borne separately on same tree. Males yellow-green, long slender drooping catkins, 5–8cm. Females dark red, small and inconspicuous solitary or in pairs originating in axils of leaves on new shoots, stalkless or very short stalked (5mm). Wind-pollinated. **Fruit and seeds:** Reddish-brown acorn up to 2.5 (3)cm. Squat acorns, flat based and ovoid, base recessed in centre, solitary or in pairs becoming dark red-brown. *Cup very shallow, 1.5 – 1.8(2.5)cm wide, curving in at rim with patterned oval tightly fitting scales, finely downy, covering less than a third of the acorn on stout stalk 1cm long.* **Identification year-round:** Acorns only reach pea size in first year, ripening in September to October of second year. Deciduous, leaves turn deep red in autumn, whiskered buds in winter. Acorns present on tree or on ground.

STATUS: Naturalised in a few places throughout England and Wales. Frequently self-sown but also spreads by suckering and regeneration from cut stools. Grey Squirrels (non-native) have been implicated in the dispersal of acorns.

HABITAT: Widely planted as an ornamental tree in parks, estates, gardens and roadsides, and occasionally for forestry, hedging and screening especially on shallow sandy soils.

IMPACT: Encroaches into open grassland and displaces native species.

Evergreen Oak

Quercus ilex

J F M A M J J A S O N D

Native range:

Eastern North America

Introduced:

1962 (1724)

Spread:

Escape from horticulture

Other names:

Holm Oak, *Quercus borealis*, *Quercus maxima*

DESCRIPTION: Evergreen broadleaved tree up to 20 (25)m tall, diameter 1.4m, often bushy with short and sinuous trunk, densely branching. Crown broadly domed. Killed or defoliated by heavy frosts. **Bark**: Grey-black to blackish, rough and finely fissured, cracking in to small squares. **Leaves**: 4–10 (15)cm long, evergreen, alternate, thick, rigid and leathery, very variable shape from oval or elliptical to lanceolate, upper side glossy, bright green, darkening with age, underside white and downy or felt-like. Untoothed or with few small spiny teeth. Young leaves and leaves on lower branches tend to be more toothed with spiny edges, like young Holly. **Flowers**: Male and female catkins borne separately on same tree. Males in dense sprays of drooping catkins, 4–7cm long, pale green, yellow and pink in bud, pale gold against silvery-grey opening leaves and black old leaves in mid-June. Female flowers tiny, in clusters of 2–3, 2mm long on stout woolly flower stalk 1cm long in outer axils, green-grey, pubescent, inconspicuous, tipped pink. April-May. Wind-pollinated. **Fruit and seeds**: Acorns small, light green, short-stalked singly or in pairs, narrowly oval and pointed, up to 1.5–2 (3)cm long. Softly hairy or felted cup, 12mm wide, with scales closely pressed together, enclosing from a third to half of the acorn. September-October. **Identification year-round**: Can be identified year round from leaves. Acorns ripening in first year in September to October.

STATUS: Widely naturalised in southern and central England and Wales especially on Cotswold limestone, and as far north as Cumbria. Spreading in southern and central England and Wales. Seed production can be prolific. Grey Squirrel (non-native) and Jay implicated in the dispersal of acorns, which germinate fairly readily.

HABITAT: Planted in parks, large gardens, churchyards and cemeteries, particularly near the coast. Frequently self-seeded in urban and brownfield sites, chalk grassland, lowland heath, mild coastal woodlands and sand dunes.

IMPACT: Colonising natural habitats aggressively and displacing native vegetation.

Sitka Spruce

Picea sitchensis

Native range:

Eastern Asia

Introduced:

1957 (arrived in GB 1832)

Spread:

Escape from forestry

Other names:

Coast Spruce

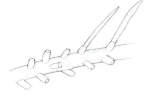

DESCRIPTION: Fast-growing evergreen coniferous tree, up to 55m, crown conical becoming cylindrical with age; trunk stout, diameter 1.1m, occasionally with buttresses. **Bark:** Thin, greyish-brown, becoming darker purplish-grey, looks smooth but feels rough, flaky, breaking away in thin scales, 5–20cm wide. **Leaves:** Needles, *sharply pointed*, rough to touch, thick and rigid, *flattened*, woody peg-like stalk, 15–25mm long, *spread all round twig*, dark or bright bluish or slate-grey green above, with *two broad whitish stripes on lower side*. **Flowers:** Male and female flowers borne separately on same plant. Males pale yellow, occurring sporadically as blunt ovoids, shed pollen in May. Females pale red, crowded around the top of some trees. Wind-pollinated. **Fruit:** Hanging, short-stalked, oblong-cyclindrical short cones, blunt at top, *6–10cm* long, thin scales with crinkly edge irregularly short-toothed above middle, pale to olive green in summer ripening to cream or pale brown. Scales elongated, rhombic, tapering to squarish with irregularly toothed apex. August to September. **Seeds:** Black, very small, 3mm long, with slender, 7–9mm long pale brown wing. **Identification year-round:** Recognisable from leaves, cones and bark.

STATUS: One of the most important forestry crops in Britain. Self-seeding, wind-dispersed.
HABITAT: Widely planted forestry tree; well adapted to cool wet conditions of uplands, but also planted in lowlands.
IMPACT: Can be invasive in upland heaths and bogs, especially those restored from forestry.

Key differences between similar species

Norway Spruce (or Common Spruce) *Picea abies* (non-native). Large conical conifer (up to 46m in height) commonly used for Christmas trees. In contrast to Sitka Spruce it has pointed branches growing in whorls. Reddish-brown, scaling bark. Mid-green needles *pointed but less sharply* than Sitka Spruce, *four-angled*, 10–25mm long. Shiny brown *cones hanging, 10–20cm long*.

29

Lodgepole Pine

Pinus contorta

Native range:

Eastern Asia

Introduced:

1968 (arrived in GB 1851)

Spread:

Escape from forestry

Other names:

Beach Pine, Shore Pine, Coast Pine

DESCRIPTION: Medium-sized, conical to rounded evergreen conifer 25 (30)m tall, diameter 1–3m, with 8m spread: young trees with broad bushy base and a vigorous central shoot; older trees tall and narrow crowned, densely bushy-domed or spired. A very variable species. **Bark:** Rich brown small square plates divided by fissures (coastal) or brown and scaly (inland) becoming brown above. **Leaves:** Needles 3–8cm long, 1–2mm wide, bright mid-green, *twisted*, sharply pointed, *in pairs. Closely clothing long vigorous shoots* of young trees. **Flowers:** Male and female flowers borne separately on same tree. Males in dense whorl, shed pollen in April. Females dull dark red, 2–4 at or just below tip of shoot. Wind-pollinated. **Fruit:** Pale brown-yellow, shining, cone somewhat egg-shaped, up to 6cm long and 2–3cm wide, each scale with a *slender fragile sharp prickle* at tip; in whorls of 2–4 *pointing back down stem*, sometimes remaining on tree, opening to blunt ovoid. **Seeds:** 4–5mm long, with a wing up to 8mm long. **Identification year-round:** Recognisable from leaves and cones.

STATUS: North and west Britain. Self-seeded, wind-dispersed.
HABITAT: An extensively planted forestry tree adapted to wet conditions and poor soils; invading suitable habitats through self-seeding, particularly heathland and blanket bog, even found on remote cliffs.
IMPACT: Displaces native species in bogs and heathland especially in Scotland and creates management problems in such habitats.

Key differences between similar species

Possible to confuse with other pines with paired needles.

	Lodgepole Pine *Pinus contorta* (non-native)	Scots Pine *Pinus sylvestris* (native)	Austrian or Corsican Pine *Pinus nigra* (non-native)	Maritime Pine *Pinus pinaster* (non-native)	Dwarf Mountain Pine *Pinus mugo* (non-native)
Height	Up to 25 (30)m	Up to 30m	Up to 50m often less	Up to 40m	Up to 4 m
Leaves (needles) – all in pairs	*3–8cm* long; bright mid-green, *twisted*	*2.5–8cm* long; grey-or blue-green	*6–18cm* long; grey-green, straight or somewhat twisted	*10–25cm*; long; pale grey-green, rigid and spine-tipped	*3–8cm long*; bright green, curved, often twisted
Cones	*2–6cm* long; *pale brown-yellow* cone, with *slender, fragile prickle* on end of cone scale	*2–8cm* long; pale brown, mature to darker brown; end of exposed part of scale flat	*5–8cm* long; yellowish-brown or pale brown, shiny, scarcely stalked; scale keeled at exposed end with persistent prickle	*8–22cm*; long, egg-shaped, symmetrical, pale shiny brown, expoed part of scale rhombus-shaped, keeled with prominent prickly protruberance	*2–5cm* long; egg-shaped, end of exposed part of scale flat
Bark	Rich brown small square plates divided by fissures (coastal) or brown and scaly (inland)	Reddish or greyish-brown, fissured into irregular longitudinal plates	Greyish or dark brown, very rough when mature, deeply fissured	Thick, deeply fissured, dark red-brown	Grey-black and scaly

Scots Pine
Pinus sylvestris

Austrian and Corsican Pines *Pinus nigra**

Maritime Pine
Pinus pinaster

Dwarf Mountain Pine
Pinus mugo

* Two subspecies

Leyland Cypress

Chamaecyparis nootkatensis x *Cupressus macrocarpa* (x *Cupressocyparis leylandii*)

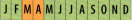

Native range:

Hybrid first formed in Wales

Introduced:

1911 (arrived in GB 1888)

Spread:

Escape from horticulture

Other names:

Leylandii

DESCRIPTION: Hybrid between Nootka Cypress (*Chamaecyparis nootkatensis*) and Monterey Cypress (*Cupressus macrocarpa*), narrowly conical evergreen tree 30 (35)m with numerous regular branches ascending almost vertically, foliage remaining alive at the base. New shoots appear in June–July *leaning at tip*. **Bark:** Dark reddish-brown with shallow, vertical fissures. **Leaves:** Dark green (some varieties yellowish or bluish-green), small, scale-like, pointed, closely pressed together overlapping like roof tiles, opposite, *adjacent pairs at right-angles to each other*, 0.5–2mm long, no leaf stalk. *Branchlets more or less square, rounded or triangular as opposed to flat, without white markings beneath*. **Flowers and fruit:** Male and female flowers borne separately on each tree. Wind-pollinated but very rarely self-seeds. Flowering largely confined to the cultivar Leighton Green (with Nootka Cypress as female parent). Male and female cones are rare. Male flowers yellow, 3mm wide, occurring at tips of twigs, shed pollen in March. Females green, becoming brown and shiny, (1) 1.5–2 (3)cm wide, spherical, 4–8 scales each with a prominent central conical spine. **Seeds:** 5–6 per scale. **Identification year-round:** Recognisable from leaves and cones (when present)

STATUS: Scattered distribution, mainly in lowland England and Wales. Despite its vigour and ubiquitous use for hedging, it is relatively uncommon in the countryside. Increasingly self-sown.
HABITAT: Widely planted as a fast-growing suburban hedging plant and in parks and gardens as a specimen tree and increasingly for screening various agricultural, commercial and industrial sites in rural areas.
IMPACT: Can cause poisoning in animals and allergic contact dermatitis in humans.

Key differences between similar species

Lawson's Cypress (opposite) and Western Red Cedar *Thuja plicata* which is non-native with a fruity pineapple scent. Larger, broader shining leaves. Obvious oblong translucent raised resin gland. Erect leading shoot. Stringy bark.

Lawson's Cypress

Chamaecyperis lawsoniana

J F **M A M** J J A S O N D

Native range:

Western North America

Introduced:

1958 (arrived in GB 1854)

Spread:

Escape from horticulture

Other names:

Lawson Cypress

Key differences between similar species

Leyland Cypress (page 32) and Western Red Cedar *Thuja plicata.*

DESCRIPTION: Tall evergreen coniferous tree, narrowly conical, 38 (45)m, diameter 1m. There is a wide range of cultivars, each with a characteristic shape. Numerous small branches, *young leading shoots drooping and forming flattened sprays*. Forked stems frequent, often repeatedly forked. **Bark:** Smooth, becoming purplish-red/grey-brown, *very spongy, cracked or fissured into long vertical grey-brown plates* raised at ends in oldest trees. **Leaves:** Dark green above, pale green beneath, ultimate branchlets flat with white markings beneath, scale-like, conspicuously glandular, 0.5–2mm long, opposite, adjacent pairs at right-angles to each other, closely pressed together, the smaller vertical pairs with obvious *translucent oval resin gland*, can be linear or absent, no leaf stalk. *Crushed foliage gives a resinous smell.* **Flowers and fruit:** Abundant male and female flowers borne separately on same tree. Wind-pollinated. Male cones small with slate black scales edged white, becoming purple/pink-red at end of March, 4–5mm long, occurring at tips of finest twigs. Female cones green, spherical, terminal on small twigs well behind tips of twigs, slate blue, often with blue-white bloom, 5mm, open in April and a few throughout summer turning green then opening as spherical woody cone, purple/yellowish-brown, relatively small, 7–8mm, 4 pairs of shield-shaped scales with edges touching each other each depressed in centre; scales wrinkled each with a small central spine. **Seeds:** 2–5 seeds on each scale, with broad wings and noticeable resinous swellings. **Identification year-round:** Male flowers/cones shed pollen in March–April, wither and then fall off. Evergreen, very hardy, can be browned by cold dry winds in severe winters.

STATUS: Widely naturalised in southern parts of lowland England and in Wales, apparently less so in Scotland and Ireland. Frequently self-sown, plants establishing opportunistically on banks, walls, heathlands, woodlands and their margins.
HABITAT: A species of town and suburban parks, gardens and churchyards throughout Britain and planted in shelter-belts and as screens, less commonly encountered in rural environment but sometimes recommended for underplanting in plantations or planted singly.
IMPACT: Potentially displaces native vegetation.

Shrubs

The term shrub usefully describes any woody plant that has several stems, none of which is dominant (as in a tree), which is usually less than 3m tall and grows from a single rootstock. The usefulness of the term is limited with some shrubs, for example some cotoneaster species grow into small trees. This field guide describes more than 15 shrub species (pages 35–59).

Shrubs come from several different plant families and hence have a number of useful characteristics to help in their identification.

Leaves: The evergreen leaves of shrubs such as Rhododendron, Prickly Heath and Shallon assist identification year round. All leaves have other useful characteristics including shape, texture and some have characteristic odours when crushed, for example Escallonia and Flowering Currants. Others such as Prickly Heath are, as the name suggests, prickly.

Bark: Colour and texture are useful aids in differentiating species in the winter: Red Osier-dogwood twigs are shiny dark red or greenish-yellow, while those of Tamarisk are purplish-brown to blackish-brown. Texture ranges from smooth to flaky.

Thorns and prickles: The presence of thorns distinguishes species such as Firethorn from other similar species; likewise with prickles in Japanese Rose.

Flowers: When present, the flowers of invasive non-native shrubs are often very characteristic from Fuchsia, Buddleia and Japanese Rose to Rhododendron, Yellow Azalea and Garden Privet. Other species have less obvious flowers.

Fruits: Although the main form of fruits are berries, the range of colours helps distinguish the species: white in Snowberry, black in Garden Privet and orange-red in Firethorn and cotoneasters. Remember fruits will change colour as they mature, typically from green, for example, green to red to purplish-black in Portuguese and Cherry Laurels. Some have stalks, others are stalkless.

Rhododendron *Rhododendron* x *superponticum* has been used for game cover in heathland areas but can overwhelm the native flora to completely dominate the landscape.

Buddleia

Buddleja davidii

J	F	M	A	M	J	J	A	S	O	N	D

Native range:

South-west China

Introduced:

1922 (arrived in GB 1896)

Spread:

Escape from horticulture

Other names:

Buddleja, Butterfly Bush

DESCRIPTION: *Partially deciduous*, perennial tall shrub, up to 3 (5)m, *woody trunk, diameter 0.2m, long arching branches*. **Bark:** Pale, flaking and fissured on older stems. **Leaves:** *Opposite, elliptical*, 10–30cm long, 2–8cm wide, slightly toothed edges, *dark green and leathery* on upper surface, *white and downy* on lower surface. Some leaves remain attached throughout winter. **Flowers:** *Pale purple-lilac*, ranging from white to dark purple. *Many small tubular flowers* arranged in *long spikes* at ends of shoots up to 25cm long. Delicate scent. Insect-pollinated. *Dead brown-blackish flower/seed heads, persisting* over winter. **Roots:** Pale grey-whitish extending away from plant. **Fruit:** Sharply pointed two-segmented capsule 3–6mm long with many winged seeds **Seeds:** *Tiny*, up to 8mm long, *very light*, opening by two sutures. Can persist in soil for >5 years. **Identification year-round:** Recognition is easy from leaves and bark.

STATUS: Very common throughout Britain, invasive and increasing steadily. Garden escape from abundant seed dispersed by wind and draught behind vehicles.

HABITAT: Ubiquitous in dry urban habitats: brownfield sites, railway sidings, built structures, even masonry high on buildings, and in old quarries forming dense shrubberies.

IMPACT: Structural damage to buildings, rooting in cracks in masonry. Carries cucumber mosaic and tomato ringspot viruses, cross-contaminating crops and landscape plants. Valuable source of nectar, especially for butterflies.

Key differences between similar species

- **Alternate-leaved Buddleia** *Buddleja alterniflora*. Non-native. *Arching or 'weeping' stems. Alternate leaves.* Sweetly scented purple-lilac flowers in *small clusters along stem*.
- **Orange-ball Tree** *Buddleja globosa*. Non-native. Opposite dark green leaves. *Dense spherical clusters of orange flowers* in early summer.
- Hybrid between Butterfly-bush and Orange-ball-tree, **Weyer's Buddleia**. *Buddleja* x *weyeriana*. Non-native. Opposite leaves. Dull yellow to greyish- or purplish-yellow honey-scented flowers in long clusters, midway between the two parents. Long flowering.

Red-osier Dogwood

Cornus sericea

Native range:

North America

Introduced:

1905 (arrived in GB 1683)

Spread:

Escape from horticulture

Other names:

Cornus stolonifera, Thelycrania sericea, Swida sericea

DESCRIPTION: A deciduous shrub up to 3m with numerous stolons, stem diameter up to 4.5cm, branches prostrate, purple-red or greenish-yellow, hairless; pith white. **Bark:** First-year twigs shiny dark red or greenish-yellow in winter. Bitter tasting, gives off unpleasant smell when bruised. **Leaves:** Mid to dark green above, pale bluish-white below; turning yellowish in autumn, opposite, ovate to elliptic, 4–10cm long, tapering-acuminate, rounded at base, many larger leaves with *5–7 pairs of lateral/secondary veins* and many tertiary veins (leaves pulled slowly from each end split leaving 'veins' joining the two pieces). Leaf stalk (1) 1.5–2.5cm. **Flowers:** Umbels, *dull white-yellow;* four petals 2–4mm and four sepals. Insect-pollinated. **Fruit and seeds:** *Dull white to cream berry* 4–8mm in diameter, often not ripening, with one 2-celled ridged stone 5mm long, 4.5mm wide, flattened to almost spherical with round base. **Identification year-round**: Deciduous, but identifiable from other shrubs (apart from some other dogwoods) by opposite buds on stem and red or greenish-yellow stems in winter.

STATUS: Widespread in England, Wales and Ireland, less so in Scotland. Spreads mainly by suckering.
HABITAT: Widely used in landscaping and in parkland and naturalised in lowland woodland, waste ground, around lakes and along riversides.
IMPACT: Extensive thickets can be produced through suckering, displacing native vegetation.

Key differences between similar species

Similar to other dogwood (or cornel) species.

	Red-osier Dogwood *Cornus sericea* (non-native)	White Dogwood *Cornus alba* (non-native)	Cornelian Cherry *Cornus mas* (non-native)	Dogwood *Cornus sanguinea*[1] (native)[3]	Dwarf Cornel *Cornus suecica* (native)[4]
Leaves	Ovate-elliptic, 4–10cm long, many larger leaves with 5–7 pairs of lateral veins and many tertiary veins	Ovate-elliptic, 4–8cm long, many larger leaves with 6–7 pairs of lateral veins	Ovate-elliptic, 4–10cm long with 3–5 pairs of lateral veins and many tertiary veins	Ovate-elliptic, (4) 6–8cm long. Rarely with >5 pairs of lateral veins and few tertiary veins	Ovate-elliptic, 1–3cm long. 5–7 pairs of lateral veins
Twigs and shrub height	Round in cross-section. Shrub to 3m	Shrub to 3m	Square in cross-section. Shrub or small tree to 4(8)m	Round in cross-section. Shrub to 4m	Low shrub to 0.2m
Flowers	White-yellow (no purple petals). Petals 2–4mm. *May–November*	White-yellow (no purple petals). Petals 2–4mm. *May–June (October)*	Tiny, yellow-white petals (no purple petals), 2–2.5mm, appear before leaves; acid scent. *February–March*	White-yellow (no purple petals). Petals 4–7mm. Faintly foetid scent. *June–July (September)*	Very small, dark purple in tight umbel surrounded by four conspicuous white petal-like bracts. Petals 1–2mm. Faintly foetid. *June–August*
Berries when ripe	White-cream, often not ripening. 4–8mm in diameter	Whitish-pale blue, 7–8mm[2]	Red, usually not ripening, 12–20mm long	Purplish-black, 5–8mm in diameter	Bright red, shiny, 4–10mm in diameter
Stem colour (first year twigs in winter)	Dark red or greenish-yellow	Bright red (despite scientific name *alba* (white))	Dull greenish-grey	Coral-red at least on one side	Green

[1] subspecies *sanguinea* (Southern Dogwood *Cornus sanguinea* subspecies *australis*) is non-native
[2] one 2-celled stone longer than wide, flattened to ellipsoid, tapering at both ends
[3] non-native in parts of northern England and Scotland
[4] largely restricted to Scotland (very local in northern England)

White Dogwood
Cornus alba

Cornelian Cherry
Cornus mas

Dogwood
Cornus sanguinea

Dwarf Cornel
Cornus suecica

Currants

Ribes species

J F **M A M J** **J A S O** N D

Blackcurrant
Ribes nigrum

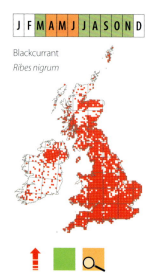

Blackcurrant

Native range:

Europe (see table)

Introduced:

1660 (post-1600)

Spread:

Grown for food

Blackcurrant

Redcurrant

Buffalo Currant

DESCRIPTION: Erect deciduous perennial shrubs, 1–2m tall. No spines apart from Gooseberry (spines present on branches). **Leaves:** Alternate, palmately lobed, toothed. **Flowers:** Solitary or in inflorescences on short side branches. Insect-pollinated. **Fruit:** Berry, typically characteristic in colour and/or size, smaller in the wild than in cultivated plants. **Seeds:** 3–5mm long and 1–3mm wide. **Identification year-round:** Difficult to identify in winter without leaves and fruits.

STATUS: A number of species present in Britain and Ireland are considered to be non-native. Seeds frequently spread by birds and also grows from garden throw-outs.
HABITAT: Woodland, scrub, rough grassland, beside roads and railways.
IMPACT: Some are invasive and extensive growth can blanket and shade out native species in sensitive habitats.

Blackcurrant

38

Key differences between similar species

Table summarises differences between currants and Gooseberry. The only pair that is particularly difficult to separate is Red Currant and Downy Currant. Buffalo Currant *Ribes odoratum* (non-native) is a shrub (2.5m high), leaves 2–5cm, not scented. Flowers bright yellow, fragrant. Berry dark red to purplish-black. Waste ground, hedgerows and river banks in and around London, rare elsewhere in England and Scotland.

R. odoratum

	Mountain Currant *Ribes alpinum* (native in parts of England, elsewhere non-native)	Flowering Currant *Ribes sanguineum* (non-native)	Blackcurrant *Ribes nigrum* (non-native)	Redcurrant *Ribes rubrum* (native in England, Scotland and Wales; non-native in Ireland)	Downy Currant *Ribes spicatum* (native)	Gooseberry *Ribes uva-crispa* (probably native)
Leaves	*Longer than wide, 2–5cm long,* not scented when crushed	*Downy, bluntly lobed, smelling of cats when crushed,* 3–10cm	5–lobed, *green, smelling of blackcurrant when crushed,* orange glands on lower side, 3–10cm	*Net-veined, hairless,* 3–5–lobed, blunt-toothed, 3–10cm long, shiny and pale yellowish-green, not scented when crushed	*Net-veined, softly hairy on both sides,* matt and dull, dark green, 8cm wide (wider than long) not scented when crushed	3–lobed, blunt-toothed, downy, 2–5cm, not scented when crushed *(spines on stems)*
Flowers	Green to yellowish-green, male and female on separate plants, April–May	*Bright pink to red, rarely white, in hanging clusters,* March–May	Reddish-green to yellowish-green, April–May	Green to yellowish-green, purple-edged, April–May	Green to yellowish-green, mid-April	Greenish-yellow or red-tinged, often edged in purple, in clusters of 1–3, March–May
Fruit/ berries (diameter)	*Red, 6–10mm.* Insipid taste	*Purplish-black with whitish bloom, 6–10mm,* rarely produced. Insipid taste	*Shiny black, 8 (15)mm.* Blackcurrant taste	*Red or rarely whitish, 6–10mm, in drooping stalked spikes of 10–20.* Sour taste	*Red or rarely whitish, 6–10mm.* Sour taste	*Greenish-yellow, sometimes bronze, hairy,* 10–20mm. Sour-sweet taste*
Seeds (length x width)	2–3, yellow, ovoid, 3mm x 1.5mm, vertically ribbed and irregular in outline	Approx. 20, light olive-green, oval, flattened with corrugated surface 3mm x 2.5mm	Yellow-brown marked with vertical ribbing, 2.5mm x 1.2mm	3.5mm x 3mm, pointed, oval and yellow with honeycombed surface	3.5mm x 3mm, pointed, oval and yellow with honeycombed surface	Many, 3–4 x 1.2mm, enclosed in transparent jelly, brown, wrinkled and bluntly angled
Origin	Native	Western North America	Europe	Europe	Native	Probably native
Habitat and distribution	Rocky habitat (woodland, streamsides and cliffs), mainly on limestone. Mainly northern England, Scotland and Wales. Very rare in Ireland	In woods, hedgerows, rocky places and sand dunes. Frequently naturalised in Scotland	Wet woodland, hedgerows, shaded streamsides. Throughout Britain and Ireland	Wet woods, fen carr and streamsides and waste ground. Widespread, less so in southern Ireland	Woods, rocky places, mainly on limestone. Scarce. Northern limestone areas, rare elsewhere	Woodland, scrub, streamsides and waste ground. Widespread, less so in southern Ireland

* = much larger in cultivars

Cotoneasters

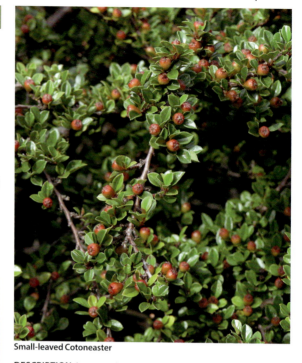
Small-leaved Cotoneaster

Cotoneaster species

| J | F | M | A | M | J | J | A | S | O | N | D |

Small-leaved Cotoneaster
C. microphyllos

Native range:

Mainly East Asia

Introduced:

Small-leaved Cotoneaster (*Cotoneaster microphyllus* aggregate) 1892 (arrived in GB in 1820s)

Spread:

Escape from horticulture

Small-leaved Cotoneaster

DESCRIPTION: Low-growing or erect perennial evergreen, semi-evergreen or deciduous shrubs with some small trees; low-growing shrubs up to 1m, medium-sized shrubs up to 2–3m and small trees up to 4m. *No thorns.* **Bark:** Pale, becoming reddish-brown. **Leaves:** Usually *elliptical to oval*, simple and *entire* (not serrated); *alternate along stem. Usually shiny and hairless on upper leaf, slightly to very hairy on lower leaf.* **Flowers:** White to pink, usually in small clusters, 5 petals. Insect-pollinated. **Fruit:** Small, globular, like a *haw berry*, mostly *red* but can be *yellow or black*. April to June. **Identification year-round:** In order to distinguish one cotoneaster from another, studying fruits/flowers and leaves is necessary. Often more than one species grow together in suitable conditions. It can take some years for a plant to mature before identification can be made.

STATUS: Many species present in Britain, all non-native, most with limited distribution. Seeds from plants in gardens and landscaping are frequently spread by birds.

HABITAT: More than 100 species are widely used as ornamentals and/or for landscaping. Many of these are becoming naturalised and can be found in a range of habitats, especially on chalk including woodland, scrub, rough grassland, beside roads and railways, in hedgerows and increasingly in heathland and on cliffs.

IMPACT: Some are invasive, for example Wall Cotoneaster *Cotoneaster horizontalis* invades coastal cliff limestone habitats competing with rare native species; extensive growth blankets and shades out native species in sensitive habitats such as heathland.

Key differences between similar species

The table shows the differences between cotoneasters and other similar shrub species (Firethorn, Escallonia, barberrys, honeysuckle shrubs (see page 48), Common Sea-buckthorn and certain aromatic wintergreens). There are more than 50 species of cotoneastesr growing in Britain, only three of the commonest are described here. All cotoneaster species can be difficult to distinguish from each other and need suitable identification books and botanical expertise to properly determine a species.

	Thorns	Leaves	Growth form	Alternate leaves	Flowers	Berry
Himalayan Cotoneaster *Cotoneaster simonsii* (non-native)	No	1.5–3cm, *not serrated*, shiny and flat on upper surface, sparsely hairy on lower surface	Deciduous erect shrub	Yes	*Pink* flowers; anthers *white*, in groups of 1–4.	*Orange-red,* slightly four-sided, 8 to 11mm, ovoid, loose drooping clusters of 4–10, stalks 2–3mm, stalk, berry base and apex all with long felted hairs
Small-leaved Cotoneaster *Cotoneaster microphyllos* (non-native)	No	0.5–0.8cm long, *not serrated*, shiny and flat on upper surface, hairy (hairs parallel to surface) on lower surface	Evergreen, low-growing and spreading shrub	Yes	*Pink flowers;* in groups of up to 5, anthers *purple to black,*	*Crimson/bright scarlet,* 5 –9mm, spherical, sometimes slightly elongated with minutely pitted skin, singly or in pairs on short stalk, 2mm
Wall Cotoneaster *Cotoneaster horizontalis* (non-native)	No	0.6–1.2cm long, *not serrated*, shiny and flat on upper surface, lower surface almost hairless	Deciduous, arching to horizontal shrub, stems spread out in a herring bone shape	Yes	*Pink* flowers; solitary, occasionally in threes; anthers *white.*	*Orange-red,* dumpy, 4–7mm, spherical, apex puckered in by 5-pointed scar, almost stalkless
Firethorn *Pyracantha coccinea* (non-native) (see page 45)	Yes	2–7cm long, shiny, serrated, opposite	Evergreen shrub	Yes	*White*	Orange to *scarlet*
Escallonia *Escallonia macrantha* (non-native)	No	1–8cm long, shiny, *serrated, scented*	Evergreen shrub	Yes	*Pinkish-red*	No berry (fruit is a capsule)
Barberrys *Berberis* species (a native species (*Berberis vulgaris*) and non-native species)	Yes	2.5–6cm long, *numerous small teeth or finely spined*	Deciduous to semi-evergreen or evergreen shrub	Yes	*Yellow*	Red to purple-black
Honeysuckle shrubs *Lonicera* species (all shrub species non-native) (see pages 48–49)	No	0.8–3cm long, *glossy,* oval to narrow, lanceolate, *opposite*	Evergreen to semi-evergreen shrub	No	*Cream*	*Violet/purple-red*
Common Sea Buckthorn *Hippophae rhamnoides* (native in eastern England)	Yes	2–8cm long, narrow lanceolate, silvery scales on surface of young leaves	Large, deciduous shrub	Yes	*Green (minute)*	Orange
Aromatic wintergreens *Gaultheria* species (non-native) (see pages 46–47)	No	Variable in length, elliptical, leathery, shiny, toothed to spiny edges	Evergreen shrub	Yes	*White* to pink	*White to purple or black*

Himalayan Cotoneaster
Cotoneaster simonsii

Wall Cotoneaster
Cotoneaster horizontalis

Firethorn
Pyracantha coccinea

Escallonia
Escallonia macrantha

Barberry
Berberis vulgaris

Box-leaved Honeysuckle
Lonicera pileata

Sea Buckthorn
Hippophae rhamnoides

Prickly Heath
Gaultheria mucronata

Garden Privet

Ligustrum ovalifolium

J F M A M J J A S O N D

Native range:
Japan

Introduced:
1939 (arrived in GB 1842)

Spread:
Escape from horticulture

Other names:
Oval-leaf Privet,
Japanese Privet

DESCRIPTION: A bushy rhizomatous perennial *evergreen* or semi-evergreen shrub, erect, 3 (5)m, much branched. *1-year old stems and branches of flower stem are hairless* (use a hand lens). **Bark:** Rough, pale greyish-brown. **Leaves:** Dark green, often yellowish, opposite, *usually oval, acute to rounded at apex*, (2)3–6 (10)cm long, 1–5cm wide. **Flowers:** *Very small ivory white flowers* 4–5mm across, borne in short dense spikes, almost stalkless. Free part of petals longer than joined part. Rather unpleasant scent. Insect-pollinated. **Fruit:** *Small berry, green turning shiny black*, 5–8 (10)mm across with oily flesh and a single black seed. Present September–October but can remain on bush till following year, shrivelled. **Identification year-round**: Easiest to identify when flowering or fruiting.

STATUS: Scattered throughout much of lowland Britain and Ireland, especially on calcareous soils. Garden throw-out. Plants very occasionally arise from bird-sown seed.

HABITAT: Very widely planted for hedging, especially in urban and suburban areas, occurring as a garden throw-out in hedges, rubbish tips, waste land and on railway banks.

IMPACT: Dense patches can displace native flora. Berries and leaves poisonous to humans and livestock. In Wild Privet, bruised leaves and crushed berries can cause acute dermatitis in humans.

Key differences between similar species

● When not flowering, leaves can resemble shrub honeysuckle species such as Fly Honeysuckle (*Lonicera xylosteum*), non-native (page 48) or Snowberry (*Symphoricarpos albus*), non-native (page 44) both of which, as with the privets, have opposite leaves. Use fruits or flowers to confirm identification.

● **Wild Privet**, *Ligustrum vulgare*. Native. Semi-deciduous shrub up to 3m tall. Bark reddish-brown, often covered in algae. Leaves often become bronze in winter, are more lanceolate than oval, typically three times longer than wide. The free part of the flower equals the joined part of the four petals. *1-year old stems and branches of flower stem have very short hairs* (use hand lens). Glossy black berries.

Snowberry

Symphoricarpos albus (variety *laevigatus*)

Native range:

North America

Introduced:

1863 (arrived in GB 1817)

Spread:

Escape from horticulture and planted in woods for game cover

Other names:

Lardy Balls, *Symphoricarpos racemosus* and *Symphoricarpos rivularis*

DESCRIPTION: Bushy rhizomatous, thicket-forming perennial deciduous *erect then arching* shrub 2 (3)m; many slender stems, little branched. Stem very hard to break, often with dark core. Twigs hairless. **Bark:** Light to reddish-brown, splitting as though stem has outgrown bark. Green/yellowish-brown to grey and smooth when younger. **Leaves:** Opposite, *oval to almost circular*, 2–6 (8)cm long, (1) 3–5 (6)cm wide with *occasional lobes, sometimes deeply lobed*; dark-dull green above, paler below, smooth, untoothed, rarely persist through winter. Leaf stalk 0.5–1cm long. **Flowers:** Inconspicuous *rosy-pink bell-shaped* flowers, whitish inside, 4 or 5 petal lobes, 5–8mm. Insect-pollinated. **Roots:** Rhizomatous extending up to several metres. **Fruit:** *White spongy spherical waxy berry*, 10–15mm, virtually stalkless, persists throughout the winter. Flesh like soft meringue. September–November. **Seeds:** Two, 3.5 (6)mm long, 2.5 (3.5)mm wide, ivory white to pale brown, finely striate, oval with one flat surface. **Identification year-round**: Easy to recognise when in leaf, flower and fruit. During winter, thickets have grey-brown colour and untidy appearance.

STATUS: Frequent throughout England and Wales, less so in northern Scotland. Suckers readily, fruiting freely and eaten by birds but rarely regenerates from seed.
HABITAT: Widely planted as cover for game in woodland and for hedging in urban and suburban areas, naturalising over time into woodland, scrub, hedgerows and waste ground.
IMPACT: Displaces native species by forming dense thickets by suckering. Berries poisonous to humans (no reports of poisoning in animals).

Key differences between similar species

- **Coralberry** (*Symphoricarpos orbiculatus*). Non-native. *All-pink berries* and *leaves 1–2cm long*. Twigs hairy when young.
- Hybrid of *Symphoricarpos microphyllus* and *Symphoricarpos orbiculatus* (*Symphoricarpos x chenaultii*). Non-native. *Berries pink on one side only* and *leaves 2–2.5cm long*. Twigs hairy when young. Leaves hairy at least on underside and stoloniferous.

Firethorn

Pyracantha coccinea

| J | F | M | A | M | J | J | A | S | O | N | D |

Native range:

Southern Europe and South-west Asia

Introduced:

Early 1900s (arrived in GB 1629)

Spread:

Escape from horticulture

Other names:

None.

DESCRIPTION: *Very thorny evergreen* shrub up to 3m tall. **Bark**: Shiny, bronze-green to deep red. **Leaves:** Dark green, *opposite*, lanceolate, shiny, hairy beneath, finely toothed, 2–5(7)cm long pointed tips with *downy stalks*. **Flowers:** White, 5–petalled, 7–9mm across, borne in clusters on downy stalks. Insect-pollinated. **Fruit:** Orange to red berry, sometimes yellow, 10mm across. Five seeds. September onwards. **Seeds:** Smooth, wedge-shaped, light brown, 2.5–3mm. **Identification year-round:** Combination of leaves and spines enables identification throughout year.

STATUS: Associated with urban and suburban areas of England, rarely elsewhere. Garden throw-out, reproduces readily from seed and increasingly spread by birds.

HABITAT: Popular ornamental for landscaping or in hedges. Naturalised in lowland areas as a garden escape, throw-out or relic of cultivation in hedgerows and amenity areas and on roadsides, banks, railways and waste ground, and in walls, pavement cracks and quarries.

IMPACT: Invasive in parts of North America.

Key differences between similar species

- **Asian Firethorn** *Pyracantha rogersiana*. Non-native. Smaller, narrower leaves, hairless beneath, 2–4(5) cm long bluntly toothed, rounded tips, and flower clusters on more or less hairless stalks. Much less frequent. The hybrid cultivar of this species and Firethorn exists and might also become naturalised.

- **Hawthorn** *Crataegus monogyna* and **Midland Hawthorn** *Crataegus laevigata*. Both native. They and their hybrids have thorns and similar clusters of 5-petalled flowers but are deciduous and the leaves are characteristically lobed.

Shallon

| J | F | M | A | M | J | J | A | S | O | N | D |

Native range:

Western North America

Introduced:

1914 (arrived in GB 1826)

Spread:

Escape from horticulture and planted in woods for game cover

Other names:

Salal, Salal-berry, American Blueberry

DESCRIPTION: A low-growing *evergreen suckering thicket-forming shrub*, 1.5 (2)m with dense array of erect branching shoots. Twigs green-reddish. **Leaves:** 5–10cm long, up to 6 (7)cm wide, alternate, broadly *oval, dark green*, rough and *leathery*, rounded to heart-shaped at base, minutely toothed, each tooth with long fragile bristle (use a hand lens), no distinctive smell when crushed. Leaf stalk 5–7mm. **Flowers:** *Pinkish-white*, 8–10mm long, *bell-shaped* in clusters 5–12cm long. Insect-pollinated. **Fruit:** *Deep purple to black, slightly hairy, juicy* berries, 0.5(1)cm in diameter. **Identification year-round:** Moderately difficult to identify during winter without flowers or berries; produces berries in autumn.

STATUS: Scattered in Britain and Ireland (also Prickly Heath *Gaultheria mucronata*). Garden throw-out. Grazed by cattle and deer and berries eaten by birds, all potentially spreading the plant. Also spreads by suckers.
HABITAT: Used as cover and food for game birds, becoming locally naturalised in lowland woodlands and open heathland on moist acid, sandy and peaty soils.
IMPACT: Out-competes native species and is a serious pest, especially on lowland heath in Scotland, where it regenerates rapidly after vegetation clearance.

Key differences between similar species

Other aromatic wintergreen species, bilberries and Bearberry, all of which are evergreen.

	Shallon *Gaultheria shallon* (non-native)	Prickly Heath *Gaultheria mucronata* (*Pernettya mucronata*) (non-native)	Bilberries *Vaccinium* species (native)	Bearberry *Arctostaphylos uva-ursi* (native)
Leaves	*5–10cm*, not spine-tipped, *leaf stalk 5–7mm*	*0.8–2cm, spine-tipped, leaf stalk up to 2mm*	*1–3cm*, not spine-tipped, leaf stalk up to 3mm	*1–3cm*, not spine-tipped, leaf stalk up to 3.5mm
Flower	Pinkish-white	White	Variable	Pinkish-white
Berry	*Deep purple to black*	*White to purple*	*Red, black or purple*	*Shiny red*

Prickly Heath
Gaultheria mucronata

Bilberries
Vaccinium species

Bearberry
Arctostaphylos uva-ursi

Honeysuckle shrubs

Lonicera species and *Leycesteria formosa*

Box-leaved Honeysuckle
Lonicera pileata

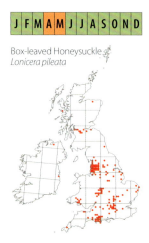

Native range:

China

Introduced:

1959 (arrived in GB 1900)

Spread:

Escape from horticulture and planted in woods for game cover

Other names:

None.

Box-leaved Honeysuckle

DESCRIPTION: Deciduous or evergreen perennial shrubs 1–2m tall, some exhibiting twining; stem becoming hollow in some species. No spines. **Bark**: Typically grey or tan, *when older often peeling*. **Leaves:** Simple, *opposite*, entire, sometimes lobed, untoothed with short stalk. **Flowers:** Stalkless, often sweet-scented flowers borne along the stem in pairs produced in leaf axils, darkening with age after pollination. Insect-pollinated. **Fruit:** Several seeded spherical or almost spherical berry. **Seeds:** Oval to wedge-shaped, shiny, hard, 2mm long. **Identification year round:** Evergreen species recognisable year round. Flowers needed for species identification in some cases. In Himalayan Honeysuckle previous year's flowers remain over winter on dead hollow canes.

STATUS: Widely naturalised in habitats ranging from widespread in west and south-west England, Wales and in Ireland for Wilson's Honeysuckle, to quite rare for Californian Honeysuckle. Used for hedging, landscaping and for game cover. Seed sown by birds and mammals or from stem or roots in garden throw-outs.

HABITAT: Hedges, woods, rough ground and scrub.

IMPACT: Potential to dominate sections of hedgerow and form thickets, displacing native species. Although some species are currently not invasive in Britain and Ireland, they are in other parts of the world in which they are non-native. Berries may cause stomach upset if ingested.

Box-leaved Honeysuckle

Box-leaved Honeysuckle

Key differences between similar species

See also Honeysuckle creepers page 64.

Species	Growth habit	Leaves	Stem	Flowers and flowering period	Fruit	Origin, invasiveness and distribution in Britain
Tartarian Honeysuckle *Lonicera tatarica* **(non-native)**	Deciduous, much branched, 1.5–2.5(4) m	Ovate to elliptic, 3–8cm long, young leaves (and stems) hairless; leaf stalk 0.3–0.8cm long	Green to reddish or brown, hairless, brittle, soon hollow, becoming rough and peeling	*Deep pink or white*. May–July	*Dark red berry*, 6.5–7.5mm. Bird-sown seed	Western and central Asia. Invasive in parts of North America. Rare in Britain
Maack's or Amur Honeysuckle *Lonicera maackii* **(non-native)**	Deciduous, upright, multi-stemmed, up to 5(6)m	Oval to elliptic, with at least some rough hairs, 5–8(9) cm long not held in horizontal plane; leaf stalk 0.8 cm long	Ashy grey, brittle, dense covering of short cottony hairs, typically hollow	White turning yellow or light orange, several pairs grouped together in clusters. May–June(July)	*Red berries*, 6mm. Bird-sown seed	Eastern Asia. Invasive in eastern North America. Very rare in Britain
Wilson's Honeysuckle *Lonicera nitida* **(non-native)**	Evergreen, up to 2m tall	Small, glossy, oval, rounded to sub-cordate at base, held at right-angles to twig, (0.4) 0.6–1.6cm long without obvious midrib; leaf stalk 0.1cm	Pale brown-grey, solid; older stems with flaky bark	*Small, creamy-green* in pairs in leaf axils, very rarely produced. April–May	*Violet berry*, 4–7mm, but very rarely fruiting. Bird-sown seed	China. Widely established and spreading especially in southern Britain
Box-leaved Honeysuckle *Lonicera pileata* **(non-native)**	Evergreen to semi-evergreen, rarely >1m tall	Narrow, lanceolate, glossy, held at 45° to twig, (0.6) 1.2–3.2cm long with obvious midrib; leaf stalk 0.1cm long	*Tendency to grow out horizontally* rather than vertically, solid; older stems with flaky bark	*Long funnel-shaped, small, creamy-white* in pairs in leaf axils, produced only occasionally. April–May	*Translucent, purplish-violet berry*, 5–8mm. Self or bird-sown seed	China. Mainly in urban areas in Britain and possibly spreading
Himalayan Honeysuckle (Flowering Nutmeg) *Leycesteria formosa* **(non-native)**	Deciduous, up to 2m. Stems can remain green over winter	Oval, with long point at tip, 5–18cm long, *opposite, joined by a ridge across stem*; leaf stalk 2(5cm long	Many green, tall bamboo-like, waxy coating, hairless, brittle, soon becoming hollow, rough and peeling	*Creamy-white to purple petals* surrounded by purple bracts *in crowded 10cm long hanging terminal tassels*. June–August	*Purple or red-purple, almost spherical berry*. Bird-sown seed, suckers freely	Himalayas. Invasive in parts of Australia. Scattered in Britain, more frequent in south and south-west
Californian or Twinberry Honeysuckle *Lonicera involucrata* **(non-native) CS&T**	Deciduous, up to 1(2) m, with arching stems	Oval, pointed, at least some rough hairs, not held in horizontal plane, (4)5–8(9)cm long; leaf stalk 0.8cm long	Slender, light yellow-green and ribbed when young becoming reddish brown	*Pale yellow, often tinged red-light orange, several pairs grouped together in clusters*. May–June	*Purple-black berry with red-purple bracts*; 5–12mm in pairs. Bird-sown seed	Western North America. Scattered across Britain, rare, apparently increasing
Purpus's or Shrubby Honeysuckle *Lonicera purpusii** **(non-native)**	Deciduous or semi-evergreen, up to 2m with arching stems	Oval, bright–dark green, not hairy or slightly hairy, 4–8(10)cm long, sub-cordate at base, held at right-angles to stem, without obvious midrib; leaf stalk 0.8cm	Becoming brown, hairless with flaky bark	Sweet scented, creamy-white honeysuckle tubular flowers with prominent yellow anthers, winter flowering prior to leaf formation. *December–March*	Berries rarely produced	Hybrid. Invasive in south-eastern North America. Very rare in southern England
Fly Honeysuckle *Lonicera xylosteum* **(non-native)**	Deciduous, up to 2(3)m	Oval, grey-green, held in horizontal plane, 3–6 (7)cm long at 45° to stem, obvious midrib; young leaves and stems downy; leaf stalk 0.5(2)cm	Pale greyish-brown, brittle, soon hollow	Yellowish-cream, sometimes tinged pink or red, delicate. Unscented. Late May–June	*Dark red berry*, 6–8mm. Purgative and emetic. Bird-sown seed, does not sucker	Euro-Siberia or possibly native. Widely distributed in Britain

Cherry Laurel

Prunus laurocerasus

Native range:

Balkan peninsula

Introduced:

1886 (arrived in GB 1629)

Spread:

Escape from horticulture

Other names:

Cerasus laurocerasus,
Laurocerasus officinalis

DESCRIPTION: Glossy-leaved evergreen, densely growing shrub, up to 8(14)m, diameter 25cm. Layering can occur when branches of old trees lie on the ground. Twigs green. **Bark:** Brown-grey, smooth with pores (lenticels). **Leaves:** Alternate, oblong or oblong-oval, (5) 10–15 (20)cm long, up to 6cm wide, *glossy yellowish-green to dark green* above, paler below, *leathery, slightly toothed*, blunt with *bitter almond scent*, edges of leaves can be rolled under, base rounded or tapering. Stout leaf-stalk, green, 1.2 (2)cm long. **Flowers:** White, fragrant, 7–9mm, flower tube funnel/bell-shaped; in slender, erect, *short candle-like spikes*, 8–13cm long of about 30 scented flowers, equalling or slightly longer than leaf in axil from which it grows; 5 petals, interior orange (use hand lens). *Flower bud spikes begin to appear as early as January* but do not open until early April. **Fruit and seeds:** *Large berry*, 1.5–2cm in diameter, smooth, turning from green to orange-red becoming purplish-black to black in August. Spherical stone, 1–1.2cm in diameter, smooth with faintly keeled margin. **Identification year round:** Evergreen; identifiable year-round.

STATUS: Increasing steadily throughout lowlands. Often planted, spreading rapidly by suckers and seeds spread by birds.

HABITAT: Commonly planted in gardens and parks and as hedges in urban and suburban areas. Naturalised and widely spreading in woods and scrub especially in coastal districts.

IMPACT: Shades out most other vegetation. All parts contain poisonous hydrogen cyanide, usually present in too small a quantity to do serious harm but seed or fruit should not be eaten.

Key differences between similar species

● See table on page 53.

50

Portuguese Laurel

Prunus lusitanica

Native range:
Iberian peninsula

Introduced:
1927 (arrived in GB 1648)

Spread:
Escape from horticulture

Other names:
None.

DESCRIPTION: A glossy-leaved evergreen shrub or rarely a small tree, 8 (12)m, diameter 16cm; branches spreading widely. Twigs dark red above, pale green beneath. **Bark:** Black and smooth, can become somewhat scaly. **Leaves:** Narrowly ovate to oblong-lanceolate, 8–13cm long, 2.5–7cm wide, odourless, smooth, rather leathery, upper surface very dark green, glossy; underside yellowish-green, obviously toothed, tapering to pointed, rounded base, margin with regular, shallow, pointed or rounded teeth. Leaf-stalks, 2cm long, hairless flushed wine-red. **Flowers:** Creamy-white petals, 4–7mm long *grooved dark red*, bell-shaped flower tube; *elongated inflorescence, 15–28cm* long with up to 100 fragrant flowers, longer than leaf in axil from which it grows. **Fruit and seeds:** 0.8 (1.3)cm, more egg-shaped than Cherry Laurel, abundant small green berries becoming red and then turning purplish-black or black, few fully ripening on each spike. Stone smooth, almost spherical, up to 1cm in diameter with faintly keeled margin. **Identification year-round:** Evergreen; identifiable year round.

STATUS: Scattered, occasionally becoming naturalised mainly in south and west. Fed on by birds, more frequently self-sown than Cherry Laurel.
HABITAT: Frequently planted in parks and gardens, and now well-established in woods, scrub and on waste ground, commonly occurs in shrubberies and woodland. More tolerant of chalk than Cherry Laurel.
IMPACT: Suppresses native woodland understorey but less aggressively than Cherry Laurel.

Key differences between similar species

- See table on page 53 which compares Portuguese Laurel with similar non-native species: Cherry Laurel (page 50), Rhododendron (page 52) and Shallon (page 46), all evergreen and growing in similar habitats, and Yellow Azalea (page 54), deciduous.

Rhododendron

Rhododendron x superponticum*

Native range:
South-east Europe and south-east Asia (most plants in Britain from Spanish stock)

Introduced:
1894 (arrived in GB 1763)

Spread:
Escape from horticulture and planted in woods for game cover

Other names:

Wild or Pontic Rhododendron, *Rhododendron ponticum*

DESCRIPTION: A large, densely branched, spreading to upright *evergreen* shrub up to 3–5(8)m tall, with solid stems forming into a trunk when mature, diameter 15cm, often dense and twisted. Bushes merging to form *smooth hemispherical colonies*. Twigs hairless, round. **Bark:** Smooth with reddish-brown tinge, often with algal covering. **Leaves:** Alternate, leathery, elliptical to oblong, 6–20cm long, 3–5cm wide, dull, dark green on upper surface, pale green on underside, hairless, midrib raised below; *arranged in a spiral at end of stem*. Leaf stalk up to 1.8cm, channelled. **Flowers:** *Showy mauvish-pink*, occasionally whitish, 4–6cm across, 5 petals joined to form a bell-shaped flower. Grouped in rounded heads. Flowering begins between age 10–20 years. Insect-pollinated including by bees, butterflies and hoverflies. **Roots:** Relatively shallow-rooting, forming dense mats with fine hair roots. **Fruit:** Dry, woody oblong seed pod/capsule, 3cm long. **Seeds:** Very small and light (0.06 milligrams), 3,000–7,000 per flower head. Ripen in December, disperse February–March. Remain viable for several years. **Identification year-round:** Identifiable from leaves year round and characteristic tightly closed cone-shaped buds in winter.

STATUS: Widespread across Britain, most common in the south and west. Spread widely in the 20th century, distribution now relatively stable. Still widely planted by gardeners. Regenerates from seed dispersed by wind and from suckers to form dense thickets. Stem layering is slow but an important means of expansion.

HABITAT: Often used for game cover. Common on acid, peaty or sandy soils in upland and lowland areas in broad-leaved woodlands, heathlands, sand dunes, river banks, parks and ornamental gardens.

IMPACT: Often reduces biodiversity by shading out native species in understorey of woodlands and out-competing by allelopathy. An individual plant can extend into unfavourable habitat by virtue of its size. A host for phytophora, fungal pathogens. All parts poisonous to humans and a range of animals including livestock.

* Naturalised populations of *Rhododendron ponticum* represent part of a complex variable hybrid swarm involving *R. ponticum* and *R. catawbiense* (particularly with eastern Scottish populations of *R. ponticum*, possibly conferring improved cold tolerance), *R. maximum* and perhaps *R. macrophyluum*. It has been proposed to name these naturalised plants *Rhododendron x superponticum*.

Key differences between similar species

There are a large number of other rhododendron species, varieties and hybrids though it is unusual to encounter any of them in the wild. Similar to Yellow Azalea, (deciduous) Cherry and Portuguese Laurels and Shallon (all evergreen growing in similar habitats) (see table).

	Rhododendron *Rhododendron ponticum* (non-native)	Yellow Azalea *Rhododendron luteum* (non-native) (see page 54)	Cherry Laurel *Prunus laurocerasus* (non-native) (see page 50)	Portuguese Laurel *Prunus lusitanica* (non-native) (see page 51)	Shallon *Gaultheria shallon* (non-native) (see page 46)
Height	Up to 8m	Up to 2m	Up to 14m	Up to 12m	Up to 1.2m
Leaves	6–20cm, *dull* dark green, *no teeth*, arranged alternately *ending in spiral*. Leaf stalk up to 18mm	6–12cm, with *shallow teeth, slightly hairy. Leaf stalk chanelled, 0.8–1.5cm long*	Weakly almond-scented when crushed, 5–20cm, *shiny* dark green, with *up to 15 very small teeth each side; arranged alternately ending in a single leaf.* Leaf stalk green *up to 15mm*	Odourless, 8–13cm, dark green, thinner than Cherry Laurel, with tapering point, with 20–35 shallow pointed or rounded teeth each side; *arranged alternately ending in a single leaf.* Leaf stalk reddish to dark red, 15–25mm	5–10cm, rounded to *heart–shaped at base*, with *tiny teeth. Leaf stalk 5–7mm*
Evergreen/ deciduous	Evergreen	Deciduous	Evergreen	Evergreen	Evergreen
Flowers	Showy mauvish-pink	Showy yellow	White in erect candle-like spikes, 8–13cm long each with about 30 flowers equalling or very slightly exceeding the leaf of the axil in which it grows	White in elongated head 15–28cm long with up to 100 flowers, exceeding the leaf of the axil in which it grows	White to pink
Fruit	Capsule	Capsule	Purplish-black, fleshy, oval berry, 2cm	Purplish-black, fleshy, egg-shaped berry, 1cm	Purplish-black, fleshy, 1cm

Rhododendron
Rhododendron ponticum

Yellow Azalea
Rhododendron luteum

Cherry Laurel
Prunus laurocerasus

Portuguese Laurel
Prunus lusitanica

Yellow Azalea

Rhododendron luteum

J F M A M J J A S O N D

Native range:

Eastern Europe, Turkey and the Caucasus

Introduced:

1939 (arrived in GB 1793)

Spread:

Escape from horticulture

Other names:

Azalea pontica

DESCRIPTION: Upright *deciduous* perennial shrub up to 2m. Twigs bristly glandular-hairy when young, round to angled in cross-section. **Leaves:** Alternate, flat, oblong to narrow and pointed, 6–12cm long, 3–5cm wide, with *shallow teeth, aromatic, both sides slightly sticky with glandular bristles. Dark green turning red, purple and orange.* Leaf stalk channelled, 0.8–1.5cm long. *Young leaves with both margins rolled equally downwards.* **Flowers:** *Showy, very fragrant and fruity, yellow* smaller than Rhododendron (page 52) (about 5cm across) with 5 petals, fused to form a bell-shape. **Fruit:** Capsule 2–2.5cm becoming hairless. **Identification year-round:** Easily identifiable when in flower. Difficult in winter as deciduous.

STATUS: Scattered in Britain, rare in Ireland. Reproduction by seed through birds and suckering.
HABITAT: Commonly grown in gardens; naturalised on acidic soils on lowland heathland, moorland and in open woodland.
IMPACT: Grows in heathlands, woodlands and dunes reducing biodiversity. Inhabits woodland regeneration. Toxic to humans and animals if ingested.

Key differences between similar species

- Similar to Rhododendron (page 52), Cherry Laurel (page 50) and Shallon (page 46), all non-native, grow in similar habitats but evergreen. For table see Rhododendron (page 53).

Tamarisk

Tamarix gallica

Native range:
Western Mediterranean region and south-western Europe

Introduced:
1796 (arrived in GB 1597)

Spread:
Planted as windbreak and to stabilise sand, also an escape from horticulture

Other names:
French Tamarisk, *Tamarix anglica*

DESCRIPTION: A spreading deciduous shrub, or rarely a small tree 3–8m, *feathery appearance* with slender branches and reddish twigs. **Bark:** Purplish-brown to blackish-brown bark with small slender projections (papillae) becoming stringy with close vertical ridges. **Leaves:** Feather-like, light green, occasionally grey-green, *scale-like, alternate*, simple 1.5–2mm long, pointed, *closely overlapping like roof tiles*, pitted with tiny salt glands. **Flowers:** Small, pink to white sprays, 5 petals 1.5–3mm long, and in *long catkin-like dense inflorescences*, 2–5cm long and 0.3–05cm wide, loosely clustered *giving a feathery appearance*, produced at end of stems. **Roots:** Deep extensive root system. **Fruit:** Three-sided capsule. **Seeds:** In Arizona, USA, 8–20+ minute seeds produced per flower, hundreds of thousands of seeds per plant but seed bank very short-lived. Tuft of hairs at apex assists wind dispersal. **Identification year-round:** Feathery appearance year-round.

STATUS: Coastal in England and Wales, rarely in Ireland. Can spread by suckering but very rarely if ever self-sown.

HABITAT: Tolerant of an extreme range of conditions, it is extensively planted in coastal habitats as a windbreak and to stabilise sand and shingle banks. Also found inland as a garden escape on waste ground and rubbish tips. Most records are of planted specimens, which can be long-lived.

IMPACT: Invasive in southern US, but has not been associated with negative impacts in Britain.

Key differences between similar species

- **African Tamarisk** *Tamarix africana*. Differs mainly in larger inflorescences (3–7cm long, 0.5–0.9cm wide) and petals (2.5–3mm). Same habitats as Tamarisk but much rarer and never self-sown.

Japanese Rose

Rosa rugosa

Native range:

East Asia

Introduced:

1927 (arrived in GB 1796)

Spread:

Escape from horticulture

Other names:

Rugosa Rose

DESCRIPTION: Suckering, deciduous, woody perennial shrub, low-growing up to 1.5 (2)m tall, *stems upright, often much branched, with many narrow straight spines*, hairy when young. Larger spines also hairy at base. **Leaves:** Alternate, shiny, dark or yellow-green above, *grey-green and hairy on underside,* blistered/wrinkled surface, coarsely toothed, divided with (5)7–9 leaflets in each leaf. **Flowers:** *Single, showy bright purplish-pink,* rarely white, *usually solitary, 6–8cm across*; notched petals. Hermaphrodite. Insect-pollinated. **Roots:** Woody rhizome, with orange-brown cortex and triangulate scale leaves. **Fruit:** A large *red hip, a smooth flattened sphere,* 1.8–2 long, 2–2.5cm wide, pointing downwards. Buoyant up to 40 weeks. **Seeds:** About 60 seeds per hip, ovoid, smooth, waxy, light brown, 4–6mm long. Buoyant for several weeks **Identification year-round:** During autumn and winter, can be recognised from spines on stems, and from hips.

STATUS: Widely distributed in England, Scotland and Wales, less so in Ireland. Spreads through suckering by rhizomes from rhizome fragments and as a garden escape. Seed is dispersed by birds and sea. **HABITAT:** Mass-planted in landscaping and widely used as an ornamental. Occurring in hedgerows, road verges, rough and waste ground and more frequently by the sea in sand dunes, shingle and cliffs. **IMPACT:** Can form extensive dense thickets, especially on fixed sand dunes and shingle, through vigorous suckering, displacing native species. Has the potential to alter the physical habitat. Occasionally forms hybrids with native species.

Key differences between similar species

Similar to other rose species with similar spines, flowers and/or fruits, which are typically also non-native species and their hybrids. Also slightly similar to Raspberry in winter. Japanese Rose is the most frequent and largest of the non-native roses but identification to species is difficult and a field guide providing more detail and identification key should be consulted.

	Japanese Rose *Rosa rugosa* (non-native)	Burnet Rose *Rosa spinosissima* (native)	Dog Rose *Rosa canina* (native)	Sweet Briar *Rosa rubiginosa* (native)	Field Rose *Rosa arvensis* (native)	Dutch Rose *Rosa* 'Hollandica' (non-native)
Prickles on stem	Many fine *straight* prickles	Many fine *slightly curved* prickles	*Strongly curved* prickles	*Strongly curved* prickles	Prickles *curved*	Many fine *straight* prickles
Flower	Bright purplish-pink, rarely white	White	Pale pink or white	Bright pink	White	Dark or mauvish-red
Fruit colour and shape	Hip large (>2cm), red, flattened sphere	Hip small, purplish-black, flattened sphere	Hip red, elongated or spherical	Hip bright scarlet, elongated or spherical	Hip red, elongated or spherical	Hip (<2cm) red, spherical to egg-shaped, often slightly drooping
Leaves	Leaflets 5–9, *hairy and grey-green on underside*	Leaflets 9–11, lighter green and slightly hairy on underside	Leaflets 5–7, not usually hairy	Leaflets 5–7, with *sweet-smelling glands*	Leaflets 5–7, usually not very hairy	Leaflets only slightly blistered/wrinkled

Burnet Rose
Rosa spinosissima

Dog Rose
Rosa canina

Sweet Briar
Rosa rubiginosa

Field Rose
Rosa arvensis

Fuchsia

Fuchsia magellanica

| J | F | M | A | M | J | J | A | S | O | N | D |

Native range:

South America (Argentina and Chile)

Introduced:

1857 (arrived in GB 1788)

Spread:

Planted as hedges and escape from horticulture

Other names:

Drop Tree

DESCRIPTION: Deciduous, hardy, spreading shrub 1.5 (3)m. Nearly all the Fuchsias in hedges in west Britain are the cultivar 'Riccartonii'. **Bark:** Twigs smooth, light brown; older stems flaky to readily peeling with a pinkish-reddish tinge. **Leaves:** *Opposite, oval, green,* 2.5–5.5cm long, *with teeth.* **Flowers:** *4 violet petals* 12mm long, *4 bright red sepals,* 24mm long, *hanging down* on solitary long flower stalks. In 'Riccartoni', flower buds are fat, squat, 17mm long and 10mm wide. In the ordinary form, buds are long, thin, 17mm long, 6mm wide. **Fruit:** 'Riccartoni': oblong, 9mm long and 4mm wide, broad flat apex, mauve-purple marked with numerous small rough green spots. Usually drops off before reaching maturity. In ordinary Fuchsia: 12–22mm long, 5mm wide, like a squat banana, plump, black to deep purple. **Seeds:** In 'Riccartoni': mature fruits contain numerous small seeds, not known if viable. In ordinary Fuchsia: numerous, about 1mm long, yellow, flat and three-angled.
Identification year-round: Easily recognised when in leaf and flower. Characteristic stems brown in colour and flaking when older.

STATUS: Widely found in western parts of Scotland, Wales and England. Reproduces by suckering, rarely self-seeds.
HABITAT: Planted as hedges but also naturalised in hedgerows, scrub, by streams and amongst rocks and on walls.
IMPACT: Potential to displace native species and vector for Fuchsia Gall Mite (*Aculops fuchsiae*).

Key differences between similar species

See notes on other shrubs with opposite leaves (page XX).
There are other *Fuchsia* species and varieties, all non-native. Large-flowered Fuchsia (*Fuchsia* 'Corallina'), a garden variety with larger leaves and flowers, is naturalised in parts of Wales and North Devon.

Oregon Grape

Mahonia aquifolium

| J | F | M | A | M | J | J | A | S | O | N | D |

DESCRIPTION: Low evergreen shrub up to 1.5m which spreads rapidly by stolons. Stout, scarcely branched spineless stem. *Twigs with yellow inner bark.* **Leaves:** Compound leaves of 2–4 opposite pairs and a terminal leaflet, 3–10cm long and 2–5cm wide, *spine-toothed and holly-like*, approximately 5–15 teeth on each side. Usually dark shiny-green above, bronzed in winter, hairless. **Flowers:** *Yellow, fragrant, in erect clusters,* each flower 8mm across. March–May, occasionally as early as January. **Roots:** Brown externally, bright yellow inside. **Fruit and seeds:** Blue-black berries, 8–9mm in diameter with fine bloom, *reminiscent of small grapes*, in loose clusters of up to 15 with a 6–7mm long stalk. Flesh reddish-purple with strong purple staining juice. 3–4 shining smooth three-angled seeds per fruit, each 4 x 1.5mm. **Identification year-round:** Evergreen.

STATUS: Increasing in distribution, probably due to frequent and widespread planting, for example as an ornamental, as shelter belts and for game-cover and feed for Pheasants. Abundantly naturalised in certain places especially in central, east and south-east England.
HABITAT: Can become well established in lowland areas in hedgerows, road verges and woodland usually in shaded or semi-shaded ,locations.
IMPACT: Not known.

Native range:

Western N. America; widely naturalised in W. and C. Europe

Introduced:

1874 (arrived in GB 1823)

Spread:

Escapes from gardens and bird-sown

Other names:

None.

Key differences between similar species

Superficially similar to seedlings and young plants of **Holly** *Ilex aquifolium* (native) but leaves of Oregon Grape are thinner and less substantial. There are various *Mahonia* hybrids: **Newmarket Oregon Grape** *Mahonia x decumbens* (*Mahonia aquifolium x Mahonia repens*) has a sprawling stem, strongly stoloniferous, up to 50cm. Leaves compound with approximately 8–22 teeth on each side, dark dull green above. *Mahonia x wagneri* (*Mahonia aquifolium x Mahonia pinnata*) has leaves with 7–13 leaflets, more than twice as long as wide, noted for changing colour during the year. Flowers bright yellow in short, clustered inflorescences in spring. **Lily-of-the-valley-bush** *Mahonia x media* (*Mahonia japonica x Mahonia lomarifolia*), an upright evergreen shrub up to 4m tall also has compound spine-toothed compound leaves of up to 10 lance-shaped, dull green leaflets. Flowers in late autumn and winter in erect, somewhat spreading inflorescences of small, cup-shaped yellow flowers.

Climbers and creepers

The native flora in Great Britain has a limited number of plants with a climbing or creeping habit. Examples are one species of honeysuckle, one of clematis (Traveller's-joy) and climbing roses (there are no invasive non-native climbing rose species). In contrast, there are about 20 well established non-native climbers and creepers, a number of which are described in this field guide (pages 61–69). A number of these species are invasive, occasionally causing significant negative impacts, ranging from smothering ground flora, shrubs and trees to damaging old or lightly built structures. The majority of non-native climbers and creepers have been introduced as ornamental plants due either to their attractive foliage especially in autumn, e.g. the Virginia creepers, or because of their attractive flowers, e.g. honeysuckles and Russian Vine.

Climbers and creepers raise themselves off the ground by climbing up other plants or on structures, either by twining, e.g. honeysuckle species, by tendrils, e.g. False Virginia Creeper, by twisting leafstalks, e.g. clematis species, or by rootlets, e.g. ivy species. They come from a number of different plant families and hence have a number of useful characteristics to help in their identification.

Russian Vine *Fallopia baldschuanica* grows extremely quickly and can establish from the smallest garden throw-outs. It will climb trees and hedges as well as other structures such as lampposts and can swamp and kill the plants on which it grows.

Tips for identifying non-native climbers and creepers in Great Britain:

- Honeysuckles, periwinkles, Russian Vine and most of the bindweeds have showy flowers which not only distinguish the different groups (or families) but assist in distinguishing between the different species.

- The Virginia creepers (pages 62–63) produce inconspicuous flowers but have relatively large leaves which usually turn dark pink to red in autumn.

- Those climbers and creepers which are perennial either form substantial stems, e.g. grape vines, Virginia creepers and Russian Vine, present year round, and/or die back to the soil surface relying on regrowth from rhizomes, e.g. bindweeds.

- There are at least four non-native honeysuckle species which can be difficult to identify when not in flower.

Greater Periwinkle

Vinca major

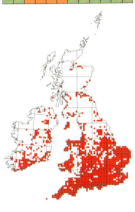

Native range:

European Mediterranean region

Introduced:

1650 (arrived in GB 1597)

Spread:

Escape from horticulture

Other names:

Blue Betsy

DESCRIPTION: Slightly woody, evergreen spreading perennial herb up to 35cm high; stems green, rarely branching, trailing and arching, up to 1.5m long rooting at the tips. The naturalised plant is the subspecies *major*. **Leaves:** *Evergreen, opposite, oval, shiny bright green, (2.5) 4–7 (9)cm long and 2cm wide,* leaf-stalk 6–12mm long. *Margins minutely hairy* (use hand lens). **Flowers:** Purplish-blue, solitary in leaf axils 3–5cm long; *flowering stems to 30cm.* Pollinated by long-tongued bees. **Roots:** Produced at tip of stem. **Fruit:** Forked, up to 2.5cm long, rarely produced. **Identification year-round:** Evergreen so identifiable year round.

STATUS: Local in southern England and Wales, spreading in Scotland. Its robust habit and vigorous growth means that it is frequently thrown out from gardens leading to vegetative spread from throw-outs and fragments of stem.

HABITAT: Naturalised in waste places, rubbish tips, rough ground, roadside verges, shaded banks, woodland and hedge banks.

IMPACT: Invasive in temperate parts of the USA, Australia and New Zealand.

Lesser Periwinkle

Key differences between similar species

- **Lesser Periwinkle** *Vinca minor*. Non-native (archaeophyte), smaller (up to 15cm high) and less invasive. Stem rooting at some nodes. Leaves are opposite, lanceolate to elliptical, pointed or blunt. *Leaf stalk is shorter, 3–4mm long.* Flowers sky-blue, 9–11mm long and 25–30mm across. March–May.
- **Intermediate Periwinkle** *Vinca difformis*. Non-native. Intermediate between the other two species.

Vinca major

Vinca minor

Virginia creepers and Boston Ivy

Parthenocissus species

Virginia Creeper
Parthenocissus quinquifolia

| J F M A M J J A S O N D |

Virginia Creeper

Native range:

Virginia and False Virginia Creeper: North America and Boston Ivy: China and Japan

Introduced:

Virginia Creeper 1927 (1629); False Virginia Creeper 1948 (pre-1824); Boston Ivy 1928 (about 1862)

Spread:

Escape from horticulture

Other names:

American Ivy, Woodbine, Fine-leaf Ivy

Virginia Creeper

DESCRIPTION: Vigorous, deciduous perennial self-clinging or scrambling woody climbers up to 20m long. *Young shoots pink-reddish green, swollen at nodes*. **Bark:** Greyish brown, rough, not peeling or flaky. **Leaves:** Simple and lobed or palm-shaped usually of 3 or 5 leaflets. *Bright bronze-green, turning red to bronze-red in autumn*. Leaf stalk up to 8cm. **Flowers:** Very small, red or greenish-white flowers, 5 petals in small clusters up stems. Pollinated by bees and wasps. **Roots:** Shallowly rooting. **Fruit:** Bluish-black spherical berries, *like small grapes*, somewhat flattened on the top. Flesh, grape-like. **Seeds:** Up to 4, dull brown, heart-shaped shaped, 3 x 4mm. **Identification year-round:** Can be identified by leaf and presence or absence of adhesive red discs at end of tendrils (see table opposite). Recognition is more difficult in winter: look for last year's tendrils and adhesive pads.

STATUS: Scattered in England and Wales, frequent in the south, rarer in Scotland. Garden throw-outs growing from stem sections or as relic of cultivation. Birds spread seeds (Virginia Creeper rarely produces berries).
HABITAT: Widely grown in gardens, found on rubbish tips, waste ground, river and railway banks, old walls, roadsides and in old hedges. Virginia Creeper is occasionally found naturalised, False Virginia Creeper is well-established and Boston Ivy more rarely encountered in lowland England and Wales.
IMPACT: Potential to swamp trees and bushes. Berries of Virginia creepers are poisonous and the plant can cause allergic reactions resulting in rashes and blisters.

Key differences between similar species

These creepers can be confused with each other and with other climbers notably ivies (some non-native), Common Grape Vine and Clematis.

	Leaves	Fruit (diameter)	Stem	Tendrils
Virginia Creeper *Parthenocissus quinquefolia* (non-native)	Palmate, most or all divided into 5 leaflets with coarse teeth, *dull green and hairy* on underside red-bronze in autumn	Bluish black berry (<1cm) with white-bluish bloom, produced rarely on a distinct central axis in a panicle	Light brown, becoming rough, swollen at nodes. Not flaky	5–8 (12) branched, ending with *adhesive disk at tips*
False Virginia Creeper *Parthenocissus inserta* (*Parthenocissus vitacea*) (non-native)	Palmate, most or all divided into 5 leaflets with sharp teeth, *shiny green and hairless* on underside turning red-bronze in autumn	Bluish black berry (<1cm) in a dichotomously branched bunch (no distinct central axis)	Light brown, becoming rough, swollen at nodes. Not flaky	(2) 3–5 branched (no or indistinct adhesive disks)
Boston Ivy *Parthenocissus tricuspidata* (non-native)	*Undivided, palmate* with 3 lobes or rarely 3 leaflets, turning red-bronze in autumn	Matt bluish black berry (<1cm) with white-bluish bloom	Grey to light brown, becoming rough, swollen at nodes, angled when young. Not flaky, becoming rough	5–9 branched, *ending with adhesive disk*
Ivy *Hedera helix* (native)	Undivided, palmate (*ivy-shaped*) lobes, evergreen	Matt black (6–8mm) in a cluster of single stalked berries	Green to grey-brown with numerous short roots. Not flaky	Absent, has aerial roots
Common Grape Vine *Vitis vinifera* (non-native)	*Undivided, palmate* lobes, turning brown and shrivelling in autumn	Green to red or black berry (grape), (6–20mm)	Light brown, swollen at nodes, round to angled, *becoming grooved and slightly flaky*	Present (no adhesive disks)
Crimson Glory *Vitis coignetiae* (non-native)	Undivided, scarcely lobed with *reddish-brown hairs*	Black berry (grape) with purple bloom, (8mm)	*Woolly rusty-brown hairs*, ribbed	Present (no adhesive disks)
Clematis species Clematis (native and non-native)	Usually divided into 3 leaflets	Dry clustered fruits with feathery 'hairs'	Light brown, *becoming grooved and flaky*	Absent, twining leaf stalks

Virginia Creeper
Parthenocissus quinquefolia

False Virginia Creeper
Parthenocissus inserta

Boston Ivy
Parthenocissus tricuspidata

Ivy
Hedera helix

Persian Ivy
Hedera colchica

Common Grape Vine
Vitis vinifera

Crimson Glory
Vitis coignetiae

Clematis species

Honeysuckle climbers

Lonicera species

Japanese Honeysuckle
L. japonica

Native range:

Eastern Asia

Introduced:

1937 (arrived in GB 1806)

Spread:

Escape from horticulture

Other names:

Woodbines, also see table

Japanese Honeysuckle

Japanese Honeysuckle

DESCRIPTION: Deciduous, semi-evergreen or evergreen perennial climbing shrubs, 4–6 (10)m, lower stem woody. Stems twining clockwise, round in cross-section sometimes becoming hollow. No spines. **Bark:** Often peeling when older. **Leaves:** *Opposite*, simple, entire, sometimes lobed, untoothed with short stalk or stalkless. **Flowers:** Stalkless, in lateral pairs produced in leaf axils or in spikes or whorls; characteristic 'honeysuckle' form, tubular with five lobes, usually divided into an upper lip with four lobes and a lower lip with one; colour varies from white and yellow to pink, orange and maroon; some are sweet 'honeysuckle'-scented, typically in the evening, some are not scented. Pollinated by nocturnal insects as well as during day. **Roots:** Shallow-rooted. **Fruit:** Spherical berry containing several seeds. **Identification year-round:** Leaves and flowers or berries combined make for easy identification, although flower colour can change with age. Recognition when only in leaf or during winter is difficult.

STATUS: Widely naturalised with distributions ranging from predominantly in the south of England for Japanese Honeysuckle to a scattered distribution in England, Wales and Scotland (but no records for Ireland) for Perfoliate Honeysuckle. Spread by seeds sown by birds and mammals and as stem sections and root fragments in garden throw-outs.

HABITAT: Hedges, woods, rough ground and scrub.

IMPACT: Stems twine around shrubs and trees and the tight grip can damage young trees. They can overwhelm shrubs with heavy growth. Potential to dominate sections of hedgerow and form dense thickets, displacing native species. Although not particularly invasive in Britain and Ireland, some species are invasive in other parts of the world in which they are non-native. Berries are mildly poisonous to humans in most species. Honeysuckles provide a source of food for a range of wildlife: insects feed on nectar and birds and small mammals on berries.

Key differences between similar species

Table summarises differences between honeysuckle creepers. (See also honeysuckle shrubs page 48.)

	Henry's Honeysuckle *Lonicera henryi* (non-native) CS&T	Japanese Honeysuckle *Lonicera japonica* (non-native) CS&T	Garden Honeysuckle *Lonicera caprifolium* x *Lonicera etrusca* (*Lonicera x italica*) (*Lonicera x americana*) (non-native)	Perfoliate or Italian Honeysuckle *Lonicera caprifolium* (non-native) CS&T	Honeysuckle (also known as Woodbine) *Lonicera periclymenum* (native)
Summary description and length	Evergreen or semi-evergreen, 5 (up to 10)m	Semi-evergreen, vigorous, 4 (up to 10)m	Deciduous, up to 4 (up to 10)m	Deciduous, 5 (up to 8)m	Deciduous, 6m
Leaves including length	Lanceolate to oblong-lanceolate, 4–12cm, dark green	Ovate to oblong, 3–8cm, dark green	Ovate to obovate, 4–10cm, shiny green on upper surface, pale and smooth beneath	Ovate to obovate, 4–8 (10)cm, clasp stem, dark green above, bluish green beneath	Ovate, elliptic or oblong, 3–7cm, usually dull greyish or bluish-green
Flowers and flowering period	Orange tinged with red to purplish-pink, in pairs in leaf axils *towards end of stem*, 15–25mm. Little or no scent. June–July	Open white and age to pale yellow tinged with purple, *in pairs in leaf axils*, 30–50mm. Scented. April–October	Open white turning yellow suffused with purple, *at end of stem*, 35–45mm. Scented. May–July(August)	Pale yellow to yellow flushed pink, *at end of stem in whorls*, often some whorls below with noticeable cup-like leaves beneath, 40–50mm. Scented. April–June	Pale yellow to yellow, *at end of stem* in whorls, 40–50mm. Scented. May–August (September)
Fruit	Blackish or purplish-blue berry with bloom, 7–8mm	Black berry, 7–8mm	Orange-red berry, 7–8mm	Orange-red berry, 7–8mm	Dark red berry, 5–8mm
Origin	China	Eastern Asia	Hybrid	East-central and south-eastern Europe	Native
Notes	Potential forest weed in Europe	Invasive in parts of North America	One of commonest garden honeysuckles	Invasive in parts of North America and Australia	

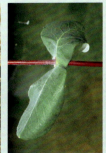

Henry's Honeysuckle
Lonicera henryi

Japanese Honeysuckle
Lonicera japonica

Perfoliate Honeysuckle
Lonicera caprifolium

Honeysuckle
Lonicera periclymenum

Russian Vine

Fallopia baldschuanica

J F M A M J J A S O N D

Native range:

Central Asia

Introduced:

1936 (arrived in GB 1894)

Spread:

Escape from horticulture

Other names:

Mile-a-minute Plant,
Polygonum baldschuanica,
Fallopia aubertii

DESCRIPTION: Vigorous, deciduous, twining and scrambling vine-like *perennial*. Woody below, *often pink-reddish near growing tips*, grows rapidly up to 5 (10)m long, clockwise climbing forming a mass of vine-like stems, green-reddish becoming grey with striations solid–hollow. **Leaves**: Light green (can be reddish-brown when young), 3–6cm long and 4cm wide, oval/triangular, wavy-edged with heart-shaped bases, a number of leaves at each node on stem. Long leaf stalk 1–3cm. **Flowers:** Individually small, 5mm in diameter, in branched showy clusters on stalk <8m long; white often turning pink on fruiting. Insect-pollinated. **Fruit:** One-seeded, dark, shiny, 2mm wide with broad decurrent wings. **Seeds:** Does not set seed in Britain and Ireland. Three-sided, dull brown, 4–5mm, with finely granular surface. **Identification year-round:** Readily identifiable in leaf and flower, less easy to recognise in winter.

STATUS: Widely distributed in England and spreading rapidly, less so in Wales, Scotland and Ireland. Grows from sections of roots or stems thrown out from gardens. Does not set seed. Can grow at a prodigious rate.
HABITAT: Climbs trees, scrub, hedges and neglected buildings. Usually occurs near lowland urban areas.
IMPACT: Overwhelms and kills shrubs and trees. Can damage structures such as fences and sheds.

Key differences between similar species

Can be confused with other native climbing *Fallopia* species and bindweeds (see Large Bindweed, page 68). Russian Vine, Black Bindweed (native) and Copse Bindweed (native) are easily recognised when in leaf, April onwards, and when in flower. Russian Vine can usually be identified from its mass of stems when not in leaf.

● Hybrids between **Japanese Knotweed** *Fallopia japonica* and **Russian Vine** have been found but are very rare. However, since the seed of this hybrid has been collected from Japanese Knotweed plants all over Great Britain and Ireland, the hybrid could turn up anywhere. Regrowth from weed-killed Japanese Knotweed has bonsai-like leaves that can look like Russian Vine.

	Russian Vine *Fallopia baldschuanica* (non-native)	Copse Bindweed *Fallopia dumetorum* (native)	Black Bindweed *Fallopia convolvulus* (native)	Bindweeds *Calystegia* and *Convolvulus* species (native and non-native)
Stems	Clockwise climbing *perennial with woody stems, green-reddish, quickly turning grey with striations*	Scrambling or clockwise climbing *annual*	Scrambling or clockwise climbing *annual*	Scrambling or anti-clockwise climbing *perennial* (no woody stems). See table on page 69
Leaves	3.5–6cm long, oval to triangular with heart-shaped base	3–6cm long, narrowly pointed, usually thinner than Black Bindweed	2–6cm long, oval to triangular with heart-shaped bases	Up to 15cm long, arrow-shaped to heart-shaped
Flowers	Small, white, often tinged pink, in showy clusters	Small, pinky-white in clusters	Small, greenish-grey and white in clusters (never as white as Russian Vine)	Large, trumpet-shaped, pink, white or pink and white
Distribution	Widely distributed in England, less so in Wales, Scotland and Ireland	Rare in south-central England (not known from Wales, Scotland or Ireland)	Common in most of Britain and Ireland	Widely distributed

Copse Bindweed
Fallopia dumetorum

Black Bindweed
Fallopia convolvulus

Bindweeds
Calystegia species

Large Bindweed

Calystegia silvatica

J	F	M	A	M	J	J	A	S	O	N	D

Native range:

Southern Europe

Introduced:

1815 (arrived in GB 1863)

Spread:

Escape from horticulture

Other names:

Great Bindweed, *Calystegia sepium* subspecies *silvatica*, *Calystegia sylvestris*, *Convolvulus silvatica*

DESCRIPTION: Anti-clockwise climbing or scrambling perennial; stems hairless, 3 (5)m long. **Leaves:** Alternate, *triangular, heart-shaped base*, 4–15cm long. **Flowers:** *Large, white, trumpet-shaped*, 6–9cm long with two *large inflated, overlapping green bracts* (18–45mm wide) at base of flower. Insect-pollinated. **Roots:** Perennial far-reaching rhizome, easily fragmented. **Fruit:** A small, almost spherical capsule, 10–15mm. **Seeds:** Smooth, black, 4–5mm in diameter, triangular-ovoid with rounded outer surface and slightly concave inner face. **Identification year-round:** Identification only when flowers present.

STATUS: Widespread in England and Wales, less so in Scotland. Commoner in urban areas. Seed-set is often very poor.
HABITAT: Garden throw-out. Hedges and waste ground. Spreads by rhizome fragments into semi-natural habitats away from habitation.
IMPACT: Out-competes native species, can hybridise with native Hedge Bindweed.

Key differences between similar species

Similar to other bindweeds (Field Bindweed, Hedge Bindweed, Hairy Bindweed, Sea Bindweed) including some hybrids and bryonies (Black Bryony, White Bryony).

	Large Bindweed *Calystegia silvatica* (non-native)	Hedge Bindweed *Calystegia sepium* (native)	Hairy Bindweed *Calystegia pulchra* (non-native) CS&T	Field Bindweed *Convolvulus arvensis* (native)	Sea Bindweed *Calystegia soldanella* (native)	Black Bryony *Tamus communis* (native)	White Bryony *Bryonia dioica* (native)
Flowers	White, trumpet-shaped	White, trumpet-shaped	*Pink or pink and white stripes*, trumpet-shaped	*Pink with white stripes*, pink or white, trumpet-shaped	*Pink with white stripes*, trumpet-shaped	*Yellow-green, small, six-petalled*	*Pale green, small, five-petalled*
Leaf shape	Triangular with heart-shaped base	Triangular with heart-shaped base	Triangular with heart-shaped base	*Arrow-shaped*	*Kidney-shaped*	*Heart-shaped*	*Deeply lobed*
Overlapping flower bract	*Yes*	No	*Yes*	No	No	No	No
Fruit	Capsule	Capsule	Capsule	Capsule	Capsule	*Red berry*	*Red berry*
Hairy stem	*No*	Sometimes	*Yes, sparsely*	No	No	No	*Bristly stem*

Hedge Bindweed
Calystegia sepium

Hairy Bindweed
Calystegia pulchra

Field Bindweed
Convolvulus arvensis

Sea Bindweed
Calystegia soldanella

Black Bryony
Tamus communis

White Bryony
Bryonia dioica

Herbs

This section includes a wide range of plants from low growing pirri-pirri-burs to the giant rhubarbs. A useful division is between those plants with long thin leaves arising from the base of the plant and with parallel veins (holding the leaf up to the light helps to show these), and broad-leaved plants with simple shapes, for example oval, to more complex compound leaves made up of a number of leaflets. The former are known as monocotyledons and include crocosmias, irises, garlics, bluebells and skunk-cabbages, as well as plants in other sections of the field guide (all the grasses and bamboos and some of the aquatic plants). The latter are dicotyledons with leaves usually coming off stems and branches and presenting a much wider range of shapes and forms, from knotweeds and goldenrods to butterburs and lupins.

The similarity in leaf form in the monocotyledons places more reliance for identification on other features including flowers and underground structures, e.g. bulbs and corms. To make the challenge greater, some have relatively short periods of vegetative growth, such as Spanish Bluebell and garlics. The leaves provide more clues than might be imagined, e.g. odours when crushed and shape of cross-sections (use lower part of leaf to determine this).

The leaves of dicotyledons provide a better basis for identification, with contrasts ranging from opposite to alternate arrangements on the stem through smooth to hairy and from toothed to smooth edges. Even when the leaves have died back, the stems and other above-ground structures are useful for identification over winter, for examples the canes of Japanese Knotweed and stems of Giant Hogweed. This diversity of form is partly due to there being one or two invasive non-native species in each of a number of plant families. Only a few families are predominantly non-native, such as the balsams.

Giant Knotweed *Fallopia sachalininsis* was introduced as an ornamental plant though less widely than Japanese Knotweed. It thrives in urban areas on brownfield sites and railway banks. It can clog streams and rivers, and, like Japanese Knotweed, can cause structural damage.

Montbretia

Crocosmia aurea x *C. pottsii* (*Crocosmia* x *crocosmifolia*)

Native range:

Hybrid species, parent plants from South Africa

Introduced:

1911 (1880)

Spread:

Escape from horticulture

Other names:

Coppertips, Falling Stars, *Montbretia* and *Tritonia* x *crocosmiiflora*

DESCRIPTION: Erect hairless deciduous vigorous spreading perennial herb up to 60cm; stem round, only visible as it emerges from topmost leaf to carry flowers. **Leaves**: *Spear-shaped (iris-like), bright green to yellow-green*, alternate, up to 60cm long, <2cm wide, *with raised midrib and at least two other raised veins, not folded into pleats or fan-like*. Dead leaves characteristically *rusty-brown with a soft texture*, slow to decay. **Flowers**: *Orange, tubular* with long stamens, yellow anthers, borne on two sides of *long spikes*, in 'nodding' clusters, persisting for up to 4 weeks. **Root**: *Flattened corm, 2.5cm in diameter* and round slender bootlace-like *stolons*. New corms continually produced on short underground stolons *forming a string of crocus-like corms with papery outer layers*. Roots of lowermost corm in a chain are contractile, dragging corm deeper into ground. Stolons may extend for some distance from corm, producing new plants at tips. Insect- or wind-pollinated. **Fruit**: A dehiscent capsule, shorter than wide.

STATUS: Most prevalent in coastal areas, south-west in particular. Extending range eastwards, limited by lack of hardiness. Rapidly forms large patches usually by corms or corm fragments from garden throw-outs, or from chains of corms being fragile, easily separated and spread by roads or agricultural works or floods. Some seed is produced.
HABITAT: Widely planted in gardens. Hedgerows, road verges, river sides, woods, wastelands especially in slightly damp conditions. Slug- and Rabbit-resistant.
IMPACT: Out-competes native species, can dominate large areas.

Key differences between similar species

Similar leaves to irises, most of which are bluish-green and often >2cm wide. **Siberian Iris**, *Iris sibirica* (non-native) is an exception (see page 76). Montbretia flowers are very different from iris flowers. Other *Crocosmia* species are rarely found outside gardens and rarely invasive. Exceptions are **Pott's Monbretia**, *Crocosmia pottsii* (non-native) naturalised in south-western Scotland; **Aunt Eliza** *Crocosmia paniculata* (non-native) widespread, and **Giant Monbretia**, *Crocosmia masoniorum* (non-native) mainly in south-west England. All three are taller, >60cm, than Montbretia; latter two have strongly pleated leaves, some leaves >3cm wide and >5 raised veins.

Garlics

J	F	M	A	M	J	J	A	S	O	N	D

Three-cornered Garlic
A. triquetrum

Native range:

Western and central Mediterranean

Introduced:

1849 (arrived in GB 1759)

Spread:

Escape from horticulture

Other names:

See table.

Three-cornered Garlic

DESCRIPTION: Bulbous perennial herbs, 40–60cm tall. Stem *triangular or rounded* in section. *All parts usually smell of garlic when fresh and crushed.* Dying away after fruiting. No above-ground parts for most of the year. **Leaves:** Green, narrow, flat to more or less cylindrical, not hollow. **Flowers:** White or pink, in a distinctive umbel at the top of the flower stalk, usually forming a star or bell-shape, some or all often replaced by small bulbs (bulbils). 6 stamens. Sheathing bracts, usually 1 or 2cm enclose flowers when in bud. Insect-pollinated. **Fruit:** A capsule with three cells usually with many seeds. **Seeds:** Black, angular. **Bulbs:** Well-formed, whitish and spherical, 5–15mm in diameter. They do not produce rhizomes. **Identification year-round:** Plants die back completely by June/July, only detectable by bulbs.

STATUS: Significantly increasing their scattered distributions in lowland Britain, Keeled Garlic apart. Reproduce by bulbils and/or seeds.
HABITAT: Found along roadsides, field margins and other waysides, usually ungrazed, and other rough and waste ground.
IMPACT: Can be very invasive in disturbed habitats, displacing native species, spring woodland species in particular.

Key differences between similar species

The common native *Allium* species, **Ramsons** and **Wild Onion**, could be confused with the non-native garlics (see also Spanish Bluebell page 74). Note: at least 20 species of *Allium* are known from habitats outside gardens and cultivation.

	Few-flowered Garlic *Allium paradoxum* (non-native)	Three-cornered Garlic *Allium triquetrum* (non-native)	Rosy Garlic *Allium roseum* (non-native)	Keeled Garlic *Allium carinatum* (non-native)	Ramsons *Allium ursinum* (native)	Wild Onion (Crow Garlic) *Allium vineale* (native)
Inflorescence	*Bulbils* (small, green, almost round) with or without flowers	*Flowers* only	*Flowers* with or without *bulbils*	*Flowers, bulbils* or *both*.	*Flowers* only	Many flowers (no bulbils), many bulbils (no flowers) or often several/few of both
Flowers	*10–15 nodding, white bell-shaped* flowers with *faint green stripe*; stalks 2–4.5cm long, *often only one flower* or none. April–May	*White* with *strong green stripe, cluster* of 3 (5)–15 flowers on longish stalks up to 2.5cm high *hanging* to one side. April–June	*Pink* (rarely white), bell-shaped, in an umbel up to 7cm across, usually many-flowered with stalks 1–4cm long. May–June	*Bright pink to purple; loose flower heads with unequal stalks 1–2.5cm, often hanging downwards.* August	*White*, an umbel, 6–28 flowers with stalks 1–2.5cm; onion-garlic odour. April–June	*Pink to dark red* or *greenish white*, in an umbel with stalks 0.5–3cm long. June–July
Bulb	Spherical, 5–10mm in diameter	Spherical, 15mm in diameter	Spherical, 10–15mm in diameter, surrounded by bulblets	Spherical, 10mm in diameter	*Narrow, slightly cylindrical bulb*, 4mm long and 1mm wide	Spherical, 10–20mm in diameter
Stem	*(10)15–40cm long, triangular*	*10–45cm long, distinctly triangular in section with sharp angles*	*10–75cm, rounded*	*30–60cm, rounded with ridges*	10–20 (50)cm, *rounded but ridged* (can be 2- or 3-angled)	*35–80 (100)cm, rounded*
Leaves	*Flat, green, long and narrow*, inner surface curving inwards; up to 30cm long and 0.5–1.5cm wide. *One leaf per bulb. No leaf stalk*	*Linear, flat, rather fleshy*, inner surface curving inwards; 10–40cm long and 0.5–2cm wide, *long, narrow and tapered with a sharp keel*, 2–5 per bulb. *No leaf stalk*	*Flat or slightly keeled, green, long and narrow* (10–35cm long, 0.5–1.5cm wide). *Matt above, glossy below.* 2–4 (6) per bulb. *No leaf stalk*	*Flat and keeled to crescent-shaped and channelled above*, dull grey-green (10–20cm long and narrow, 1.0–2.5mm wide), 3–5 *prominent veins on underside*, 2–4 per bulb. *No leaf stalk*	Dark green above, paler beneath, narrowly elliptical to narrowly ovate, inner surface curving inwards; 6–24cm long and 1.5–8mm wide; 2–3 per bulb. *Leaf stalk up to 7cm long*	*Almost cylindrical, hollow*, 15–60cm long and 0.2–0.4cm wide. 2–4 per bulb. *No leaf stalk*
Fruit (capsule) and seed	Capsule rarely produced. Seeds angular, with white appendage	Capsule 6–7mm. Seeds angular	Capsule 4–4.5mm. Seeds angular	Capsule 5mm. Seeds angular	Capsule 3–5mm. Seeds spherical	Capsule 3–4mm. Seeds almost spherical
Smell	*Garlic*	*Garlic*	*Garlic*	*Garlic*	*Onion*	*Onion*
Distribution in Britain and Ireland	Mainly eastern	Common in south-western Britain and Ireland	Common in south-west England and south Wales	Scattered throughout England and very scattered elsewhere	Frequent, often abundant, in most of Britain and Ireland	Common in southern England, frequent to scattered elsewhere
Origin	Caucasus	Western and central Mediterranean	Mediterranean	Central and south-eastern Europe	Native	Native
Date of Introduction (arrived in Britain)	1863 (1823)	1849 (1759)	1837 (1752)	1806 (1789)	Native	Native
Notes	Spread mainly by bulbils by vehicles and footwear, rarely by ant-dispersed seed. Damp woods, grassy habitats, rough ground, waysides	Spread by movement of bulbs in soil and ant-dispersed seed. Rough, waste or cultivated ground, waysides	Rough or cultivated ground, old sand dunes, waysides	Spread by seed, bulbils and movement of bulbs in soil. Grassy habitats, rough ground, waysides	Spread by movement of bulbs in soil and by ant-dispersed seed. Found in woods and other damp shady habitats	Spread by seed, bulbils and movement of bulbs in soil. Grassy habitats, rough or cultivated ground, waysides

Spanish Bluebell

Hyacinthoides hispanica

| J | F | M | A | M | J | J | A | S | O | N | D |

Native range:

South-western Europe

Introduced:

1909 (arrived in 1683)

Spread:

Escape from horticulture

Other names:

Endymion hispanicus

DESCRIPTION: Robust, medium to tall perennial herb up to 40 (60)cm high with bulbs. **Leaves:** 4–8. Spear-shaped with *hooded tips. Tough, shiny deep green on both sides, finely hairy along the margin. 1–3.5cm wide* and 20–40 (50)cm long. Initially erect but flopping over and spreading after flowering. No odour when crushed. **Flowers:** Mid-violet to blue; starry, broad flaring bell-shaped and not scented or only faintly scented in warm weather. Grouped together in a characteristic erect spike, *spiralled around stem*. Petals flaring outwards, *not rolled back or only slightly rolled back. Anthers pale to dark blue* and fused to bottom of petal. **Fruit:** A capsule, 0.8–2.2cm long, 1.5–1.8cm wide, green becoming light brown and dry. **Seeds:** Black, broadly ovoid, 3–4mm in diameter. **Bulbs:** White, spherical, 1.5–3.0cm long and 1–2cm wide, no odour when scraped or crushed. **Identification year-round:** Leaves emerge in spring, but difficult to identify until flowering. No above-ground parts visible after June/July.

STATUS: Widely distributed and increasing slowly but over-recorded, some records for Spanish Bluebell being the hybrid (see table). Spreads from throw-outs from gardens disposed of in suitable habitats. Plants send out underground runners, on the end of which new bulbs form. They also seed freely.
HABITAT: Cultivated in gardens. Naturalised in woodland edges, hedge-rows, waysides and churchyards, usually under shade.
IMPACT: Hybridises with native Bluebell leading to genetic introgression. Both Spanish Bluebell and hybrid are physically displacing Bluebell.

Key differences between similar species

Similar to the Bluebell (native) and their hybrid.

	Spanish Bluebell *Hyacinthoides hispanica* (non-native)	Hybrid Bluebell *Hyacinthoides x massartiana (Hyacinthoides hispanica x Hyacinthoides non-scripta)*	Bluebell *Hyacinthoides. non-scripta* (native)
Leaf width	Usually broad, often greater than 15mm broad and up to 35mm	Usually broad, 10 to 35mm	*Narrow, usually less than 15mm* but can be up to 20mm
Flower shape	*Broad* bell shape with petals *flaring outwards*	*Broad* bell shape with petals *slightly curled backwards*	*Narrow* tube-like shape with petals *curled strongly backwards*
Pollen colour	Pale to dark blue, pale green (not creamy-white)	Pale to dark blue, pale green (not creamy-white)	Creamy-white
Anther colour and position	*Usually pale to dark blue* and fused to *bottom of petal*	*Pale creamy-blue, occasionally creamy-white in white and pink flowers* and fused to *middle of petal*	*Usually creamy-white* and fused to *top of petal*
Flower arrangement on spike	Flower spike usually stiff and upright with flowers *spiralling* around stem. Erect when in fruit	Flowers *spiral* around stem and often droop slightly to one side. Erect when in fruit	Flowers droop from *one side* of stem. Erect when in fruit
Scent in warm weather	None to faint scent	None to faint scent	Strong, sweet scent

Hybrid Bluebell
Hyacinthoides x *massartiana*

Bluebell
Hyacinthoides non-scripta

Pitcher Plant

Native range:

East North America

Introduced:

Early 20th century (Ireland), 1940s (Britain) (1640)

Spread:

Spread from horticulture

Other names:

Purple Pitcher Plant, Northern Pitcher Plant, Frog's-britches, Side-saddle Flower

DESCRIPTION: Long-lived, insectivorous perennial herb, forming dense clumps. **Leaves:** All in basal rosette, consisting of tubular insectivorous inverted bulging cones or pitchers 10–20(30)cm long, 3–6cm at widest point, green, marbled with red, curved with a small leaf blade in form of a broad erect hood at entrance, pitchers narrowed to a short stalk-like base. Pitchers contain water which drowns trapped insects. Trailing along ground with apex turning up to become ascending or erect. **Flowers:** Large, solitary at the end of a leafless stalk up to 60cm, nodding, ill-scented; about 5cm across with 5 purplish red-purple petals and sepals with contrasting large yellow-green umbrella-like style about 3cm across. May take 4-5 years to flowering. Insect pollinated. **Roots:** A strong rhizome 0.3–1.5 cm in diameter. **Fruit:** A capsule, 10–20mm in diameter, dry – splitting open when ripe. **Seeds:** Tiny, teardrop shaped, 1.5-2(2.3)mm long, 1–1.3mm wide, 0.0002–0.0008g (data from North America); rough surface. **Identification year-round:** Does not die back over winter.

STATUS: Restricted to a few scattered locations but spreading locally at a number of sites where it has been planted in wet peat bogs. Horizontal spread by rhizome extension. Dispersed by wind and in steams and rivulets.

HABITAT: Well naturalised in raised and blanket bogs, most vigorous in wet, flushed areas.

IMPACT: Displaces other carnivorous species, such as Sundew *Drosera* species and uncommon bog species including bryophytes growing amongst or on Sphagnum tussocks and hummock tops. Potential impact on rare invertebrates caught in the pitchers.

Key differences between similar species

A singular species unlike any other plant found in the wild in Britain or Ireland except for **Trumpets** *Sarracenia flava* from south-east North America planted in a very few bogs in southern England. Differs from *S. purpurea* in its pitchers being green, straight and more or less erect, 30-60cm long with an arching hood and rarely red-veined, and yellow in its petals. Seeds 2–2.5mm long, 1–1.8mm wide.

American Skunk-cabbage

Lysichiton americanus

J	F	M	A	M	J	J	A	S	O	N	D

Native range:

Western North America

Introduced:

1947 (arrived in GB 1901)

Spread:

Escape from horticulture

Other names:

Yellow Skunk-cabbage,
Western Skunk-cabbage,
Lysichiton americanum

DESCRIPTION: Perennial stemless herb up to 1.5m with rhizomes forming large patches. **Leaves:** *Bright green, rippled surface, oval/oblong*, (30) 40–100 (150)cm long and 25–70cm wide, rolled when young, leathery. *Flat or tapered* at base. *Musky odour released from leaves (and hood) when crushed.* NB Sap from leaves and rhizomes can make skin itch. **Flowers:** *One large yellow hood* (spathe) 10–35cm long, *wrapped around a spike of greenish flowers* (spadix) 3.5–12cm long, *foul-smelling, appears as leaves are just emerging from soil.* **Roots:** *Dark, short* and erect rhizome, sparsely branched. **Fruit:** A green berry containing two seeds. **Identification year-round:** Easy when flowering, otherwise difficult to separate from Asian Skunk-cabbage. Leaves appear at about same time as flowers, die back in winter.

STATUS: Extending range eastwards. A throw-out from gardens. Spreads via rhizomes and seeds. Initially slow to establish, not flowering until sixth year, but subsequently spreading quickly by seed.
HABITAT: Increasingly planted beside ponds and streams in parks and gardens. Naturalised in wet ground, beside ponds and streams and in wet woodland.
IMPACT: Persistent and spreading, potentially dominating large areas. Out-competes native species.

Key differences between similar species
- **Asian Skunk-cabbage** *Lysichiton camtschatcensis*. Non-native. Leaves similar. Sap from leaves and rhizomes (roots) can make skin itch. Less common and has a *large white hood* (spathe). *Scentless. Flowering May–July. White*, short and erect rhizomes.
- **Eastern Skunk-cabbage** *Symplocarpus foetidus*. Non-native. Also has similar leaves but this has not been found outside of gardens.

Giant Rhubarb

Gunnera tinctoria

| J | F | M | A | M | J | J | A | S | O | N | D |

Native range:

Chile, Ecuador and Colombia

Introduced:

1908 (arrived in GB 1849)

Spread:

Escape from horticulture

Other names:

Chilean Giant Rhubarb,
Prickly Rhubarb

DESCRIPTION: Huge, clump-forming perennial herb up to 2m tall like over-sized rhubarb with *stout brown 'furry' horizontal stems* (rhizomes). **Leaves:** *Very large, up to 1.5 (2)m wide, umbrella-shaped and sized,* with 5–9 (13) jagged *toothed* lobes, weakly soap-scented with stiff bristly hairs on both sides. Leaf stalks 1.5 (up to 1.8)m long, reddish-purple except in very young plants, round in cross-section with *weak pale green spines or bristles.* **Flowers:** Large and *upright, cone-like to cylindrical structure, up to 1m tall, four times as long as wide,* 3–4 per plant, comprising many thousands of male, female and hermaphrodite stalkless reddish-green flowers, aging to reddish-brown; branches are short and stubby (<5cm). Apex compact and rounded. Wind-pollinated (insect pollination reported in New Zealand). **Roots:** Huge rhizome 6–25cm in diameter, mostly horizontal, up to 3.5 long, covered with soil and leaf litter. **Fruit and seeds:** Small, red-orange spongy berries, 2 x 3mm, containing a single oval seed with copious oil. **Identification year-round:** Over winter leaves die back but stout horizontal stems persist as well as remains of dead leaves and leaf stalks. New leaves appear in spring.

STATUS: Throughout lowland areas, especially south-west England and Isle of Man. Reproduces mainly by seed, but can form stands from vegetative growth. Seeds spread by water and birds.
HABITAT: Gardens as an ornamental. Widely naturalised in permanently damp and shaded areas with rich soil including woodland and grassland near water and often self-sown where long established.
IMPACT: Forms dense colonies up to 0.5ha and more in extent, suppressing native plants as the large leaves prevent other plants growing underneath them. Takes over hedges, roadside verges and ditches. Impedes water flow through obstruction of streams and rivers when water levels are high.

Key differences between similar species

Similar to Brazilian Giant Rhubarb, which is less common due its poor reproductive ability, and Giant Hogweed and Rhubarb.

	Giant Rhubarb *Gunnera tinctoria* (non-native) CS&T	Brazilian Giant Rhubarb *Gunnera manicata* (non-native)*	Giant Hogweed *Heracleum mantegazzianum* (non-native) see page 94	Rhubarb *Rheum* species (non-native)
Leaf	Palmately lobed, *up to 2m* across with acute tip. *Veins on underside hairy*	Palmate, *pinnately lobed*, can be *more than 2m across. Veins on underside prickly*	*Deeply lobed*, up to 2.5m across, *sharply pointed*	Palmate, *deeply lobed*, up to 1m across
Height	Up to 2m	More than 2m	Up to 3.5 (5)m	Up to 2m
Leaf stalk/ stem	*Numerous pale bristles and weak spines, reddish appearance.* 1.5–1.8m long	*Reddish-tipped, stout spines, greenish appearance, 1.5–2.5m long*	*Stem green, red-spotted,* softly hairy	*Smooth, green stalks,* often *reddish or tinged red*
Flower/ inflorescence	More compact than Brazilian, upright, cone-shaped, close to ground, four times as long as wide. Central part of main inflorescence 3–3.3cm in diameter. Branches 9.5–11cm with older flowers reddish-brown.	More open than Giant, upright, cone- to narrowly egg-shaped, close to ground, more than three times as long as wide. Central part of main inflorescence 4–4.5cm. Branches 5–7cm with older flowers greenish-yellow, usually ending in long tail	*Large umbel* (umbrella-like flower cluster) of hundreds of *tiny white flowers.* May–July	Loose panicle, *reddish, like a dock flower.* May–August

* Native range: southern Brazil. Date of introduction (arrived in GB): 1935 (1867)

Brazilian Giant Rhubarb
Gunnera manicata

Giant Hogweed
Heracleum mantegazzianum

Rhubarb
Rheum species

White Butterbur

Petasites albus

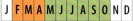

J F M A M J J A S O N D

Native range:

Europe and SW Asia

Introduced:

1843 (arrived in GB 1683)

Spread:

Escape from horticulture

Other names:

None.

DESCRIPTION: Herbaceous patch-forming perennial, flowering stems to 30 (70)cm with rolled-in leaf-like scales. Male plants much more common than female plants. **Leaves:** Rounded, heart-shaped with regular angular lobes and teeth, *green above, white-woolly beneath* up to 30 (50)cm wide, shaggy leaf stalk up to 30cm long. **Flowers:** *Fragrant, pure white or yellowish-white,* flower-head of up to 45 flowers, not much longer than broad, *appearing before the leaves.* Fragrant. **Fruit and seeds:** Yellowish brown single-seeded dry indehiscent fruit. Fruit a 'clock'. **Identification year-round:** *Leaves appear after flowers* then die down in winter.

STATUS: Increasing locally. Plants male or female. Male plant much more common in Britain.

HABITAT: Woods and waste places, on waysides and shady areas.

IMPACT: Can form large stands, displacing native flora.

Key differences between similar species

Similar to other butterburs (*Petasites*), one native and two non-native, and **Colt's-foot** *Tussilago farfara* (native).

	White Butterbur *Petasites albus* (non-native)	Winter Heliotrope *Petasites fragrans* (non-native)	Butterbur *Petasites hybridus* (native)	Giant Butterbur *Petasites japonicus* (non-native)	Colt's-foot *Tussilago farfara* (native)
Leaf width	Up to 30cm	Up to 20cm	Up to 90 (120)cm	Up to 90cm	10–20 (30)cm
Leaf shape (see page 00)	Rounded, heart-shaped with regular lobes and teeth	Kidney-shaped or heart-shaped, regularly toothed	Rounded heart-shaped, shallowly lobed, irregularly toothed	Kidney-shaped or heart-shaped, not lobed, irregularly toothed	Rounded heart-shaped, shallowly lobed or toothed with blackish teeth to margin
Leaf colour	Green above, *white-woolly beneath*	Green, *slightly hairy beneath, shiny above*	Green above, *grey-hairy beneath*	Green, *hairless beneath*	Green above, *white-woolly beneath*, with *black-tipped teeth*
Flower colour	*White or yellowish white. Not scented*	*White, tinged purple (vanilla-scented)*	*White, tinged purple. Not scented*	*Cream to white. Not scented*	*Yellow. Not scented*
Timing of flowering	February–April	*November–March*	March–May, before leaves	February–April, before leaves	February–April, before leaves
Leaves remaining in winter	No	*Yes*	No	No	No

Winter Heliotrope

Petasites fragrans

J F M A M J J A S O N D

Native range:
Central Mediterranean and north Africa

Introduced:
1835 (arrived in GB 1806)

Spread:
Escape from horticulture

Other names:
None.

DESCRIPTION: Short to medium *herbaceous hairy perennial*, flowering stem up to 30cm. **Leaves:** Heart/kidney-shaped, regularly toothed, up to 20(50)cm wide, not lobed, *slightly hairy beneath, shiny above, appearing with the flowers*. Leaf stalk up to 30cm, reddish at base, turning yellow-brown when cut. **Flowers:** Male flower heads in a broad inflorescence *white to lilac/pinkish-white, tinged purple, strongly vanilla- or almond-scented*. Male and female plants borne on separate plants, but only male plants known in Britain. **Fruit and seeds:** Fruit a 'clock'. **Identification year-round:** *Leaves appear with the flowers.* Leaves persist through the winter.

STATUS: Well established by early 20th century and still spreading in Britain. Grown as an ornamental. Spreads vegetatively and can extend 1m per year.

HABITAT: Naturalised on stream sides, banks, rough ground, roadsides and woodland edges.

IMPACT: Can form large, persistent stands out-competing native flora.

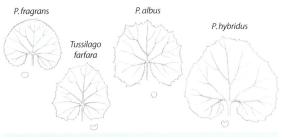

P. fragrans   *P. albus*   *P. hybridus*   *Tussilago farfara*

Key differences between similar species
See table opposite in White Butterbur.

81

Giant Butterbur

Petasites japonicus

Native range:

Japan and Sakhalin

Introduced:

1924 (arrived in GB 1897)

Spread:

Escape from horticulture

Other names:

None.

DESCRIPTION: Medium to *tall, robust* rhizomatous *herbaceous patch-forming hairy perennial*, flowering stem up to 30cm with 15 or more overlapping leaf-like scales. Only male plants known in Britain and Ireland. **Leaves:** Very large up to 90 (100)cm across, green, kidney-shaped or heart-shaped, not lobed and unevenly toothed, *hairless beneath*. Leaf stalk up to 1.5m, turning purplish when cut. **Flowers:** *Fragrant, cream to white with pale green bracts when young making flower head like a small cauliflower, elongating up to 1m before leaves* formed. **Fruit:** Up to 4mm, glabrous, pappus to 12mm. **Identification year-round:** Late winter–early summer. *Leaves appear after flowers*, die down in winter.

STATUS: Scattered throughout most of Britain, rare in Ireland. Garden throw-out or deliberately planted spreading by rhizomes.
HABITAT: Naturalised in extensive stands on stream sides, and other wet habitats, roads and in plantations, in open and shady situations.
IMPACT: Forms large, very persistent stands, shading out native flora.

Key differences between similar species

See table on page 80..

Japanese Knotweed

Fallopia japonica

Native range:
Japan, Taiwan, northern China

Introduced:
1886 (arrived in GB 1825)

Spread:
Escape from horticulture

Other names:
Japanese Bamboo,
Polygonum cuspidatum,
Reynoutria japonica

DESCRIPTION: Tall, vigorous herbaceous perennial *up to 2 (3)m* often growing in dense thickets, robust *bamboo-like hollow* pale green, slightly fleshy, *stems, flecked purple-red*, up to 4cm in diameter, *zig-zag growth form* with regular swollen nodes, becoming woody. Early frosts can cause wilting of new shoots. Tall-brown to bronze canes remain over winter. Plants build up a crown, new growth erupting from pink buds, or directly from rhizomes as small red shoots, asparagus-like in form, turning green. **Leaves:** Lush, light green, shield-shaped with *flattened base*, 10–15cm long; occasionally show wind or frost damage as pale yellow parallel bands. Underside of larger leaves without hairs. Young leaves rolled back sometimes with red-purple tinge; yellow-rusty in autumn, leaf stalk up to 3cm. **Flowers:** Tiny, clustered in loose, often branched spikes at base of upper leaves. Males (not known in Britain) erect with protruding stamens; females, with distinct stigmas, form drooping grape-like clusters. Insect-pollinated. **Roots:** Vigorous underground rhizome with *carrot-orange inner core, externally resembles Ginger*; knotty, snaps like a carrot; extending 7 (20)m from parent plant, penetrating up to 2 (3)m deep. **Fruit:** Thin, papery, three-winged, 8–9mm long. **Seeds:** Shiny, triangular, dark brown, 3–4mm long, 2mm wide, sterile. **Identification year-round:** Distinctive rhizome enables year-round recognition. Characteristic over-wintering canes (see also Giant Knotweed).

STATUS: Throughout lowland areas, especially south-west England. Introduced as an ornamental. Regenerates from rhizome fragments as small as 7g, providing a node is present, and stem sections. Dispersed very effectively in transported soil and by water.

HABITAT: Most urban habitats, particularly brownfield, railways and the banks of waterways. Thrives in damp soils.

IMPACT: Forms dense colonies, suppressing native plants. Impedes water flow through obstruction of streams and rivers when water levels are high. Can cause damage to built structures.

Key differences between similar species
Similar to other Asiatic knotweeds (pages 84–86).

Giant Knotweed

Fallopia sachalinensis

| J | F | M | A | M | J | J | A | S | O | N | D |

Native range:

Japan

Introduced:

1903 (arrived in GB 1896)

Spread:

Escape from horticulture

Other names:

Polygonum sachalinensis,
Reynoutria sachalinensis

DESCRIPTION: Tall, 2–3 (5)m, vigorous, herbaceous perennial occasionally growing in dense thickets, less aggressively than Japanese Knotweed, bamboo-like stems with regular nodes, straight growth form, pale green typically flecked with red-purple. Established plants build up a crown of stems and rhizomes, new growth erupting from pink buds in the crown. **Leaves:** Green, yellowing in autumn, *oval to oblong-shaped, up to 40cm long* with a heart-shaped base. Underside of leaves with scattered long *wavy hairs* (use a hand lens). Leaf stalk 1–4cm. **Flowers:** Greenish-white, tiny in grape-like clusters in spikes longer and denser than Japanese. Insect-pollinated. **Roots:** Orange-coloured rhizome, inner part has a carrot-like appearance, leathery outer layer appearing like Ginger, generally knotty, snaps like a carrot. **Fruit:** Thin, papery, three-winged. **Seeds:** Shiny, dark brown, sterile 4–5mm long, three-sided.
Identification year-round: Pink-red buds form on crowns giving rise to small red shoots, turning green, asparagus-like in form, becoming more like bamboo. Tall, lush green in summer, in autumn yellowing and dying back, canes are hollow and may detach from crown at surface of soil. In winter, only canes and crowns remain, characteristic brown to bronze. Distinctive rhizome enables year-round recognition.

STATUS: Throughout lowland areas, especially south-west England. Originally introduced as an ornamental though less widely than Japanese. Now spread by movement of soils containing rhizome fragments.
HABITAT: Most urban habitats, particularly brownfield, railways and the banks of waterways; thrives in damp soils.
IMPACT: Forms dense colonies, suppressing native plants. Impedes water flow through obstruction of streams and rivers when water levels are high. Can cause structural damage to buildings.

Key differences between similar species
Similar to other Asiatic knotweeds (see pages 83–86).

Hybrid Japanese Knotweed

Fallopia japonica x *F. sachalinensis* (*Fallopia* x *bohemica*)

J F M A M J J A S O N D

Native range:

Naturally occurring hybrid between Giant Knotweed and Japanese Knotweed

Introduced:

1954 (arrived in GB 1872)

Spread:

Escape from horticulture

Other names:

Reynoutria x *bohemica*

DESCRIPTION: Tall, herbaceous vigorous perennial, even more rampant than either of the parent species, up to 2.5 (4)m often growing in dense thickets, bamboo-like stems up to 4cm in diameter with regular nodes, zig-zag growth form, pale green typically flecked with red-purple. Established plants build up a crown of stems and rhizomes, new growth erupting from pink buds in the crown. **Leaves:** Green, yellowing in autumn, *oblong shield-shaped* with a heart-shaped base, 20–25cm long. Underside of larger lower leaves with numerous *short stout hairs* (use hand lens). **Flowers:** Tiny, greenish-white, clustered in loose often branched spikes at base of upper leaves/upper leaf joints. **Roots:** As Giant Knotweed (page 84). **Fruit and Seeds:** As Giant Knotweed (pages 84). **Identification year-round:** As Giant Knotweed (page 84).

STATUS: Throughout lowland areas. The distribution map under-represents actual extent. Hybrid arising spontaneously from Japanese Knotweed and Giant Knotweed plants, being spread by human activity in soil containing rhizome fragments.

HABITAT and IMPACT: As Giant Knotweed (page 84).

| *F. japonica* | *F. sachalinensis* | *Fallopia* x *bohemica* |

Key differences between similar species
Similar to other Asiatic knotweeds (see pages 83–86).

Himalayan Knotweed

Persicaria wallichii

J	F	M	A	M	J	J	A	S	O	N	D

Native range:

Himalayas

Introduced:

1917 (arrived in GB end of 19th century)

Spread:

Escape from horticulture

Other names:

Polygonum polystachyum,
Persicaria polystachyum

DESCRIPTION: Tall, stout erect patch-forming rhizomatous perennial herb, 1.5 (up to 1.8)m. **Leaves:** 8–20cm long, broad (3–8 (10)cm wide), *red-veined*, lanceolate, tapering to a long point *and tapering to base;* lower leaves truncate to cordate at base; range from hairless to densely hairy beneath, leaf-stalk short, 1–3cm, with extra-floral nectaries at the base. **Flowers:** White, long branched spikes, lax, rather leafy, at the end of the stem or in the axils of leaves. Tepals 2.5mm at flowering. Does not always produce flowers. Insect-pollinated. **Roots:** Underground rhizome, creeping brownish-orange knotted exterior, pale ivory core; fibrous roots. **Fruit:** Pale brown, much longer than perianth, rarely produced. **Seeds:** Achene, smooth, ovoid three blunt-angled, 1.5–3mm. **Identification year-round:** Large size, leaf shape and coloration are distinctive features during growing season.

STATUS: Scattered over Britain and Ireland, expanded considerably in recent years. Seed is only occasionally set in Britain, but it establishes readily by vegetative reproduction from sections of rhizome.
HABITAT: Generally lowland, growing in dense stands along streamsides, hedge banks, river banks, roadsides, railway banks and waste ground.
IMPACT: Dense patches can displace native species and, along watercourses, exacerbate flooding in high flows.

Key differences between similar species
Can be confused with other knotweeds (see pages 83–85).
● **Soft Knotweed** *Persicaria mollis.* Non-native. Leaves densely hairy (Himalyan Knotweed leaves can be hairless but may be densely hairy). Leaves are cuneate at the base. No extra-floral nectaries at the base of the leaf stalk. Tepals >2.5mm at flowering.

Red Valerian

Centranthus ruber

| J | F | M | A | M | J | J | A | S | O | N | D |

Native range:

South-western Europe and Mediterranean region

Introduced:

1763 (arrived in GB 1597)

Spread:

Escape from horticulture

Other names:

Jupiter's Beard, Keys of Heaven

DESCRIPTION: Perennial, medium-sized herb, rhizomatous, hairless and erect, 80 (100)cm; stem slightly woody, fleshy and waxy; round, becoming hollow, makes snapping sound when broken, typically breaking just above root. In winter dies back to basal leaves, dried stem and, in older plants, woody crown. Grows as an expanding clump, becoming woody over time. **Leaves:** *Rather fleshy, waxy, fragrant, usually pale bluish-green or greyish, oval* to lanceolate, opposite pairs, 3–7cm long, 1–5cm wide, pointed or blunt, slightly toothed at base, minute crenate margins. Upper leaves toothed and stalkless, clasping the stem; lowest leaves slender with leaf stalks and untoothed edges. Rolled when young. **Flowers:** *Small, 4.6mm, one stamen* (use a hand lens), *dark red, pink, occasionally white, fragrant, with long nectar-containing spur, in loose clusters. 5 petals, four facing* in one direction, fifth facing backwards, all arising from a long tube. Insect-pollinated. Long-blooming. **Roots:** Branched fleshy rootstock with taproot. **Fruit and seeds**: One seeded nut, feathery. **Identification year-round:** Dead stems and woody crown enable recognition over winter.

STATUS: Consolidating, especially in south-western England. A throw-out from gardens. Reproduces from wind-dispersed seed and quickly becomes established.
HABITAT: Naturalised in well-drained lowland areas, a wide range of disturbed and open habitats: on rocks, cliffs, limestone outcrops, shingle banks, sand dunes and pavements, waste ground, in quarries, on railway banks, old walls and buildings.
IMPACT: Displacing native species and reducing open areas for nesting birds in shingle communities, sand dunes and limestone habitats including limestone pavement.

Key differences between similar species
Valeriana species (also called valerians) are superficially similar but have pinnate or pinnately lobed leaves, flowers have 3 stamens (use a hand lens) and fruits are not feathery.

Canadian Goldenrod

Solidago canadensis

J	F	M	A	M	J	J	A	S	O	N	D

Native range:

North America and widely naturalised elsewhere in Europe

Introduced:

1888 (arrived in GB 1648)

Spread:

Escape from horticulture

Other names:

Solidago altissima

DESCRIPTION: Variable, tall, vigorous, rhizomatous upright perennial herb, developing dense stands; stem erect, unbranched, *downy and hairy at least in top half, channelled and ridged*, up to 2 (2.5)m, diameter 3–5mm, green-purplish at base. **Leaves:** Numerous, strap-shaped, lanceolate, 5–16cm long, (0.5) 1.5–2 (3)cm wide, stalkless, toothed, pointed, with two prominent lateral veins, hairy on both sides, minimally along the margin and on the veins on the underside. **Flowers:** Small golden-yellow flowers, 4–6mm on curved branches, forming a *terminal spike or pyramid-shaped* crowded one-sided spray. Pollinated by a range of insects. **Roots:** Persistent purplish rhizomes. **Fruit and seeds:** Achenes, 0.9–1.2mm, short hairs; one-seeded, pappus 2–2.5mm. Small, more or less angled cypsela, many-veined; pappus 1–2 rows of short ciliate hairs. **Identification year-round:** Very characteristic when in flower; seed heads too are a useful feature but difficult to distinguish from hybrids and cultivars and some other goldenrods.

STATUS: Expanding considerably. Very popular in gardens and throw-outs can be very persistent, spreading by rhizomes, clonal growth producing dense stands. Plants are fertile and spread by seed.
HABITAT: Naturalised in lowland rough grassland along road and rail verges and river sides, in damp wayside ground, waste ground and spoil heaps on a wide range of soil types.
IMPACT: Dense stands displace native species.

Key differences between similar species

A very variable species and similar to other non-native Goldenrod species including hybrids.

	Canadian Goldenrod *Solidago canadensis* (non-native) CS&T	Early Goldenrod *Solidago gigantea* (non-native) CS&T	Goldenrod *Solidago virgaurea* (native)
Height	*60–200cm*	*60–200cm*	*Up to 70cm*
Size and timing of flowering	*Small*, 5mm wide in curved branched spike. July–October	*Small*, 5mm wide. July–October	*Large*, 6–10mm wide in straight branched spike. July–September
Shape of compound flower head	*Pyramid*-shaped	*Pyramid*-shaped	*Loose, rather narrow inflorescence*
Stem	*Downy to roughly hairy* on the top half of stem, 3–5mm diameter	More or less *hairless* stem, often bluish-green, 5–8mm diameter	*Variable*
Leaves	*Hairy*, lanceolate, toothed margin	*Hairless, except for lowerside veins*, lanceolate, toothed margin	More or less *hairless*, weakly aromatic when crushed. Widest above middle and tapering to base
Rhizome/roots	*Creeping rhizome*	*Rhizome present*	No creeping rhizome

Early Goldenrod
Solidago gigantea

Goldenrod
Solidago virgaurea

Ragweed

J **F** **M** **A** **M** **J** **J** **A** **S** **O** N D

Native range:

North America; widely naturalised elsewhere in Europe

Introduced:

1836 (arrived in GB 1759)

Spread:

Brought in with seeds

Other names:

Common or Annual Ragweed

DESCRIPTION: Medium to tall, erect annual herb 1 (1.3)m tall. Stems stout, rough, hairy, branched with blunt ridges or round, often reddish, becoming woody at base of stem; giving *aromatic smell when broken*.
Leaves: Present May–October, mostly opposite but alternate towards top of stem, dark green above, greyish and short hairs beneath, up to 10 (15) cm long, *deeply pinnately lobed; larger leaflets with lobes divided again; lobes toothed*. Leaf stalk up to 3cm. **Flowers:** Arising from axils of leaves, male heads greenish-yellow, 3–5mm in diameter, in slender spikes; female inconspicuous at base of upper leaves, flower bracts with tiny teeth. Wind-pollinated. **Roots:** Shallow, fibrous. **Fruit:** *A bur, hard, ridged and woody*, achene-like, (3) 4–5mm long with a subulate beak 1.5–2mm long with 5–7 prickly, small erect spines near or above middle, yellowish to reddish-brown.
Seeds: A single tiny seed in each pod, 3–4mm long. **Identification year round:** Easier to identify when flowering with mature leaves.

STATUS: Fairly frequent in England, Wales and Scotland but casual (rarely persisting) from bird-seed and oilseed. Burs attach to fur and clothing.
HABITAT: Disturbed ground, rubbish tips, dockyards, arable fields and on waste ground and in places where bird-seed is scattered.
IMPACT: Causes hayfever, regarded as serious weed for this reason in North America and parts of Europe.

Key differences between similar species

Two other non-native *Ambrosia* species are found in similar habitats to Rag-weed. They are uncommon to rare and both originate in North America.

- **Perennial (or Cuman) Ragweed** *Ambrosia psilostachya* (or *Ambrosia coronopifolia*). Non-native. Perennial with stems up to 1m, arising from creeping roots. Flowers in August. *Leaves grey-green, up to 20cm. Upper leaves alternate, pinnately divided nearly to base, not aromatic. Flowers in August. Seeds warty, without spines, 4–8mm long*.
- **Giant Ragweed** *Ambrosia trifida*. Non-native **CS&T**. Annual with stems up to 2.5m. *Leaves green, up to 90cm across. All opposite, palmately lobed with 3–5 lobes (lobes > 1cm wide).* Flowers August–October. *Seed a bur 6–12mm long*.

Oxford Ragwort

Senecio squalidus

DESCRIPTION: Short-lived perennial herb, effectively annual, up to 50cm, sometimes woody at base. **Leaves:** Alternate, deeply lobed leaves, only lower leaves stalked, with narrow pointed lobes. **Flowers:** *Dense, bright yellow*, 15–20mm across, between 12 to 15 ray florets, 8 to 10mm long with black-tipped bracts. **Roots:** *Taproot.* **Fruit and seeds:** Feathery (like a simple version of a dandelion seed) and hairy. **Identification year-round:** Easiest to identify once flowering with mature leaves.

STATUS: Common in England and Wales, local in Scotland and Ireland; still spreading. Originally escaped from Oxford Botanic Garden, but rarely deliberately grown in gardens today. Reproduces from wind-dispersed seed, establishing rapidly.

HABITAT: Wasteland, road sides, railway lines, gardens and walls.

IMPACT: Out-competes native species, hybridises with native ragworts. Poisonous to livestock although livestock are less exposed to this species than Common Ragwort (see table), a native species of meadows.

Native range:
Southern Europe

Introduced:
1850s (arrived in GB 1794)

Spread:
Escape from horticulture

Other names:
Creulys Rhydychen (Welsh)

Key differences between similar species
May be confused with other ragworts.

	Leaf shape	Underside of leaf	Flower colour	Flower heads	Outer flower petals (ray florets)
Narrow-leaved Ragwort *Senecio aequidens* (native) CS&T	Slender, linear, largely undivided		Lemon–golden yellow	Loose cluster	Yes, 5–8mm long
Oxford Ragwort *Senecio squalidus* (non-native)	*Deeply lobed*, with narrow pointed lobes	*Almost hairless*	Bright yellow	*Loose cluster*	*Yes, >8mm long*
Common Ragwort *Senecio jacobea* (native)	Deeply lobed with *blunt lobes*	*More or less hairless*	Bright yellow	*Dense cluster*	*Yes, 5–8mm long*
Hoary Ragwort *Senecio erucifolius* (native)	Deeply lobed with narrow pointed lobes	*Cottony hairs* and *lobes, margins folded downwards*	Pale yellow	*Dense cluster*	Yes, 5–9mm long
Marsh Ragwort *Senecio aquaticus* (native)	*Basal leaves undivided, upper leaves with large oval end lobes*	Hairless	Golden yellow	Loose cluster	Yes, >8mm long
Silver Ragwort *Senecio cineraria* (non-native)	Deeply lobed	*White-felted underneath*	Bright yellow	*Dense cluster*	*Yes, 3–6mm long*

Beaked Hawk's-beard

Crepis vesicaria

| J | F | M | A | M | J | J | A | S | O | N | D |

Native range:

Mediterranean and south-western Asia

Introduced:

1896 (arrived in GB 1713)

Spread:

Escape from horticulture

Other names:

Crepis taraxacifolia

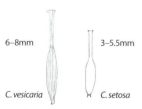

6–8mm 3–5.5mm

C. vesicaria *C. setosa*

DESCRIPTION: A usually biennial herb, sometimes annual or perennial, usually a single branched stem up to 80cm long but may have several branches arising just above basal rosette. Upperparts without stiff bristles. **Leaves:** *Dandelion-like*, 10–35cm long and 2–8cm wide, densely hairy to more or less hairless. Stem leaves not arrow-shaped. **Flowers:** *Yellow, outer florets striped brown underneath. Flower head bracts in two sets, one long, one short.* May to July. **Roots:** *Taproot.* **Fruit and seeds:** One-seeded, 6–8mm long, brown or yellowish, spindle-like shape (wide in the middle and tapering at both ends), including long beak almost as long as body of seed, ribbed (about 10 ribs), tapering towards top, with white to pale brownish unbranched pappus.

Identification year-round: Difficult at any time due to the number of hawk's-beard species and other yellow-flowered dandelion-like plants of the daisy family.

STATUS: Common in south and spreading, especially in western England and Wales. A throw-out from gardens. Reproduces from wind dispersed seed; establishing rapidly.

HABITAT: Lightly mown or grazed lowland grassy places including roadsides, lawns, railway banks and in waste places on dry calcareous soils.

IMPACT: No adverse impacts reported.

Key differences between similar species

● **Bristly Hawk's-beard** *Crepis setosa.* Non-native. Upper parts of stems and flower bracts are bristly. Stem leaves arrow-shaped with pointed ear-shaped lobes. Flowers pale yellow and flowering later, July–September.

● **Hawkweeds** *Hieracium* species. Hairy. Flower heads with bracts in two or more rows. Seeds are a good way of distinguishing between these plants.

Perfoliate Alexanders

Smyrnium perfoliatum

Native range:

Southern Europe

Introduced:

1932 (arrived in GB 1596)

Spread:

Escape from horticulture

Other names:

Yellow or Biennial Perfoliate Alexanders

DESCRIPTION: More or less hairless, tall erect biennial or perennial herb, up to 1.2 (1.5)m. Stem angled, narrowly winged on angles, pith-filled or hollow, hairy at nodes only, upper branches alternate. Odourless. **Leaves:** *Upper leaves simple, oval*, clasping stem *with heart-shaped bases, bright yellowish-green, odourless, shallowly toothed up to 10cm long. Lower leaves 2–3 pinnate or ternate with oval, toothed lobes, dying early.* **Flowers:** Small *yellow, in a flat-topped umbel*, rounded with 5–12 branches for each umbel; no bracts. Insect-pollinated. **Roots:** Swollen tuber-like taproot, resembling a small turnip. **Fruit and seeds:** Brownish-black when ripe, slender, broader than long, (2) 3–3.5mm long, 5–5.5mm wide, flattened; encased in hard, dryish coat with three prominent slender ridges, numerous *dark stripes (oil ducts)*. **Identification year-round:** Difficult to recognise until flowering stem produced in second year, although seedlings have small tubers. Recognisable from clasping leaves on stem in spring, flower heads in summer and dead stems and seed heads in winter.

STATUS: Established in a few locations. Spread by seeds.
HABITAT: A garden and flower arrangement throw-out, naturalised in grassy places and in cultivated ground, a casual in waste places.
IMPACT: Some localised impacts reported. Potential to smother adjacent native vegetation, for example in woodlands

Key differences between similar species
Leaves clasping stem distinguish Perfoliate Alexanders from all other umbellifers.

Giant Hogweed

Heracleum mantegazzianum

Native range:

South-west Asia

Introduced:

1828 (arrived in GB 1820)

Spread:

Escape from horticulture

Other names:

None.

Use gloves if handling this plant

DESCRIPTION: Very large perennial herb persisting 3–5 years, *up to 3.5 (5)m*, hollow stem *often purple-mottled*, usually with *sharp bristles, 5–10cm in diameter*. After reaching a mature stage it flowers, sets seed and dies. *All parts have strong resinous smell*. **Leaves:** Very large, up to 2.5 (3)m across, *sharply divided/serrated leaves* with bristles on underside. **Flowers:** *Umbrella-shaped* flower head very large up to 80cm across with many small white flowers pollinated by various insects; self-pollination may occur. **Roots:** *Parsnip-like taproot*. **Fruit and seeds:** Some 20,000 (up to 50,000) seeds per plant. 0.9–1.5cm long, elliptical, flattened, usually devoid of hairs, with *dark stripes (oil ducts), 2 on one side, 4 on other side*, shed August–September. **Identification year-round:** Basal leaves in spring, flower heads and mature leaves in summer and dead stems and seed heads in winter.

STATUS: Widespread. Introduced as ornamental. Spreads by seed (wind-dispersed) and via watercourses.

HABITAT: Waste ground and common on riverbanks.

IMPACT: Exposure to sap causes skin blistering if exposed to sunlight (photosensitivity). Out-competes native species. Can impede flow in rivers and streams in flood conditions and expose banks to erosion in winter.

Giant Hogweed   Hogweed

Key differences between similar species

When at full height it is difficult to confuse Giant Hogweed with any other plant. While still growing or stunted, possibly as a result of disturbance, it can be confused with **Hogweed** *Heracleum sphondylium* (native) a much shorter plant, up to 2m, stem width 1–2cm. Flower head is up to 80cm and the seed length 0.8cm.

Orange Balsam

Impatiens capensis

J	F	M	A	M	J	J	A	S	O	N	D

Native range:

North America

Introduced:

1822 (arrived in GB very early 19th century)

Spread:

Escape from horticulture

Other names:

Jewel Weed

DESCRIPTION: Tall, herbaceous, hairless annual, upright with brownish, occasionally purplish *fleshy stem*, up to 0.6 (1.5)m *with markedly swollen nodes*. Stem and leaves with yellow dye. **Leaves:** *Alternate, oval, 3–9cm, toothed with leaf stalk up to 5cm. Fewer than 12 teeth per side,* 1–2mm deep. **Flowers:** *Orange with large brownish, blood-red blotches,* 2–3.5cm, *with spur, 0.5–1.0cm long,* at base like nasturtiums. Insect-pollinated. **Roots:** Weakly rooted. **Fruit:** Capsule oblong with numerous seeds, explosive to the touch when mature. **Seeds:** About 5mm in diameter, ellipsoid; float on water. **Identification year round:** Distinguishable when in leaf. Dies back in autumn.

STATUS: Steady expansion in England, rare elsewhere. Seeds can be ejected from their capsules to a distance of a few metres and can be dispersed by water.

HABITAT: Naturalised on the banks of lowland rivers, canals, lakes and reservoirs.

IMPACT: None recorded despite its spread.

Key differences between similar species

There are three other balsam species common in Britain (two non-native and one native) and one rare non-native (Kashmir Balsam).

	Orange Balsam *Impatiens capensis* (non-native)	Touch-me-not Balsam *Impatiens noli-tangere* (native to Lake District and central Wales)	Small Balsam *Impatiens parviflora* (non-native)	Indian or Himalayan Balsam *Impatiens glandulifera* (non-native)	Kashmir Balsam *Impatiens balfourii* (non-native)
Height	60 (150)cm	60 (100)cm	60 (100)cm	200cm	100 (200)cm
Flower size	2–3.5cm	2–3.5cm	0.6–1.8cm	2.5–4cm	2.5–4cm
Flower colour	Orange with large brownish spots	Yellow with small brownish spots	Pale yellow	Deep to pale pinkish-purple or white	Pinkish-purple with white helmet
Spur	5–10mm, curving under	6–12mm, at approximately 90°	2–5mm, gradually tapered into straight spur	2–7mm, bent at >90°	7–12mm, straight or slightly curved or bent
Leaves	Alternate, 6–12 teeth on each side	Alternate, 6–15 teeth on each side	Alternate, 20–30 teeth on each side	Opposite or in whorls of 3, red-toothed, 24–75 teeth on each side	Alternate, 40–50 teeth on each side

Indian or Himalayan Balsam

Impatiens glandulifera

| J | F | M | A | M | J | J | A | S | O | N | D |

Native range:
West and central Himalayas

Introduced:
1855 (arrived in GB 1839)

Spread:
Escape from horticulture

Other names:
Policeman's Helmet,
Impatiens roylei

DESCRIPTION: Tall herbaceous hairless annual, stem upright, ridged and stout, reddish, fleshy, sappy and brittle, up to 2m, 3–4cm in diameter, sometimes with swollen nodes. Stems and leaves with yellow dye. Dead stems fall to the ground, dry and shrunken, straw-like. **Leaves:** Opposite or in whorls of 3–5, slender to elliptical, finely serrated edges, 24–75 teeth on each side, at least lower teeth red-tipped, may have reddish midrib; leaf stalk hollow, 6–15cm long, may be reddish-purple. **Flowers:** *Variable from deep to pale pinkish-purple or white,* trumpet-shaped, sweet-scented, 2.5–4cm front to back; spur green, rather stout, bent at >90°. Insect-pollinated. **Roots:** Weakly rooted with many short and fleshy, *finger-like* white to pinkish roots, *pointing down from node on thick vertical taproot,* all *persisting when plant is dead*; sometimes smelling of antiseptic. **Fruit:** Club-shaped, angled capsule, 1.5–3cm long, green, exploding on touch when ripe, sides coiling back. **Seeds:** Shining brown-black, 2–4 (5)mm in diameter, broadly ovoid with a single ridge down one side, slightly beaked at apex, truncate at base; require cold spell to break dormancy. Seedlings March to June. **Identification year-round:** Dies off in autumn leaving stringy dried stems, obvious in large stands.

STATUS: Locally common in most of Britain. Introduced as an ornamental, still popular as a garden plant. Seeds can be ejected from their capsules a few metres and can be dispersed by water, spreading rapidly both up and down waterways.
HABITAT: Very frequent on banks of lowland waterways forming continuous stands, damp woodland, flushes and mires, damp soil in waste ground.
IMPACT: Rapid and dense growth can shade out native vegetation such as Tansy *Tanacetum vulgare* and thus affect associated fauna, for example Tansy Beetle *Chrysolina graminis*.

Key differences between similar species
Similar to other balsams – see page 95.

Small Balsam

| J | F | M | A | M | J | J | A | S | O | N | D |

Native range:

Central Asia and widely natural-ised in temperate Europe

Introduced:

1851 (arrived in GB 1823)

Spread:

Escape from horticulture

Other names:

None.

DESCRIPTION: Medium, hairless, herbaceous annual, upright with *fleshy stem* up to 60 (100)cm; stems and leaves with yellow dye. **Leaves:** *Pale green, alternate, oval, stalked with saw-toothed margin, 4–20cm long, 2–9cm wide. More than 20 teeth* on each side of leaf. **Flowers:** *Small, pale yellow or cream, 0.5–1.5cm, with a short, almost straight, red-tipped spur*, 0.4–1.2cm long, at base of flower. **Roots:** Weakly rooted. **Fruit:** Capsule up to 20mm, narrowly club-shaped, hairless, with seeds, bursts at a touch when mature. **Seeds:** Whitish, 4–6mm, oblong, striated. **Identification year-round:** Distinguishable when in leaf and when in flower. Dies off in autumn.

STATUS: Steadily increasing but rare in Ireland. Spreads from seeds ejected from capsules.

HABITAT: Shady and damp places including semi-natural woodland and plantations, especially along tracks, shaded river banks, hedges and disturbed or cultivated ground.

IMPACT: None recorded although it can establish extensive patches in well-established woodland.

Key differences between similar species

Flowers of Small Balsam are much smaller than the other balsams. See Orange Balsam (page 95).

Tree Lupin

Lupinus arboreus

| J | F | M | A | M | J | J | A | S | O | N | D |

Native range:

California

Introduced:

At least 1945 (arrived in GB 1793)

Spread:

Escape from horticulture and planted to stabilise sand

Other names:

None

DESCRIPTION: Short-lived, semi-evergreen erect *perennial small shrub* (not a tree), much-branched and woody below, *up to 2 (3)m*. Twigs reddish, hairy, round in cross-section. *Only lupin not to die back in winter.* **Leaves:** *Palmate leaf* with 5–10 (12) alternate spear-shaped leaflets up to 6cm long radiating from a central point, silky hairs below, hairless above; leaf stalk has silky hairs. **Flowers:** *Sulphur-yellow or white,* sometimes tinged blue or purple, sweetly honey-scented, *pea-like, 14–17mm long arranged in spirals* in large spikes, 4–10cm. Insect-pollinated. **Roots:** Tap root with fibrous roots. **Fruit:** *Stiffly hairy brown legume or pea-pod,* 3–5 (8)cm long. **Seeds:** 8–12, dark brown, 4–5mm long, ellipsoid, mottled with pair of spots near micropyle, long-lived. **Identification year-round:** Present throughout winter though frost sensitive.

STATUS: Scattered localities concentrated around east and south coasts. Killed by heavy frosts. Copiously produced seed flung from explosive pods making gunfire-like sound on a hot day, establishing in dry, frost-free areas.

HABITAT: Garden escape widely planted on sand dunes and in land restoration. Coastal areas on sand dunes, shingle banks and cliffs, wasteland, roadsides and railways.

IMPACT: Can cover large areas, out-competing native species, especially on sand dunes.

Key differences between similar species

The only species that are similar are other lupin species.

	Tree Lupin *Lupinus arboreus* (non-native)	Nootka Lupin *Lupinus nootkatensis* (non-native)	Garden Lupin *Lupinus polyphyllus* (non-native)	Russell Lupin *Lupinus arboreus* x *Lupinus polyphyllus* (*Lupinus* x *regalis*) (non-native)	White Lupin *Lupinus albus* (non-native)	Narrow-leaved Lupin *Lupinus angustifolius* (non-native)
Height	Up to 2 (3)m	Up to 1m	Up to 1m	Up to 1.5m	Up to 0.6 (1.2)m	Up to 0.6 (1)m
Woody stems	*Yes. Does not die back in winter*	No. Dies back in winter	No. Dies back in winter	No. Dies back in winter	No. Dies back in winter. Easily uprooted	No. Dies back in winter. Easily uprooted
Stems branched	*Yes, more than 1 flowering spike*	*No, only one flowering spike*	*No, usually only one flowering spike*	*Yes, more than one flowering spike*	Yes, sparingly, a single terminal stalkless spike	*Much branched*
No. of leaflets	7–11	6–9	9–15 (17)	9–16	5–9	5–9
Leaf veins	Only midrib visible	Secondary veins visible		Secondary veins visible	All veins obscure	All veins obscure
Flower colour	Yellow or white	*Bluish-purple or mixed colour*	*Blue, purple, pink or white*	*Blue, purple, pink or white*	*White, usually tinged blue-violet*	*Blue*
Status	Scattered	*Scotland only*	Scattered	Scattered	*Rare*	*Rare*

Nootka Lupin

Lupinus nootkatensis

J F **M A M J J A S** O N D

Native range:
North-west North America and north-east Asia

Introduced:
1862 (arrived in GB 1794)

Spread:
Escape from horticulture

Other names:
Wild Lupin, Scottish Lupin

DESCRIPTION: Tall, erect robust tuft-forming hairy perennial *herb, up to 1m*, with *long shaggy hairs on stem, dying back to an underground branched woody crown*. **Leaves:** *Palmate leaf* with (6) 7–8 (9) elliptic leaflets radiating from a central point, 2–6cm long. Sparsely silky hairy below, hairless above, sometimes hairy above too. Leaf stalk longer than leaflets. **Flowers:** *Bluish-purple, sometimes almost white tinged purple, scented, pea-like flowers, 12–16mm* in a single large spike; flowering stem densely hairy. Self-fertilisation occurs, cross-pollination by bees. **Fruit:** *Silky hairy brown oblong legume or peapod*, 6–8cm long, 4–5cm wide. **Seeds:** Ellipsoid, 4mm long, 3mm wide, 15–20mg in weight. **Identification year-round:** Recognisable in spring, summer and autumn. Dies back in winter leaving characteristic seed heads.

STATUS: Restricted to parts of Scotland, probably declining in distribution. Garden escape but now rarely cultivated. Spreads mainly by seeds as lateral shoot expansion is rare. Seeds spread by water, wind and probably birds.
HABITAT: River shingle and banks of streams, and moorland.
IMPACT: Displaces native plant species. Poisonous to humans and livestock.

Key differences between similar species
The only species that are similar are other lupin species. Can be distinguished from Garden Lupin by number of leaflets. See Tree Lupin, page 98, for table.

Russell Lupin

Lupinus arboreus x *Lupinus polyphyllus* (*Lupinus* x *regalis*)

J	F	M	A	M	J	J	A	S	O	N	D

Native range:
Hybrid of Tree Lupin and Garden Lupin, garden origin

Introduced:
At least 1955 (arrived in GB 1937)

Spread:
Escape from horticulture

Other names:
None.

DESCRIPTION: Tall, erect short-lived tuft-forming perennial *herb up to 1.5m with sparingly branched stems* with *short sparse hairs, weakly angled*. **Leaves:** *Palmate leaf* with 9–15(18) leaflets, 9–15cm long, radiating from top of hairy leaf stalk. **Flowers:** Blue, purple, pink or white, scented, *pea-like flowers* in large spikes. **Fruit:** Green velvety oblong legume or pod, 2.5–5cm long, drying to a greyish-brown, splitting to reveal a row of seeds. **Seeds:** Dark brown, ellipsoid, up to 4mm long. **Identification year-round:** Dies back in winter leaving characteristic seed heads.

STATUS: Scattered throughout lowland Britain. Garden escape, a very popular garden plant. Subsequently spreads by seeds.
HABITAT: Rough ground, road and railway banks, river shingle and waste ground.
IMPACT: Seed pods and seeds are poisonous to humans and livestock.

Key differences between similar species
The only species that are similar are other lupins. Russell Lupin is difficult to differentiate from Garden Lupin and various lupin hybrids. Leaves are useful for identification. Care needs to be taken using flower colour as this is variable within lupins. See Tree Lupin, page 98, for table.

Pink Purslane

Claytonia sibirica

Native range:

Eastern Asia and western North America, widely naturalised elsewhere in north-west Europe

Introduced:

1838 (arrived in GB 1768)

Spread:

Escape from horticulture

Other names:

Montia sibirica

DESCRIPTION: Short, rather fleshy, hairless annual, sometimes perennial herb, brittle stem up to 40cm. **Leaves:** Fleshy, shiny dark green above, paler below, stem leaves stalkless, lower leaves 1–5cm long with long stalks 7–8cm. Usually present year-round. **Flowers:** *Pink, sometimes white, 16–20mm across, 5 deeply notched petals*. **Roots:** Short scaly tap roots. **Fruit:** One- or few-seeded capsule opening vertically. **Identification year-round:** Easy to recognise when in flower, less so when only leaves present.

STATUS: Scattered throughout Britain especially in north and west, rare in Ireland, has spread rapidly since 1930s through garden throw-outs, subsequently dispersing by seed including being washed downstream to new sites.

HABITAT: Damp, shady, bare areas in open woodlands or hedgerows and by streams.

IMPACT: Rapidly colonises semi-natural woodland, suppressing other vegetation by lush spring foliage which then collapses on top of nearby plants.

Key differences between similar species

- **Springbeauty** *Claytonia perfoliata*. Non-native, naturalised in sandy soils in waste ground, sand dunes, gardens and agricultural land. Increasing in its distribution. Has smaller, white flowers. Petals only slightly notched. The two stem leaves are fused into a cup-shaped structure beneath the flower.

Slender Speedwell

Veronica filiformis

Native range:

Caucasus and northern Turkey

Introduced:

1838 (arrived in GB 1808)

Spread:

Escape from horticulture

Other names:

None.

DESCRIPTION: *Low, creeping, mat-forming perennial*, up to 50cm long. Stems very slender, <1mm in diameter with minute hairs, up to 5cm high. **Leaves:** *Kidney-shaped, scalloped*, 7–10mm, rounded, bluntly toothed with leaf stalk up to 5mm. Mostly opposite on non-flowering stems. **Flowers:** *Blue* to *mauvish-blue,* 8–15mm wide with pale to *white lower lip*, solitary in axils of alternated leaves, on long slender stalks at least 2–3 times length of leaves. Poor flowering under dry conditions. **Roots:** Roots freely at the nodes. **Fruit:** Small 2-lobed capsule, lobes almost parallel, slightly hairy, rarely formed. **Seeds:** Rarely sets seed. **Identification year-round:** Combination of rooting at most nodes, leaf shape and number of teeth enable identification year-round. Easily recognisable when in flower due to long flower stalk.

STATUS: Throughout most of Britain and Ireland. Originally an alpine garden escape, now often treated as a weed. Regenerates from cut or broken fragments spread by wind after mowing and possibly by birds; rarely from seeds.
HABITAT: Damp grasslands, margins of watercourses, roadsides and wasteland.
IMPACT: Displaces native species and is a weed of lawns and gardens.

Key differences between similar species

Similar to other speedwell species, some of the more similar species are included in the table.

	Leaf shape and number of teeth	Flower colour and flower stalk	Hairiness	Habit	Annual or perennial
Slender Speedwell *Veronica filiformis* (non-native)	*Kidney-shaped*, 3–4 teeth on each side	*Blue* to *mauvish-blue* with *white lower lip, flower stalk 2–3(4) times length of leaves*	*Not hairy*	*Creeping*, stems rooting at most nodes	*Perennial*
Ivy-leaved Speedwell *Veronica hederifolia* (non-native)	*Ivy shaped, lobed, 2–3 deep teeth on each side*	Pale blue, flower stalk shorter than leaves	*Hairy*	Creeping, rooting only near base of stem	Annual
Wall Speedwell *Veronica arvensis* (native)	*Oval/triangular, coarsely toothed, (1) 2–5 teeth on each side*	All blue, borne at end of stem	*Downy*	*Erect to prostrate: low, often very low*	Annual
Common Field Speedwell *Veronica persica* (non-native)	*Oval/triangular, coarsely toothed, 5–7 teeth on each side*	Bright blue, lower lip white, *flower stalk up to 2 times length of leaves*	*Hairy*	Creeping, rooting only near base of stem	Annual
Grey Field Speedwell *Veronica polita* non-native)	*Oval/triangular, coarsely toothed, 4 obtuse teeth on each side*	*All blue, flower stalk hairy similar length to leaves*	*Hairy*	Creeping, rooting only near base of stem	Annual
Green Field Speedwell *Veronica agrestis* (non-native)	*Oval/triangular, coarsely toothed, 3–4 teeth on each side*	*Pale blue* with white lower lip, flower stalk long and slender	*Hairy*	Creeping, rooting only near base of stem	Annual
Thyme-leaved Speedwell *Veronica serpyllifolia* (native)	*Small, oval and thyme-like, untoothed*	*White or pale blue, borne in leafy spike at end of stem*	Not hairy	Creeping, rooting at nodes	Perennial

Ivy-leaved Speedwell
Veronica hederifolia

Wall Speedwell
Veronica arvensis

Common Field Speedwell
Veronica persica

Grey Field Speedwell
Veronica polita

Green Field Speedwell
Veronica agrestis

Thyme-leaved Speedwell
Veronica serpyllifolia

Pirri-pirri-bur

Acaena novae-zelandiae

| J | F | M | A | M | J | J | A | S | O | N | D |

Native range:

South-east Australia and New Zealand

Introduced:

1901

Spread:

Escape from horticulture

Other names:

Acaena anserinifolia

DESCRIPTION: Creeping perennial *mat-forming dwarf hairy shrub* up to 11 (17)cm high; short, erect leafy stem pink flushed but mainly green, woody at base, trailing up to 1m often partially buried, growths appearing crowded. **Leaves:** Bright green, glossy, 3–10cm long, *pinnate* with 5–13 (15) deeply toothed leaflets. Leaflets (3) 5–10 (20)mm long, those near tip of leaf 2–2.5 times as long as broad, *5–6 teeth* on each side of a single leaflet, oblong, smooth to slightly wrinkled, bright glossy green on upper surface, paler underneath. **Flowers:** *Greenish-white spherical* dense flower head, 3.5cm in diameter, densely packed with inconspicuous petalless flowers, on long erect pale green stem (up to 11cm), holding flower heads well above leaves, sometimes flushed with red. *Each flower with 4 spines, 6–10 (12)mm long* but often with 1 or 2 much shorter, *soft becoming barbed.* **Roots:** Rooting at nodes, many secondary roots, up to 3mm diameter, black, dark red-brown inside with many fibrous roots. **Fruit:** *Spherical* burr-like head, *stem up to 25cm.* **Seeds:** Inverted cone-shaped, hairy, 4mm long, 2mm wide with 4 long slender *reddish spines, barbed at tip.* **Identification year-round:** Flowers and seed heads are characteristic, the latter remaining over winter.

STATUS: Scattered with local concentrations. Garden throw-out. Reproduction is from seed which sticks to clothes (socks and trouser legs in particular) and animals' fur, and sometimes from pieces of rooted stolon.

HABITAT: Dry open ground: sand dunes, heaths, cliffs, roadsides and disused railway lines on sandy soil. Forms tough mats, resistant to trampling.

IMPACT: Displaces native species.

Key differences between similar species

There are three other species of *Acaena* in Britain, also occurring on bare ground, Pirri-pirri-bur being one of the larger species. Hybrids, for example between Pirri-pirri-bur and Spineless Pirri-pirri-bur, occur in gardens. Pirri-pirri-burs might also be confused with other members of the rose family with pinnate leaves and similar seed heads..

	Leaflets	Woody stem	Flower	Seed head
Pirri-pirri-bur *Acaena novae-zelandiae* (non-native)	2–6 pairs. Deeply toothed (7–8 (12) teeth on each side), smooth, bright green on upper surface, paler underneath, smooth oblong leaflets, those near tip of leaf 2–2.5 times as long as broad	Only at base	*Greenish-white, spherical head of very small flowers; up to 4 spines per flower, 6–10mm long, often 1 or 2 much shorter*	Spherical burr with 4 *red barbed spines*
Two-spined Acaena *Acaena ovalifolia* (non-native)	(3) 4 (5) pairs, apical pair 10–30mm long, 1.5 to twice as long as wide. Finely wrinkled, green beneath	Yes	*Spherical, up to 4cm in diameter, 2 spines per fruit, 8–10mm, barbed, red*	
Bronze Pirri-pirri-bur *Acaena anserinifolia* (non-native)	4–6 (7) pairs, apical pair 3–10mm long. Matt, markedly bronzed, end leaflet rounded, leaflets near tip of leaf not twice as long as broad	Yes	*Spherical, 12–16mm in diameter, 4 spines per flower, up to 9mm, barbed*	
Spineless Pirri-pirri-bur *Acaena inermis* (non-native)	5–7 pairs, 11–13mm, apical pair 2–3mm, about as long as wide, with 5–10 teeth on each side. Matt, bluish- or greyish-green, tinged brown to orange with age, end leaflet rounded, leaflets near tip of leaf not twice as broad or broader than long	Yes	*Spherical, 2.5cm in diameter, no spines, barbs, up to 4 stout, red spines, up to 13mm but sometimes none*	Spineless burrs 1.6cm across (some forms with short, thick, soft-tipped spines)
Agrimony *Agrimonia eupatoria* (native)	3–6 pairs of main leaflets with *smaller leaflets in between*	No	*Yellow, long spike*	Individual seed heads with *erect hooks*
Salad Burnet *Sanguisorba minor* subspecies *minor* (native)	3–12 pairs of rounded leaflets	No	*Green, spherical head of very small flowers on erect stems*	Spherical seed head with *netted ridges*
Great Burnet *Sanguisorba officinalis* (native)	3–7 pairs of oval leaflets	No	*Dull crimson, oblong head of very small flowers on erect stems*	Oblong seed head
Silverweed *Potentilla anserina* (native)	4–8 (12) pairs, silvery hairs beneath	No	*Yellow, individual flowers*	Small dry fruit

American Willowherb

Epilobium ciliatum

J	F	M	A	M	J	J	A	S	O	N	D

Native range:

North America also widely naturalised in central and northern Europe

Introduced:

1891

Spread:

Escape from horticulture

Other names:

Fringed Willowherb,
Northern Willowherb,
Epilobium adencaulon

DESCRIPTION: Erect *perennial* herb, 75 (100)cm, often reddish, without stolons with short leafy basal rosette. Stem with 4 raised lines (2 at base), upper part with hairs and in autumn producing leafy overwintering rosettes with stalkless leaves. **Leaves:** *Mostly opposite, oblong-lanceolate, 3–10cm long, 1–3cm wide,* shiny, yellowish-green above, paler beneath, sometimes tinged red, *hairless, toothed with slightly heart-shaped base and short leaf stalk,* 0.1–0.5cm. **Flowers:** *Pale purplish-pink or white,* 0.8–1cm, 4 deeply lobed petals that can appear as four pairs, *gap between petals,* stigma club-shaped. Self-pollinated. **Fruit:** Elongated 4-sided pod that splits when ripe. **Seeds:** Egg-shaped, flattened, about 1mm long, with plume of long silky hairs, longitudinal papilose ridges with extra appendage 0.05–0.2mm long at hairy end (use hand lens - x20 essential). **Identification year-round:** Easy with flowers and seeds (use a hand lens), less so when not flowering or seeding. In winter look for overwintering rosettes.

STATUS: Very common, rapidly spreading to north and west. Spreads readily by wind-dispersed seed, establishing rapidly.

HABITAT: Disturbed ground especially in urban areas (roadsides, waste ground, gardens, on walls and in pavement cracks), damp woodland, cultivated land, occasionally grows in semi-natural habitats, including marshes.

IMPACT: Although one of the most frequent non-native species, none recorded for Britain but a serious weed in parts of North America.

Key differences between similar species

Similar to other erect willowherbs (up to 75cm) and their hybrids of which a number can be confused with American Willowherb.

New Zealand Willowherb

Epilobium brunnescens

| J | F | M | A | M | J | J | A | S | O | N | D |

Native range:

New Zealand

Introduced:

1904

Spread:

Escape from horticulture

Other names:

Epilobium nerterioides

DESCRIPTION: Creeping perennial almost hairless herb, up to 20cm long, prostrate and forming mats up to 2m across with slender stems rooting at nodes. Up to 4cm high. Much branched, branches often with ascending tips. **Leaves:** *Rounded, opposite, 0.3–7 (10)mm long, 3–6mm wide, slightly toothed, bronzy green above, often purplish beneath, short leaf stalk, 0.5–3mm long.* **Flowers:** Pale pink to white, solitary, petals 0.3–0.4cm, in leaf axils, 4 deeply notched petals and sepals often reddish, on long erect stalk, up to 4cm. Self-pollinated. **Roots:** Weakly rooted. **Fruit:** Elongate 4-sided pod that splits when ripe, long stalk, 2–6cm. **Seeds:** 0.7mm, uniformly papillose, truncate at hairy end, with tuft of hairs persistent or dropping off. **Identification year-round:** Can be recognised by characteristic creeping form, present thoughout the year.

STATUS: Widespread and increasing in upland areas in west, north and north-west Britain. Originally introduced as rock-garden species. Spreads by seeds and fragments, rooting at the nodes.

HABITAT: Damp bare ground from acidic to very base-rich, on gravel, sandy, gritty or stony soils, streamsides, ditches, tracks and paths, scree, quarries, damp stone walls and banks. Well naturalised in many remote localities.

IMPACT: Occupies large patches of wetland areas including beds of standing or flowing waterbodies which might otherwise support native plants.

Key differences between similar species

Similar to hybrids of New Zealand Willowherb and other willowherbs, and other creeping willowherbs (up to 20cm).

- **Rockery Willowherb**, *Epilobium pedunculare*. Non-native. Known from only a few places in England, Scotland and Wales. Forms loose mats up to 0.5m across. Larger, rounder, more sharply toothed leaves. Long fruit stalks, 5–10cm.
- **Bronzy Willowherb**, *Epilobium komarovianum*. Non-native. Known from only a few places in England and Scotland. Forms mats up to 0.5m across. Untoothed elliptical leaves. Bronzy above, usually green beneath.

Hottentot Fig

J F M A M J J A S O N D

Native range:

South Africa.

Introduced:

1886 (arrived in GB about 1690)

Spread:

Escape from horticulture

Other names:

Sour Fig, Sally-my-handsome, *Mesembryanthemum*

DESCRIPTION: Low, trailing, *succulent, mat-forming evergreen* perennial up to 3m long, woody stem, 8–13mm in diameter, 25cm high. **Leaves:** *In opposite pairs, united at the base, 3-angled, tapered, slightly curved, 4–12cm long, 1–1.5cm wide.* Dark yellowish-green, turning reddish in autumn and when older. **Flowers:** *Striking large silky and daisy-like*, stalked, numerous petals, yellow fading to pale pink; pinkish-purple; or pink with yellow bases, 4.5–10cm in diameter, usually with *yellow centre, only open in afternoon.* Pollinated by a range of insects. **Roots:** New roots form at each node giving a dense fibrous shallow root system. **Fruit:** Fleshy, indehiscent, slightly fig-like, edible. **Seeds:** Embedded in mucilage. **Identification year-round:** Can always be identified from leaves. Flowers are very obvious.

STATUS: Limited to coastal areas. Planted to stabilise sand dunes and as a garden throw-out. Subsequently spreads by vegetative propagation by runners rooting at nodes, and through seeds ingested by Rabbits, deer and rodents and spread in droppings. Ingestion enhances germination. **HABITAT:** Mild coastal areas, sea cliffs and sand dunes. **IMPACT:** Forms large dense mats, displacing native vegetation of cliff tops and other coastal habitats. Even if damaged can regrow from fragments or seed. Alters soil conditions, increasing nitrogen and organic carbon.

Key differences between similar species

There are several other introduced species, including Purple Dewplant (page 110), also a mesembryanthemum and found in the same habitat as Hottentot Fig. In west Cornwall and the Scilly Isles there are even more species of this family.

	Hottentot Fig *Carpobrotus edulis* (non-native)	Sally-my-handsome *Carpobrotus acinaciformis* (non-native)	Angular Sea Fig *Carpobrotus glaucescens* (non-native)	Purple Dewplant *Disphyma crassifolium* (non-native)
Flowers	*Large*, 4.5–10cm in diameter, usually *yellow* fading to pink (not white or yellow at base) with yellow centre	*Large, 8–12cm in diameter, always pink to purple, numerous petals with purple centre*	*Small, 3.5–6.5cm in diameter, pink to purple, white* or yellow at *base* of petals, more or less without stalk	*2.5–5cm in diameter, white below, purple above. Fewer petals*
Leaves	In *pairs, three-angled*, equally thick for most of length, 5–*12cm*	In *pairs, three-angled, noticeably curved, broadest above middle, narrowing abruptly to a sharp tip, 4–10cm*	In *pairs, three-angled, 2–7cm long*	*Cylindrical, smooth, curved like jelly beans, dark green to reddish-green. 1.5–4cm long*
Fruit	*Not longer than wide*		*Longer than wide*	Rather spongy, opening by 5 winged valves
Distribution	See distribution map	Mainly in coastal south-west England	Scattered round coast in a few locations	Scattered round coast in a few locations

Sally-my-handsome
Carpobrotus acinaciformis

Angular Sea Fig
Carpobrotus glaucescens

Purple Dewplant
Disphyma crassifolium

Purple Dewplant

Disphyma crassifolium

J	F	M	A	M	J	J	A	S	O	N	D

Native range:

North America; widely naturalised elsewhere in Europe

Introduced:

1836 (arrived in GB 1727)

Spread:

Escape from cultivation

Other names:

Rounded Noon-flower

DESCRIPTION: Low-growing, *mat-forming, succulent* perennial up to 1m long, stem woody at base, well branched, 9cm high. **Leaves:** *In pairs, cylindrical (slightly flat on upper surface), smooth, 1.5–4cm long, 0.5–1cm wide, curved like jelly beans, dark green to reddish-green with translucent dots.* **Flowers:** Bright reddish or pinkish-purple, 2.5 to 4 (5)cm in diameter, *white below, purple above*, numerous petals. Insect-pollinated. **Roots:** Rooting at nodes. **Fruit:** Rather spongy woody capsule, opening by 5 winged valves. **Identification year-round:** Can always be identified from leaves. Flowers are obvious.

STATUS: Scattered round coast, mainly in southern England. A throw-out from gardens, also originating from wool shoddy (inferior woollen yarn), subsequently spreads by vegetative propagation by runners rooting at nodes. Viable seed is produced in Britain but seedlings have not been seen in the wild.

HABITAT: Mild coastal areas, sea cliffs and sand places. Less susceptible to frost damage than other mesembryanthemums.

IMPACT: Forms dense mats displacing native vegetation.

Key differences between similar species

Several other introduced mesembryanthemum species are similar including Hottentot Fig (page 108), and found in the same habitat.

Thorn Apple

Native range:

Central and South America

Introduced:

1777 (arrived in GB 1597)

Spread:

Escaped from cultivation for alkaloid harvesting

Other names:

Jimsonweed, *Datura tatula* and *Datura inermis*

Use gloves if handling this plant

DESCRIPTION: Erect and stout hairless annual with an *unpleasant musky smell*, stem tough with round cross-section, 1 (1.5)m tall, stem >0.5cm in diameter. **Leaves:** Alternate, shiny dark green on upper surface, pointed, diamond to oval, *coarsely lobed,* jaggedly toothed, often asymmetric at base, 5–10 (18)cm long, 4–15cm wide, on long stalks 7(11)cm. **Flowers:** *White* (rarely purple), solitary, *trumpet-shaped, 6–8cm across, 5–10cm long, five pointed lobes*. Self-fertilising, also cross-pollinated by insects (mainly hawkmoths and honeybees). **Fruit:** *Large, oval*, green erect *capsule containing 100 or more seeds with 100–200 almost equal sharp spines or tubercles up 15mm long,* nauseating odour, rarely smooth, (3) 4–5 (7)cm long, opening by 4 flaps, like a Horse Chestnut. **Seeds:** Black or grey, kidney-shaped 3–4mm, strongly compressed, with regular small depressions. **Identification year-round:** Flowers and fruit enable easy identification; not easy to recognise after dieback.

STATUS: Naturalised or casual throughout Britain but not in northern Scotland and Ireland. Overall, may be declining. Spread as garden escape, via bird seed and as contaminant of bags of South American fertiliser. Can reappear after long periods from dormant seeds.
HABITAT: Waste ground, rubbish tips, manure heaps, field margins and other disturbed ground. Irregular in its appearances.
IMPACT: All parts of the plant are very poisonous. Can cause dermatitis on contact with skin.

Key differences between similar species
- **Angels Trumpets** *Datura ferox*. Capsule erect with <60 spines of unequal length.
- **Recurved Thorn Apple** *Datura innoxia*. Capsule bent sharply downwards.

Variegated Yellow Archangel

Lamiastrum galeobdolon subspecies *argentatum*

Native range:

Origin uncertain, thought to be a subspecies of *Lamiastrum gale-obdolon* subspecies *montanum*

Introduced:

1974 (late 1960s)

Spread:

Escaped from cultivation

Other names:

Aluminium Archangel,
Galeobdolon argentatum,
Lamium galeobdolon variegatum

DESCRIPTION: Erect hairy perennial with long *creeping leafy runners rooting at nodes, square stem*; flowering stems 20–60cm tall. **Leaves:** Opposite, hairy, oval, pointed, 4–7cm long, rounded at base and coarsely toothed, *10–14 teeth each side* with large distinctive permanent *silvery-whitish blotches* throughout the year turning *brownish-maroon along midrib and lateral veins in winter.* Smell slightly of paraffin. Leaf stalk 1–3cm long. **Flowers:** *Yellow with hooded upper petal* and *three lobed lower petal* streaked with *reddish-brown lines* and two-lipped in whorls in leaf axils arranged around leaf stalk. Self-fertilising, also cross-pollinated by insects. **Roots:** Weakly rooted with pale brown fibrous roots, 10–15cm long. **Fruit and seeds:** 3 x 2mm, obovoid, up to 800 seeds per plant, hidden inside remains of flower. **Identification year-round:** Leaf variegation is characteristic, flowers obvious.

STATUS: Scattered over Britain especially south-west. Garden throw-outs subsequently spreading vegetatively. In parts of USA, seeds dispersed up to 70m by ants attracted to specific oils within the seed.
HABITAT: Gardens, roadsides, woodland, shaded streamsides, woodland edges, tracksides, often in shady conditions and on a range of soils.
IMPACT: Creeping runners can overwhelm other species. Rampant, aggressive and can quickly form extensive patches. Genetic transfer with native subspecies and possible dilution and loss of native genetic diversity.

Key differences between similar species
Similar to native **Yellow Archangel** (*Lamiastrum galeobdolon* subspecies *montanum* and subspecies *galeobdolon*) and White Dead-nettle (*Lamium album*). Both can have same creeping form, but all lack the distinctive variegated leaves.

Grasses and bamboos

The grass family (Poaceae or Gramineae) contains more species than any other family of flowering plants and they grow on all continents in a wide range of habitats. Surprisingly there are relatively few invasive non-native grass species in Great Britain. They comprise annuals or herbaceous and, in the case of bamboos, woody perennials.

None of the bamboos (sub-family Bambusoideae) is native to Great Britain. A number of bamboos have naturalised and some are invasive. They are evergreen woody (or herbaceous) perennials, the leaves staying green through an average winter. The stems of these bamboos are round and the leaves are <3 (4)cm wide.

This field guide describes two grass species and bamboos (pages 114–117). Grasses have a number of useful characteristics to help in their identification.

Leaves The leaves are arranged on the stem in two alternating rows distinguishing them from sedges, the leaves of which are arranged in three rows. A leaf comprises a long narrow blade and a sheath around the stem. The blade is typically linear, flat and thin, often rolled or folded along the long axis. Sheaths begin at nodes and wrap firmly or loosely around the internode, usually split with overlapping edges. In bamboos, the leaves often have a false leaf-stalk separating them from the sheath. At the junction of the blade and the sheath is the ligule, a membrane or line of hairs.

Flowers The small greenish flowers lack petals and sepals, are located between two bracts and are arranged into units called spikelets, clustered together to form a flower head or spike.

Stem Usually round, hollow, interrupted at intervals by nodes, cylindrical (rarely flattened and not 3–angled) and may grow upright or be bent at their bases.

Roots All originating from a node, fibrous and relatively shallow, typically penetrating much less than a metre into the ground, often greatly branched and with rhizomes or stolons.

An aerial view of the great area covered by clumps of Pampas Grass *Cortaderia seloana* which has become a seriously invasive species in the Camargue, Southern France.

Pampas Grass

| J | F | M | A | M | J | J | A | S | O | N | D |

Native range:

South America

Introduced:

1925 (1849)

Spread:

Escaped from horticulture

Other names:

Silver Pampas Grass, Uruguayan Pampas Grass

DESCRIPTION: Very large densely tufted, perennial tussock-forming grass more than *1m across*. Stems erect up to *3m*. **Leaves:** 1–3m long, *bluish-white or bluish-green*, flat, hard, linear, acute at the apex with *cutting serrated edges and marked longitudinal ribs; a line of hairs for a ligule*. **Flowers:** *Very large spreading many-branched seed head 30–100 (120)cm long*; hairy mass when fruiting *silvery-white or purple-tinged*. **Roots:** Can extend deep into the soil. **Seeds:** A grain covered in hairs. Wind-dispersed. **Identification year-round:** Flower heads remain which coupled with the plant's size make it easy to identify.

STATUS: Naturalised in unevenly dispersed small populations mainly in south-west England, increasing at a steady rate. Most populations result from garden throw-outs or deliberate planting. Seed easily carried by the wind. Seedlings are increasingly common. Also spreads by rhizomes. **HABITAT:** Mainly found on roadsides, railway banks, maritime cliffs and dunes in the south. Can tolerate saline conditions and thrives in moist soils. **IMPACT:** Forms dense stands and displaces other plants. Leaf litter is substantial, slow to decompose and smothers other plants. Provides a suitable habitat for vermin, has sharp leaves and is highly flammable.

Key differences between similar species

Distinguished from **Early Pampas Grass** *Cortaderia richardii* (non-native) by the latter's flowering stems and heads (>60cm) drooping to one side and leaf blades being dark green on both sides with a strong midrib and strong veins on either side but lacks longitudinal ribs. Inflorescence has a pale gold to cream colour. June–September. Found in moist conditions. During early stages of growth, both look very similar and make it very hard to distinguish between them.

Miscanthus grasses

Chinese Silver Grass *Miscanthus sinensis* and
Elephant Grass *Miscanthus sacchariflorus* x *Miscanthus sinensis* (*Miscanthus* x *giganteus*)

J F **M A M** J J **A S O** N D

Native range:

East Asia

Introduced:

Miscanthus sinensis 1983 (19th century); *Miscanthus sacchariflorus* 1973 (19th century)

Spread:

Escaped from horticulture

DESCRIPTION: Very tall herbaceous perennial grasses. Elephant Grass stems up to 4m. Chinese Silver Grass 0.8–2 (4)m. **Leaves:** Elephant Grass: 40–120cm long, 1–2 (4)cm wide; leaf sheaths reddish at base, ligule up to 1.5mm. Chinese Silver-grass: 18–75cm long, 0.3–2 (4)cm wide; leaf sheaths not reddish at base, ligule up to 4mm. *Ligule membranous, fringed with hairs.* **Flowers:** Purplish; late October (Elephant Grass) and September (Chinese Silver Grass). **Roots:** Short and shallow. **Seed:** Plumed grain; wind-dispersed. **Identification year-round:** The plants remain standing when dead, so identifiable in all seasons.

STATUS: Possible escape from gardens and biofuel crops.
HABITAT: Open and disturbed ground including gravel workings.
IMPACT: Could potentially outcompete native species if they were to produce dense stands. Invasive in North America.

Species	Chinese Silver Grass *Miscanthus sinensis* (non-native) *Eulalia japonica*	Elephant Grass *Miscanthus sacchari-florus* x *Miscanthus sinensis* (*Miscanthus* x *giganteus*) (non-native)	Common Reed *Phragmites australis* (native)	Giant Reed *Arundo donax* (non-native)	Pampas Grass *Cortaderia selloana* (non-native)
Height	Up to 2(4)m	Up to 4m	Up to 3.5m	Up to 6m	Up to 3m
Flower colour	Purplish*	Purplish*	Purplish*	Light green/whitish to silvery purple	Silvery white
Ligule	Membranous with fringe of hairs, up to 1.5mm long	Membranous with fringe of hairs, up to 4mm long	Fringe of hairs only	Large papery with small hairs along margin	Dense fringe of silky hairs only
Habitat	Clump-forming and tussock-forming	Clump-forming	Clump-forming	Clump-forming	Tussock-forming

* Ornamentals can have various colours

Bamboos

| J | F | M | A | M | J | J | A | S | O | N | D |

Native range:

Mostly southern hemisphere especially East Asia. No native bamboo species in Europe

Introduced:

1960s onwards (1860s onwards)

Spread:

Escape from horticulture

Identification of bamboos to species or even genus is very difficult. It is dependent on flower structure and many bamboos rarely flower in Britain. The taxonomy of bamboos is unsettled and the names of the genera and species may change.

DESCRIPTION: A group of woody perennial rhizomatous evergreens in the grass family, most of which are large up to 6m or more. More than 20 species known in Britain. Woody stems hollow between nodes. **Leaves:** Flat, longitudinal veins often with conspicuous cross veins, tough. Most have a distinct short leaf stalk between the blade and the sheath. **Roots/rhizome:** A useful division is between the clump-forming species and the creeping bamboos. The latter are more likely to become invasive. **Identification year-round:** As evergreens bamboos are present in all seasons.

Clump-forming bamboos such as Chinese Fountain Bamboo *Fargesia spathacea*. **Rhizome:** Relatively short and thick curving upwards in close proximity to the main plant; each rhizome terminates in a new shoot producing a single stem or culm; horizontal growth by short distances each year, new rhizomes or roots can be produced at nodes. New culms can only form at the very tip of the rhizome causing them to curve upwards and exhibit the clumping behaviour.

Running (or creeping) bamboos such as Broad-leaved Bamboo *Sasa palmata* and Simon's Bamboo *Pleioblastus simonii*, adapted to rapidly colonising areas of suitable ground. Culms are more widely separated from each other. **Rhizome:** Long and thin, usually growing and branching away from main plant in straight lines each forming buds that produce new culms at regular intervals; some species can send rhizomes up to 7m away in a single growing season. Buds can be produced at the nodes forming either new culms or rhizomes. Running bamboos are typically spaced over a wide area and are invasive.

STATUS: Seldom escape beyond the parks and gardens in which they have been and continue to be widely grown. Can persist in locations for decades. All bamboos reproduce largely vegetatively by sending up new shoots from rhizomes. Flowering is very rare in most species.
HABITAT: Planted and naturalised in lowland areas in woodland, by rivers and in parks and estates in moist and shaded conditions and found as a relic of cultivation.
IMPACT: Vigorous and extensive growth can displace native species; can be extremely difficult to remove a well established plant.

	Description	Distribution	Date of introduction (arrived in GB) and origin
Arrow Bamboo (Metake) *Pseudosasa japonica* (non-native)	Large with very short running rhizomes, stem 2.5–2 (5)m. Mostly with one branch at each upper node only: stem round cross-section except just above nodes. Leaves broad (8)15–30cm long, 2–4cm wide, partly hairless on underside, mostly 5–9 veins either side of midrib, ¾ underside bluish-white, can brown in cold snaps. Flowers freely and regularly	Increasing, mostly due to deliberate planting and ability to persist; long established in numerous localities. Widespread in south and south-west England and west Wales; rare in Scotland and Ireland	1955 (1850) Japan and Korea
Broad-leaved Bamboo *Sasa palmata* (non-native)	Large with far creeping running rhizomes: stem 2–3m, 1cm in diameter, mottled purple, round cross-section except just above nodes; nodes mostly with one lateral branch. Leaves large up to 40cm long, 3.5–7 (9)cm wide, shining green above, paler beneath, leaf stalk usually green 8–14 veins either side of midrib. Flowers fairly frequently	Established in widely scattered localities across Britain and Ireland, occasionally in very large thickets. Increasing, mostly due to deliber-ate planting	1964 (about 1889) Japan and Sakhalin
Square-stemmed Bamboo *Chimonobambusa quadrangularis* (non-native)	Large with running rhizomes: stem 3–8m, square in cross-section, grey-green colour with a matt appearance and rough edges and faces, nodes mostly with 3 branches. Leaves 8–29cm long; 2–3cm wide and glossy, 8–14 veins on either side of midrib with distinct cross-veins	Naturalised in thickets in south-west England and Ireland.	1993 (about 1892) China
Chinese Fountain Bamboo *Fargesia spathacea* (non-native)	Very large, clump-forming, stem 4–6m, slender, arching canes, round cross-section except just above nodes: nodes with 3 or more lateral branches with 45° upward slope. Leaves many, small, 6–9cm long; 8–11mm wide, hairless with short stalk, 3–4 veins either side of midrib, can brown and fall in cold snaps	Can spread and has persisted for more than 80 years in a woodland in Leicestershire, where it was originally planted	1964 (1889) West China
Maximowicz's Bamboo *Pleioblastus chino* (non-native)	Large with running rhizomes, stem 1–2 (3)m, 1.5cm in diam-eter, 2 to many branches per node, round cross-section except just above nodes. Leaves mostly >10 (20)cm long, narrow, uniformly green on both sides, occasionally variegated, 2–7 veins on each side of midrib	Rarely encountered in the wild (mainly southern England and Wales) but may be under-recorded	1964 (1876) Japan
Dwarf Bamboo *Pleioblastus pymaeus* (non-native)	Running rhizomes, stem 0.5–1m, 0.3cm in diameter 1–2 branches per node, stem round cross-section except just above nodes. Leaves all <10cm long, 0.3–1.5cm wide, with 2–3 veins on either side of midrib	Popular in gardens and can be persistent. Only recently been recorded from the wild in southern and south-west England	Recent (1860s) Japan
Simon's Bamboo *Pleioblastus simonii* (non-native)	Running rhizomes, stem 3–5 (7)m, arching when mature, 2 to many branches per node, round cross-section except just above nodes. Leaves mostly >10cm long, 1.5–2.5cm wide, usually half bluish-white on underside, 4–7 veins on each side of midrib	Rarely persistent. Only known from south coast	1965 (about 1862) Japan
Veitch's Bamboo *Sasa veitchii* (non-native)	Running rhizomes, stem 0.5–1.5m, 0.7cm in diameter, purplish, round cross-section except just above nodes, nodes mostly with one lateral branch. Leaves 2.5–6cm long, 1.5–3.5 (6)cm wide, blunt with broad whitish and withered margins in winter, stalks often purplish, (5) 6–9 veins either side of midrib	Increasingly popular in gardens, despite being extremely vigorous and invasive. Occasional in southern and south-west England, rare elsewhere	1962 (about 1880) Japan
Hairy Bamboo *Sasaella ramosa* (*Arundinaria vagans*) (non-native)	Far-creeping running rhizomes, stem up to 1(1.5)m, slightly zig-zag, 1 branch at each node on top half of stem only; sheaths persistent. Leaves 12–20cm long, 1–2.5cm wide, hairy on underside, held in distinctive palm-like fan shape	Increasingly popular in gardens forming dense patches. Southern England, Surrey in particular, rare in Wales, not known from wild in Scotland or Ireland	1983 (1892) Japan
Narihira Bamboo (Narihiradake) *Semiarundi-naria fatuosa* (non-native)	Clump-forming with very shortly creeping rhizome, stem erect, 3–6(8)m, green aging to red-purple, sometimes flattened or grooved at top, nodes of mid-region of main stems mostly with 3–5 branches. Leaves 10–15cm long, 1–2.5cm wide, often purplish	Popular in gardens but rare in wild	1967 (1892) Japan
Indian Fountain Bamboo *Yushania anceps* (non-native)	Clump-forming but can behave more like running species. Large, stem 3–4 (6)m, often purplish, short plants upright but weight of foliage causes taller stems to arch over. 15cm long; 18mm wide, but often considerably smaller with short leaf stalk. Unusually reproduction by seed has been reported	Increasingly popular in gardens, can be persistent, forming thickets and may be increasing	1961 (about 1865) Central and north-west Himalayas

Mosses and liverworts

The mosses and liverworts, or bryophytes (Bryophyta), are a well-defined group of green non-flowering plants. They are mostly small (2–5cm tall) and simple, lacking highly developed structures such as flowers, seeds and roots, and spread by spores. There are 600 species of mosses and 280 species of liverworts in Great Britain, living in a wide range of habitats but they are most abundant in humid environments and some are aquatic.

A moss plant consists of leaves and stem, the leaves being organised more or less spirally around the stem, and most have a midrib or nerve. The leaves are never lobed or divided.

A liverwort is either undifferentiated into stem and leaves, consisting of a flattened frond or thallus, or in the case of the leafy liverworts, the leaves are usually divided into segments and lack a midrib or nerve.

In both mosses and liverworts, root-like threads or rhizoids attach the plant to its growing surface.

There are relatively few invasive non-native species of bryophytes, most of these being mosses. This field guide describes five moss and liverwort species (pages 119–121 and on page 139 for aquatic species).

Mosses and liverworts have a number of useful characteristics to help in their identification. In order to see these clearly it is necessary to use a hand lens:

*   General appearance, for example growing in tufts, carpets or mats
*   Leaves including colour, size, shape including nature of the tip
*   Shape, size and surface texture of capsules when present

Heath Star-moss *Campylopus introflexus* forming a dense carpet on peat.

Heath Star-moss

Campylopus introflexus

| J | F | M | A | M | J | J | A | S | O | N | D |

Native range:

Southern hemisphere, also widespread elsewhere in north-west Europe

Introduced:

1941

Spread:

Spreads by spores

Other names:

None.

DESCRIPTION: *Moss*, often abundant, forming *dark green or blackish, rather hoary tufts* or carpets up to 5 (10)cm tall but usually much less. Conspicuously white-grey when dry due to *white 'stars'* formed by long silvery hair points on upper leaves. Stems erect with swollen nodes, clusters of short branches commonly form dense heads (use a hand lens). **Leaves:** Olive-green to green, 2.5–6.5mm long, erect, stiff and straight with a sheen when moist; *a toothed white hair* at tip, the latter bending back markedly when dry (use a hand-lens). **Fruit:** *Capsules*, oval-cylindrical 1–1.4mm long, deeply furrowed and shrunken when dried; stem *curves down strongly*; frequently formed in wetter areas, often in considerable quantities, ripening in spring–early summer. **Identification year-round:** Plant present in all seasons.

STATUS: Locally plentiful, commonest in north and west, less so in central and east England. Spreads easily by spores even over long distances, locally by vegetative propagation from leaves or shoot tips. **HABITAT:** Bare peat especially after peat-cutting, burning or ploughing for forestry. As an early colonist, spreads rapidly to cover large areas. Occasionally on rotting logs, old fence posts, roof tiles, thatch, sand dunes, shingle, thin soil in woodland at edges of tracks, railway ballast, mine waste but rare on rocks and trees. **IMPACT:** Out-competes and displaces other mosses and lichens. Carpets on peat can reduce regeneration of heathland preventing establishment of native species.

Key differences between similar species
Stiff Swan-neck Moss, *Campylopus pilifer* (native) grows in small dark green patches; stem uniformly thick; leaf hair points are straight or slightly curved back when dry; very scarce, restricted to cracks and crevices in dry rocks and thin stony soil overlying rocks, mostly near west coast.

Cape Thread-moss

Orthodontium lineare

J	F	M	A	M	J	J	A	S	O	N	D

Native range:

Southern hemisphere, also spreading eastwards in continental Europe

Introduced:

1910

Spread:

Spreads by spores

Other names:

None.

DESCRIPTION: *Moss*, forming *extensive low, silky dull green tufts or carpets* up to 1cm tall. **Leaves:** Very fine, soft with plain margins, 3–4mm long; lower leaves much shorter, with slight sheen and slightly curved back when dry, acute apex, pointing down characteristically below the horizontal, often weakly curved in one direction when moist (use a hand lens). **Fruit:** *Narrow, club-shaped capsule, gradually taper into a stalk*, smooth when wet, often produced in vast numbers in late spring, ripening in early summer. Stalk *about 5mm long, green-yellow, arcuate*, thin, characteristically curved so capsules held below horizontal. *When green and young, capsules held at an oblique angle with characteristically upturned beak*. Mature and empty capsules erect, turning reddish-brown, becoming distinctly and deeply furrowed (use a hand lens). **Identification year-round:** Plant present in all seasons.

STATUS: Widely distributed and spreading by spores, locally abundant.
HABITAT: Wide range of acidic habitats, particularly on vertical surfaces, pollution-tolerant, in both shady and sunny places, on sandy and peaty banks, dry peat, logs, stumps, tree roots and rotting wood, on siliceous cliffs and crags, particularly sandstone, forming extensive patches.
IMPACT: Out-competes and displaces other species with similar habitat requirements, such as mosses and lichens.

Key differences between similar species
Similar to other delicate, native fine-leaved mosses.
- **Orthodontium gracile.** Very rare. *Dull, silky, light green leaves. Pale, smooth capsule when mature and empty. Transverse sections of well-developed leaves viewed under a microscope can be used to separate the two species although differentiation is difficult.*
- **Dicranella heteromalla.** Slightly more robust moss. *Leaves tapering, finely pointed usually markedly turned in one direction. Furrowed brown capsule is abruptly contracted into its stalk.*
- **Campylopus flexuosus.** Much wider nerve. More rigid leaves.

Southern Crestwort

Lophocolea semiteres

Native range:

Southern hemisphere, also spreading elsewhere in north-west Europe

Introduced:

1955

Spread:

Spreads by spores and regenerants

Other names:

Chiloscyphus semiteres,
Jungermannia semiteres

DESCRIPTION: A *delicate, translucent, slightly aromatic, pale green leafy liverwort* looking somewhat like a moss, sometimes forming extensive mats. Male plants very conspicuous and much commoner than females. Shoots 0.5–3mm wide. **Leaves:** *Overlapping each other and completely hiding stem* use a hand lens), almost all turning in one direction, pale or yellowish green, delicate, translucent, entire or slightly and bluntly notched, up to 1.8mm wide, 1.5mm long growing in an unusual, flat pattern. *Underleaves bilobed with spreading lobes*, toothed edges and often partly fused with lateral leaves on one or both sides. When drying, leaves tend to curl upwards and plant appears much yellower and narrower. Aromatic scent. **Fruit:** Capsules rare. Spring. Sporophytes locally abundant. October-March. Spores 16–19µm. **Identification year-round:** Plant present in all seasons.

STATUS: Frequent and spreading in England, less frequent in Wales and Scotland. Sporophytes rare, but older leaves found to produce abundant vegetative propagules.

HABITAT: Grows in extensive often almost pure carpets in open habitats such as acid heaths, on peaty soil, heathy cliff tops and non-basic dunes, and in shady habitats such as pine forests and tree bases, rotting logs, especially under conifers.

Impact: Displaces native liverworts, mosses and lichens in a variety of habitats.

Key differences between similar species

Lophocolea semiteres is larger than **Bifid Crestwort** *Lophocolea bidentata* and **Variable-leaved Crestwort** *Lophocolea heterophylla* (both native). In the latter lower leaves bilobed. **St Winfred's Moss** *Chiloscyphus polyanthus* and **Pale Liverwort** *Chiloscyphus pallescens* (both native) can be very similar, but underleaves are small, bilobed, with lobes close to and parallel to one another, pointing straight towards the shoot tips, and not partly fused with adjacent lobes. *Lophocolea brookwoodiana* is rare, unscented unlike other *Lophocolea* species.

Aquatic plants

Aquatic plants are those plants which are adapted to living under, on or growing up through water. They come from a number of different plant families and their leaves have adapted in different ways to the aquatic environment. Hence, they have a number of useful characteristics to help in their identification. This field guide describes more than 20 aquatic plant species, which are usefully divided into:

Submerged plants in which the leaves are found below the water surface exhibiting a variety of forms from divided through to oval and linear in shape (pages 124–133)

Floating plants in which the leaves float on the water surface, ranging from the tiny free floating duckweeds to the oval-shaped leaves of pondweeds (pages 134–147) and

Emergent plants in which the leaves grow up and out of the water, with leaf shapes ranging from strap-like through oval to arrow-shaped (pages 148–151).

New Zealand Pigmyweed *Crassula helmsii* can thrive in a range of aquatic habitats. It may displace other aquatic plants as well as reducing the amenity value of a water body.

Some plants span more than one of the three types, for example Carolina Water-shield which sometimes has floating as well as submerged leaves, and the arrowheads, some of which have submerged, floating and emergent leaves.

Non-native aquatic plants make up a disproportionately large proportion of the invasive plants found in Great Britain, an observation which holds true in other parts of the world. A number of these invasive species have been introduced as ornamental pond plants and/or for use in cold water aquaria, excess growth being thrown out and finding its way into a variety of waterbodies.

Invasive non-native aquatic plant species cause significant problems in aquatic systems, from displacing native flora and fauna to impeding flow in streams, rivers and canals and disrupting water sports including angling.

Aquatic plants do not always produce flowers and even when they do, most are relatively insignificant.

Floating Pennywort *Hydrocotyle ranunculoides* can rapidly form very dense mats of vegetation which not only overwhelm native species but can reduce the amount of oxygen within the water, causing harm to air-breathing insects and to native aquatic plants.

Parrot's-feather *Myriophyllum aquaticum* reproduces effectively and can quickly dominate ponds, as well as larger slow-moving water bodies such as reservoirs and canals.

Carolina Water-shield

Cabomba caroliniana

Native range:
Eastern areas of North and South America

Introduced:
1969

Spread:
Escape from horticulture

Other names:

Fanwort

DESCRIPTION: Submerged multi-branched perennial herb, stems long up to 2m rooted in bed of waterbody. Whole plant can have a tubular appearance when submerged, sometimes reddish in colour. Stems fragile, detach easily; with white or reddish-brown hairs. **Leaves:** Submerged leaves bright green, sometimes dark red or purple beneath, 3–5cm long, *in pairs, fan-shaped, finely divided, more than three times leaf stalks; 1–3cm long*. Occasionally also with inconspicuous floating leaves borne on flowering branches, linear, oval-triangular, occasionally split at tip with stem attached in centre, 0.6–2cm. **Flowers:** Solitary, white, small, 6–10mm, six petals with bright yellow centres, slightly above or floating on water surface. **Roots:** Short rhizomes with fibrous roots. **Fruit and seeds:** An indehiscent, usually 3-sided follicle. **Identification year-round:** Dies back in winter but remains submerged and so identifiable year-round.

STATUS: Very occasional outside of gardens. Present in a canal in Hampshire since 1990. A popular aquarium plant and occurrences so far have probably been by intentional introductions or throw-outs. Can set seed, but usually spreads by vegetative reproduction from stem fragments. **HABITAT:** Ponds, lakes, canals and slow flowing rivers, growing down to 3m on a silty bed.
IMPACT: Forms dense stands in The Netherlands that can displace native species as well as clog up waterways. Spreads quickly via stem fragments, making management difficult.

Key differences between similar species

Can be confused with other aquatic species with finely divided leaves and/or whorls.

	Carolina Water-shield *Cabomba caroliniana* (non-native)	Milfoils *Myriophyllum* species (native and non-native)	Water-crowfoots *Ranunculus* species (native)	Hornworts *Ceratophyllum* species (native)
Habit	Submerged aquatic (except for flowers)	Submerged (except for flowers) and, in some species, *emergent* leaves	Submerged aquatic (except for flowers), sometimes with floating leaves	Submerged aquatic (including flowers)
Leaves	*Finely divided* submerged leaves in pairs with fan shape and leaf stalk. Occasionally small floating leaves (0.6–2cm)	*Herringbone-shaped* pinnate leaves, 4–6 in *a whorl*. No floating leaves	Submerged leaves *finely divided* in threes, alternate (never opposite), with 6–30 segments; no leaf stalk. Can have *small broad, floating buttercup-shaped* leaves	Divided leaves in *whorls* with *'tuning fork' ends*. No floating leaves
Flowers	*Obvious at surface, white* with six petals, *solitary/in clusters* not spike, 6–10mm	At surface, in short spike, 4–6 in a whorl, tiny, *red with yellowish or green tinge*	Obvious at surface, solitary, white with five petals (7–30mm)	Submerged, minute, rarely produced, *solitary* in leaf axils, green to whitish

Milfoils
Myriophyllum species

Water-crowfoots
Ranunculus species

Hornworts
Ceratophyllum species

Parrot's-feather

Myriophyllum aquaticum

Native range:

Central South America

Introduced:

1960 (arrived in GB 1878)

Spread:

Escape from horticulture

Other names:

Parrot-feather, Water-milfoil

DESCRIPTION: *Emergent and submerged perennial (submerged only in fast flowing water).* Long trailing stems up to 2m, 3–4mm in diameter, brittle. Emergent stem up to 30cm. **Leaves**: In whorls of 4–6, emergent leaves feathery, pale blue-green, finely pinnate with 8–30 segments and covered with a waxy coating. Submersed leaves limp and brownish, often in a state of deterioration. **Flowers**: Inconspicuous, 2mm in diameter, only female, white, 4–6 in a whorl; borne in the axils of the emergent leaves. July-August. **Roots**: Rooting at lower nodes. **Fruit and seeds**: None produced in Britain and Ireland. **Identification year-round:** Frost-tolerant and present throughout the year.

STATUS: Becoming common in southern Britain, spreading northwards. Rare in Scotland and Ireland. Garden throw-out. Spread is only by vegetative reproduction from stem fragments.
HABITAT: Small, sheltered, nutrient-rich water bodies, especially ponds and ditches. Also grows in reservoirs, canals and flooded quarries.
IMPACT: Choking waterbodies and waterways.

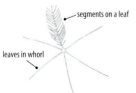

segments on a leaf

leaves in whorl

Key differences between similar species

Can be confused with native species of water-milfoil, hornwort, Mare's-tail, Water Violet and the non-native Carolina Water-shield.

	Flowers	Leaves		Habit
Parrot's-feather *Myriophyllum aquaticum* (non-native)	Submerged and emergent stems. Spreading in England and Wales, rare in Scotland and Ireland	Blue-grey, herring-bone pattern with 8–30 segments, 4–6 in a whorl		In spike, 4–6 in a whorl, tiny, white. July–August
Unevenleafed Feather-weed *Myriophyllum heterophyllum* (non-native)	Submerged and emergent stems. Very rare	Emergent leaves narrowly oval and pointed, edges may be toothed; submerged leaves with 5–12 segments; transitional leaves pinnately cut; in whorls of 4 or 6		In a spike, 4–6 in a whorl; 4 stamens (other *Myriophyllum* species have 8 (use a hand lens)). July–August.
Whorled Water-milfoil *Myriophyllum verticillatum* (native)	Submerged stems (except for flowers). Scattered in England, Welsh borders and Ireland	Herring-bone pattern with 24–35 segments, 5 in a whorl		In spike, 5 in a whorl, greenish. July–August
Spiked Water-milfoil *Myriophyllum spicatum* (native)	Submerged stems (except for flowers). Throughout Britain and Ireland	Herring-bone pattern with 13–38 segments, 4 in a whorl, often encrusted		In spike, 4 in a whorl, tiny, reddish petals. June–July
Alternate Water-milfoil *Myriophyllum alterniflorum* (native)	Submerged stems (except for flowers). Throughout Britain and Ireland, more common in west	Herring-bone pattern with 6–18 segments, 4 in a whorl often pinkish		In spike, 2–4 in a whorl with upper flowers opposite or alternate, tiny, petals yellow. May–August
Mare's-tail *Hippuris vulgaris* (native)	Submerged and emergent stems. Throughout Britain and Ireland	Strap-shaped (not divided), in whorls of 6–12		Tiny, pink at base of leaves on emergent stem. June–July
Hornwort *Ceratophyllum* species (native)	Submerged and emergent stems. Throughout Britain and Ireland	Divided leaves in whorls with 'tuning fork' ends		Flowers submerged, small, solitary in leaf axils, green and white. July–September
Water Violet *Hottonia palustris* (native)	Submerged stems (except for flowers). Scattered in England and Wales, very locally naturalised in Scotland and Ireland	Divided leaves arranged alternately		Obvious lilac-pink, in a whorl. May–June
Red (or Australian) Water-milfoil *Myriophyllum verrucosum* (non-native)	Submerged stems (except for flowers). Very rare	Short, upward curved, with 14–20 segments 3 or 4 in a whorl, often deep reddish, rarely >1cm		Solitary

New Zealand Pigmyweed

Crassula helmsii

J F M A M J J A S O N D

Native range:

Australia and New Zealand

Introduced:

1956 (arrived in GB 1927)

Spread:

Escape from horticulture

Other names:

Australian Swamp Stonecrop,
Tillaea recurva, Tillaea aquatica

DESCRIPTION: Perennial submerged and/or amphibious/emergent herb with three growth forms. *Terrestrial plant with stems up to 30cm long and 8cm high trailing or creeping on mud with densely packed fleshy leaves; emergent plant with leaves intermediate between terrestrial and submerged forms; submerged plant with elongated stems up to 3m, relatively sparse leaves, able to form extensive mats on the bed of a water body. Stem round and fleshy* in all three forms. **Leaves:** *Narrow, 4–15 (20) mm long, in opposite pairs. Fleshy when emergent or terrestrial, flatter when permanently submerged. Leaf bases joined around the stem to form a collar.* **Flowers:** *Minute, whitish-green to slightly pink, 4 petals, 1–2mm, solitary* at leaf-stem junctions, with stalks 2–8mm; often absent. **Fruit:** Cluster of few-seeded carpels, rarely seen. **Seeds:** 2–5 tiny elliptical seeds per flower, 0.4–0.5mm long **Identification year-round:** Present throughout the year though dies back in winter.

STATUS: Widespread in England and Wales. Spreading northwards though relatively uncommon in Scotland. Very common in the south-east of England. Garden throw-outs. Spreads by vegetative reproduction from stem fragments. Viable seed not known in Britain.

HABITAT: Submerged in sheltered lowland waters up to 3m deep or as an emergent on soft, damp substrates in a variety of habitats, including ponds, lakes, reservoirs, canals and ditches.

IMPACT: Can form dense stands and can impede drainage and exacerbate flooding. Displaces other aquatic plants and can reduce the amenity value of a water body.

Key differences between similar species

Similar to water-starwort species (native), Water-purslane (native) and Pigmyweed (native).

	New Zealand Pigmyweed *Crassula helmsii* (non-native)	Water-starworts *Callitriche* species (native)	Water Purslane *Lythrum portula* (native)	Pigmyweed *Crassula aquatica* (native) – very rare
Leaf description	*Succulent*, narrow, pointed	*Not fleshy*, leaf tips typically *notched*	*Not fleshy*, oval	*Succulent*, narrow, pointed
Flowers	1–2mm, with *4 white* petals, on 2–8mm *stalk*	Inconspicuous, with up to *2 green* bracteoles (no petals)	Petals *up to 6*, 1mm long, *purplish*	1–2mm, *4 white* petals, *no stalk*
Distribution	*Widespread in England and Wales*	*Very common throughout Britain and Ireland*	*Scattered throughout Britain and Ireland*	*Very rare*

Water-starworts
Callitriche species

Water Purslane
Lythrum portula

Pigmyweed
Crassula aquatica

Large-flowered Waterweed

Egeria densa

J F M A M J J A S O N D

Native range:

South America

Introduced:

1950

Spread:

Escape from horticulture

Other names:

Large-flowered Water-thyme,
Elodea densa

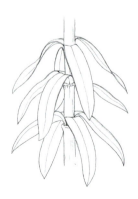

DESCRIPTION: *Submerged* evergreen perennial herb. Stem round, 1–3mm in diameter and 2 (3)m from bed of waterbody; regularly branched. Usually much larger than *Elodea* pondweeds. **Leaves**: *Whorls of (3)4–6(7).* Dark green and occasionally streaked reddish. Minutely serrated, 15–40mm long, 1.5–5mm wide, narrowly oblong to linear, abruptly acute; bent back, not twisted. *Small teeth present along central vein on underside of leaf* but not rough to touch. **Flowers**: Rarely flowers unless water is unusually or artificially warmed. White, up to 2cm across (only male plants in Britain). August–November. **Roots**: White or pale, slender, unbranched. Adventitious roots freely produced from double nodes on the stem. **Identification year-round:** Often present throughout year.

STATUS: Only naturalised in a few locations. Grown in ponds and aquaria, deliberate release or as throw-outs. Reproduces vegetatively from fragments which root readily from nodes on stem.
HABITAT: Waterbodies such as rivers and canals, where it is often naturalised especially if waters are artificially heated, and in ponds and pools, where it may only be casual.
IMPACT: Little impact yet recorded in Britain. In other parts of Europe, can overwhelm waterbodies and out compete native species; chokes up waterways impeding drainage.

Key differences between similar species

May be confused with other waterweeds.

	Large-flowered Waterweed *Egeria densa* (non-native)	Curly Waterweed *Lagarosiphon major* (non-native)	Canadian Waterweed *Elodea canadensis* (non-native)	Nuttall's Waterweed *Elodea nuttallii* (non-native)	South American Waterweed *Elodea callitrichoides* (non-native)	Esthwaite Waterweed *Hydrilla verticillata* (non-native)
Stem (all have round stems) (use hand lens)	1–3mm in diameter with stele not purple	2–2.5mm in diameter with aerenchyma around central stele (use hand lens)	1mm in diameter. Several hollows around central stele like a cartwheel (use hand lens)	1mm in diameter. Several hollows around central stele like a cartwheel (use hand lens)	1mm in diameter	1–2mm in diameter with purple stele
Leaf arrangement (look at leaves lower down the stem)	Whorls of (3)4–6(8) leaves	Lower leaves spiralled, rarely in whorls of 3(4) towards apex of stem	Whorls of 3(4) leaves	Whorls of 3–4 leaves	Upper leaves in whorls of 3 which are often distant	Upper leaves in whorls of (3)4–5(8), leaves in spiral lower down stem
Leaf shape						
Leaf description (all lack a leaf stalk)	15-40mm long, more pointed than Elodea, 5mm wide. Minutely toothed (use hand lens). Reddish streaked. Midrib not rough to touch on leaf underside	Strongly bent back (not twisted), 6-30mm in length, 3mm wide. Minutely toothed (use hand lens). Translucent midrib	Widest in middle, tip is rounded or broadly acute. <17mm in length (measurements from upper leaves). Mainly parallel sided. Not strongly bent back nor twisted. Toothed, often minutely (use hand lens). Midrib visible	Widest at base and tapering to the tip which is narrowly acute or acuminate. <25mm in length; broadest at base and tapering gradually to apex. Usually some leaves bent back and/or twisted. Toothed, often minutely. Midrib visible	Narrowly oval and pointed or narrowly triangular; not strongly bent back or twisted, 9-25mm in length, 0.5-2mm wide. Minutely toothed (use hand lens)	6-20(40)mm in length, 2.25(5)mm in width with obvious toothed edge. Straight not twisted. Midrib, 2-3mm wide, rough to touch on leaf underside, reddish when fresh
Flowers (all have three petals)	+ White, large, 12–20mm in diameter. June–August	* White but inconspicuous, 3mm in diameter. July–August	* White but inconspicuous, 4–5mm in diameter. May–October	* White but inconspicuous, 2–3.5mm. May–September	* White, more conspicuous, 6–7mm in diameter. September–December	* White, 6–10mm in diameter. June–August
Notes		Roots unbranched, white to rusty brown, 0.6–0.8mm in diameter, up to 40(50)cm long	Roots unbranched, thread-like.		Root tips red when fresh. Known as casual from only a few sites in Britain	Only waterweed in Britain to produce tubers

Canadian and Nuttall's Waterweeds

Elodea canadensis and *Elodea nuttallii*

| J | F | M | A | M | J | J | A | S | O | N | D |

Nuttall's Waterweed
Elodea nuttallii

Native range:

North America

Introduced:

Canadian Waterweed 1842
Nuttall's Waterweed 1966

Spread:

Escape from horticulture

Other names:

American Pondweed

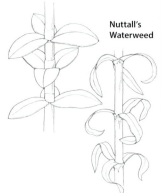

Canadian
Waterweed

Nuttall's
Waterweed

Canadian Waterweed

DESCRIPTION: *Submerged* evergreen perennial herbs. Stems to 3m from bed of water body, branching and often forming dense masses. **Leaves:** Canadian Waterweed in *whorls of 3*, 4.5–17mm long, 1.4–5.6mm wide, *widest in middle*. Nuttall's Waterweed in *whorls of 3–4*, 5.5–35mm long, 0.8–3mm wide, *widest at base* and tapering to the ends. **Flowers:** White, solitary, inconspicuous, 1–6mm across, borne on long thread-like stalk. Only female plants in Britain. **Roots:** Fine and white, developing only at nodes. **Identification year-round:** Present in same form year-round.

STATUS: Canadian Waterweed is fairly common throughout Britain and Ireland except in north and north-west Scotland. Nuttall's Waterweed is common in England, scattered in Wales, Scotland and Ireland, replacing Canadian Waterweed in many localities. Grown in ponds and aquaria, deliberately released or thrown out. Reproduces vegetatively from fragments.

HABITAT: Still or slow-flowing, shallow or deep water.

IMPACT: Can overwhelm water bodies and out-compete native species; chokes up waterway, impeding flow and navigation; interferes with angling.

Nuttall's Waterweed

Key differences between similar species

For similar species see **Large-flowered Waterweed** (page 130).

Curly Waterweed

Lagrosiphon major

J F M A M J J A S O N D

Native range:

Southern Africa

Introduced:

1944

Spread:

Escape from horticulture

Other names:

Curly Water-thyme

DESCRIPTION: *Submerged aquatic*, stems to 3m from bed of water body. **Leaves:** *Strongly curved* with small teeth, 6–30mm long, 1–3mm wide. Minute basal scales at base of leaves; variously whorled or spiralled, *lowest always spiralled*. **Flowers:** Solitary, inconspicuous, white, borne on long thread-like stalk. **Roots:** Unbranched, >1 developing at nodes; up to 45cm long, 0.6–0.8mm wide. **Identification year-round:** Present in same form year-round.

STATUS: Locally frequent in England and Wales, less so in Scotland and Ireland; spreading in all regions. Grown in ponds and aquariums, deliberately released or thrown out. Reproduces vegetatively from fragments.

HABITAT: Water bodies such as lakes, ponds and canals.

IMPACT: Can overwhelm water bodies and out-compete native species; chokes up waterways.

Key differences between similar species
For similar species see **Large-flowered Waterweed** *Egeria densa*.

Giant Salvinia

Salvinia molesta

J	F	M	A	M	J	J	A	S	O	N	D

Not recorded in Britain

Native range:

South America

Introduced:

No records outside of horticulture

Spread:

Escape from horticulture

Other names:

Kariba Weed, *Salvinia rotundifolia*

Tiny hairs on upper surface of fronds: split at tips but rejoining above in Great Salvinia; split at tips but branches remaining free in Floating Water-moss (use hand lens).

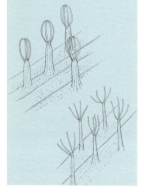

DESCRIPTION: Free-floating, annual fern (perennial in tropical regions). **Leaves:** Light to medium green, oval, velvety and spongy, sometimes with reddish-purplish tinge, growing on a long central stem. Fronds 2cm long, up to 6cm wide in whorls of 3, two floating and one submerged, the latter being finely dissected and dangling, resembling roots. Fronds round to oblong in shape with a distinctive fold in the centre. Eggwhisk-shaped hairs on the upper surface of fronds (use hand lens) make frond like a cat's tongue, water-repellent. Fronds become folded and compressed into upright chains and plants aggregate into floating mats. **Roots:** Feathery structures, profusely hairy, in fact a finely dissected frond. **Identification year-round:** Dies off in winter persisting in larger water bodies in mild winters.

STATUS: Very occasional outside of gardens. Used in aquariums and garden ponds. Discarded material can grow during summer, dies off in winter. Reproduces vegetatively. Does not produce viable spores. **HABITAT:** Still or slow-flowing water, lakes, ponds, ditches, wetlands. Grows optimally at a water temperature of 20–30°C, frost-sensitive (killed below -3°C).

IMPACT: Unable to establish and so likely to cause significant impacts in Britain without considerable climate change. Causes significant impacts elsewhere in the world.

Key differences between similar species
Superficial resemblance to **Water Fern** (non-native page 137) but fronds are very different. **Floating Water-moss** *Salvinia natans*, fronds up to 1cm long, is used as an ornamental plant and found rarely in the wild in Britain. Fronds have hairs on the upper surface that are separated at the apex like little hands (use hand lens).

Least Duckweed

Lemna minuta

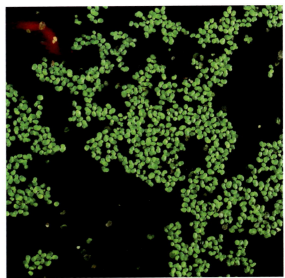

J F M A M J J A S O N D

Native range:

Temperate and subtropical North and South America. Widely naturalised in Europe

Introduced:

1977 (arrived in GB 1977)

Spread:

Escape from horticulture

Other names:

Lemna minuscula

Common Duckweed

DESCRIPTION: Aquatic perennial plant reduced to a frond floating on water surface; sometimes stranded on mud. Duckweeds should only be identified from well-grown spring or summer fronds, as autumn and winter fronds can be smaller than usual with fewer veins or roots. **Leaves**: Pad-like delicate, *thin, translucent frond*, usually 1–3 fronds per cluster, symmetrical and uniform in size at 0.8–4mm long and 0.5–2.5mm wide, widest just above mid-point, pale greyish-green to bluish-white, elongate, elliptic, flattened on both surfaces, with *one indistinct vein* (use a hand lens) *extending less than 2/3 way from root of apex of frond*; most noticeable in dense patches. **Flowers**: Rarely produced; tiny, in hollows on the fronds. **Roots**: Each frond with *one simple white root*. **Identification year-round**: Difficult to identify at any time due to similarity with other small duckweeds. Present all year although some die back in winter.

STATUS: Rapidly spread since the late 1980s. Probably under-recorded, as easily misidentified as Common Duckweed. Dispersal probably by waterfowl, cattle and other livestock. Reproduction by vegetative budding.

HABITAT: Surface of ponds, ditches, lakes, slowly flowing rivers, canals and ditches. Reasonably shade-tolerant: can occur on ponds shaded by marginal trees or woodland.

IMPACT: Forms dense mats covering the surface of the water that block out light, causing deoxygenation, preventing air-breathing insects from reaching the surface and reducing water temperatures. Dense and continuous stands can be a safety hazard as the water surface appears solid. Has potential to accumulate in a dense mass in drainage channels, block conduits and impede water flow.

Key differences between similar species

See table overleaf.

135

Key differences between similar species

Care needs to be taken to distinguish Least Duckweed from native duckweeds, Common Duckweed in particular. Use mature fronds. Duckweeds can vary in size and colour during the year depending on growing conditions, for example light and nutrients. Two or more duckweeds can be found growing together.

	Roots per frond	Frond shape	Veins	Front colour	Size of frond (mm)	Other features
Least Duckweed *Lemna minuta* (non-native)	1	Flat	1 (difficult to see)	Bluish or greyish-white (hard to discern when fronds in low density)	Small: 0.8–4 x 0.5–2.5	1–3 fronds per cluster, floating on surface throughout year. Widely distributed in southern England and spreading
Common Duckweed *Lemna minor* (native)	1	Flat	3	Green	Medium: 1–8 x 0.6–5(7); widest at middle or toward base	Widely distributed in England, Scotland and Wales
Valdivia Duckweed *Lemna valdiviana* (non-native)	1	Flat	1 (indistinct)	Translucent, pale green, thin and delicate	Small: 0.8–4 x 0.5–3	4+ fronds per cluster, often submerged just below surface in winter. Not yet established outside cultivation
Red Duckweed *Lemna turonifera* (non-native)	Several	Flat	Usually		Medium: 1–4 x 0.8–3.5	Only in a few places
Fat Duckweed *Lemna gibba* (native)	1	Swollen on lower side at least in some fronds	4–5	Green above, white-green below; reddish colour developing from margin of frond	Medium: 1–8 x 0.8–6; widest toward apex	Widely distributed in England
Greater Duckweed *Spirodela polyrhiza* (native)	Many	Flat	Many (>7)	Green above, purple below	Largest: 1.5–10 x 1.5–8	Central and southern England
Rootless Duckweed *Wolffia arrhiza* (native)	None	Rounded, swollen both sides	None	Green	Smallest: 0.5–1.5 x 0.4–1.2	Southern England very local

Greater Duckweed *Spiroldela oligorhiza*, a duckweed from eastern Australia, is found in horticultural and aquatic plant outlets in Britain but not naturalised. *Lemna aequinctialis*, a subtropical to tropical species, has been found in aquatic plant tanks in a garden in Britain.

Images of frond shape taken from Lansdown, R. 2009. *A Field Guide to the Riverine Plants of Britain and Ireland*. Privately published, Ardeola, Stroud, Gloucester.

Water Fern

Azolla filiculoides

J F M A M J J A S O N D

Native range:
Western North and Central America; widely naturalised elsewhere in Europe

Introduced:
1883

Spread:
Escape from horticulture

Other names:
Fairy Fern, American Water Fern

DESCRIPTION: Very small water fern *free-floating on the surface* forming dense mats but can also be present as a few fronds amongst emergent or other floating vegetation. **Stems:** floating, short, very slender obscured by scales on fronds. **Leaves:** Fronds composed of *densely overlapping scales* 1–1.5mm, arranged on *two opposite sides of stem*. Fronds branching with two lobes 1–2 (5)cm long and 1.5cm wide, *green to bluish green* in early part of the season but *becoming bright red* when exposed to stresses such as cold, brackish water or shading; rough, granular appearance, non-wettable surface. **Roots:** Hair-like, hanging, simple roots, *dark brown to black*, not conspicuously hairy, easily break off. **Sori:** (structures producing spores (singular: sorus) – no flowers): on lower lobe of first leaf of each branch (use hand lens). **Spores:** Held in sori, tiny, produced in pairs at base of side branches. Ripe June-September. **Identification year-round:** Unmistakable all year round when in its red form and relatively easy to distinguish from duckweeds in its green form, but can die back in winter.

STATUS: Sporadic distribution in southern and central England since rapid spread post mid-20th century. Widely cultivated for ornamental use in ponds and aquaria. Garden and aquarium throw-out and as a contaminant on other plants that might be brought or exchanged. Spreads mainly vegetatively from fragments though can produce minute spores. Populations can fluctuate greatly during the year and from year to year.

HABITAT: Lowland standing or slow-moving water, canals, ditches, ponds and sheltered bays in lakes and rivers. Frequent in calcareous water and near the sea.

IMPACT: Forms dense mats covering the surface of the water and blocking out light, causing deoxygenation, preventing air-breathing insects from reaching the surface and reducing water temperatures. Dense and continuous stands can be a health hazard as the water surface appears solid. Dense masses in drainage.

Key differences between similar species

Can be confused with floating liverworts.

Floating Crystalwort *Riccia fluitans* (native) and Pond Crystalwort *Riccia rhenana* (probably non-native and rather rare), two very similar liverworts *floating at the surface* usually as a mesh-like mass of *narrowly and equally forked green parallel sided leaves* (thalli). Found in stagnant water in ponds, clay pits and marl pits, or slow-moving water in canals and ditches, often with duckweeds (see pages 135–136) and sometimes Fringed Heartwort (see below).

Floating Crystalwort has thalli 2–3cm long and about 1mm wide, each forked 2–6 times into two nearly equal branches, each branch forking at 60–90° to each other, slightly translucent, bright or yellowish-green and sometimes tinged violet or reddish. They lack a groove above or become very weakly grooved only at the extreme tip, which is broad and almost truncate with a central notch. Spore producing capsules are very rare: spread is by thallus fragments. Frequent in England and Wales, less frequent in Ireland and rare in Scotland.

Pond Crystalwort is very similar, but is never reddish. The thallus forks 2–4 times into two nearly equal branches, with each branch forking at 80–105° to each other. First recorded in England in 1952 and now scattered mainly in south-east England (rare in Ireland). This aquatic liverwort is favoured by aquarists and occurrences are considered to be introductions from aquaria.

Fringed Heartwort, *Ricciocarpos natans* (sometime *Ricciocarpus natans*) a liverwort (native) *free-floating on the surface* like Water Fern with floating *tongue or rosette-like thallus* (0.5–1.5cm) *in partial rosette* or *intricate mats*, bright yellow-green to dark green with a conspicuous fringe of violet, sometimes thallus is reddish to pale dark brown; undersurface covered with dense short purplish root-like structures (scales) projecting to the sides and visible from above).

Carolina Azolla (*Azolla caroliniana*) and **Mexican Azolla** (*Azolla mexicana*) (non-native) have been reported from north-western Europe and could be found in Britain.

Water Fern
Azolla filiculoides

Floating Crystalwort
Riccia fluitans

Pond Crystalwort
Riccia rhenana

Fringed Heartwort
Ricciocarpos natans

Water Hyacinth

Eichhornia crassipes

Native range:
South America

Introduced:
At least 1982

Spread:
Escape from horticulture

Other names:
None.

DESCRIPTION: *Free-floating* aquatic plant, 0.5 (1)m long including roots and flowering stalk. Stolons round in cross-section. Can form extensive floating mats. **Leaves:** *Glossy, thick, rounded with swollen expanded bases*, 5–15cm long, with numerous parallel veins. Leaf stalk 2–30cm. **Flowers:** Pale purple, clustered in a large striking spike reminiscent of a hyacinth. **Roots:** *Long black feathered.* **Fruit:** A capsule. **Seeds:** 4mm long, 1mm wide, hundreds contained within a capsule. **Identification year-round:** Recognisable from leaves from spring to autumn. Dies off in winter as not frost-hardy.

STATUS: Not able to persist in Britain. Occasional occurrences as a casual. Garden or aquarium throw-out. Vegetative reproduction from stolons allows it to form dense mats. Also flowers and produces seeds year-round in milder climates.

HABITAT: Still to slow-moving water including ponds and canals.

IMPACT: Unable to establish and so unlikely to cause significant impacts in Britain without considerable climate change. Causes significant impacts elsewhere in the world.

Key differences between similar species
There are no other species that look like Water Hyacinth.

Water Lettuce

Pistia stratiotes

J	F	M	A	M	J	J	A	S	O	N	D

Native range:

Native distribution uncertain

Introduced:

At least 1983

Spread:

Escape from horticulture

Other names:

Water or Nile Cabbage

DESCRIPTION: *Free-floating* aquatic perennial which can form dense mats. Stolons round in cross-section. **Leaves:** *Rosette of light green and velvety-hairy fan-shaped leaves,* 5–10 (15)cm long with *many parallel veins and wavy margins.* Leaf stalk indistinct. **Flowers:** Small, concealed in rosette. Flowers in late summer to early winter. Can flower all year round in warm climates. **Roots:** Long, feathery, hanging green roots. **Fruit:** Green berry. **Identification year-round:** Leaves present in Britain during growing season. Dies off completely in winter as not frost-hardy.

STATUS: Not able to persist in Britain. Occasional occurrences as a casual. Garden or aquarium throw-out. Vegetative reproduction allows it to form dense mats.

HABITAT: Still to slow-moving water including ponds and canals.

IMPACT: Unable to establish and so unlikely to cause significant impacts in Britain without considerable climate change. Causes significant impacts elsewhere in the world.

Key differences between similar species
There are no other species that look like Water Lettuce.

140

Floating Pennywort

Hydrocotyle ranunculoides

J F M A M J J A S O N D

Native range:

North America; widely naturalised in Central and South America

Introduced:

1990 (arrived in GB 1980s)

Spread:

Escape from horticulture

DESCRIPTION: Fleshy stems up to 20cm high, *often floating*, can form *emergent dense mats* either rooted or occasionally free-floating. **Leaves:** *Circular to kidney-shaped, bluntly toothed with branching veins*, up to 70mm across, *divided halfway to base, with leaf stalk (up to 50cm) joining at the end of the apex between the lobes*. **Flowers:** White-green, tiny, in miniature umbels of up to 10 flowers. **Roots:** Fine, hair-like roots up to 10cm at nodes along stem. **Fruit:** Flattened globe shape, 2–3mm across, on stalk shorter than leaf stalk. **Seeds:** Brownish with ribs, the two halves with persistent short stalk. **Identification year-round:** From leaves which vary little throughout the year. In winter plants are most likely to be found at the water's edge.

STATUS: Common in south and east of England, spreading to other parts of Britain. Spreading rapidly from garden throw-outs and by fragments. **HABITAT:** Still or slow-moving water including lakes, ponds, canals, ditches and rivers. Grows across the surface of water bodies from margins. **IMPACT:** Can rapidly form very dense mats and can grow up to 20cm per day, restricting water flow and amenity use, excluding native species, causing deoxygenation, obstructing air-breathing insects from reaching the water surface and reducing water temperatures.

Key differences between similar species

- **Marsh Pennywort** *Hydrocotyle vulgaris* (native) has leaves like a parasol with leaf stalk attached to leaf centre, 0-8-5cm in diameter and grows at edges of water in damp ground (never floating).
- **New Zealand Pennywort** *Hydrocotyle novae-zelandiae* (non-native) has very small leaves, 1cm across with leaf stalk attached at apex of the space between the lobes. It is not a water plant and is found only very rarely (CS&T).
- **Frogbit** *Hydrocharis morsus-ranae* (native) is a free-floating water plant of lowland waterbodies and has leaves, 4cm in diameter, rounded in outline with an indentation where the leafstalk is attached.
- **Celery-leaved Buttercup** *Ranunculus sceleratus* has similar leaves that can be floating but does not root at the nodes..

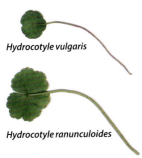

Hydrocotyle vulgaris

Hydrocotyle ranunculoides

Hydrocotyle novae-zelandiae

Cape Pondweed

Aponogeton distachyos

| J | F | M | A | M | J | J | A | S | O | N | D |

Native range:

Southern Africa

Introduced:

1889 (arrived in GB 1788)

Spread:

Escape from horticulture

Other names:

Water Hawthorn and Vleikos

DESCRIPTION: Floating-leaved aquatic tuberous perennial, with *stems rooted in* mud, up to 2m growing from bed of water body. **Leaves:** Floating on water, *6–25cm long, 7–8cm wide*, elliptic-lanceolate to oblong-elliptic, tip obtuse to pointed; 5–9 parallel veins with ladder-like cross veins; *abundant reddish streaks on undersurface*. Long leaf stalks up to 80 (100)cm with purple-black stamens. **Flowers:** Up to 10 white small flowers, each with two petals in a *forked spike* to 6cm at the surface of the water. Borne on a long stalk. **Roots:** Roots not septate, produces tubers. **Fruit:** Egg-shaped with a curved or straight beak. **Seeds:** Does produce seed in Britain. **Identification year-round:** Leaves present April–October. Flowers very characteristic.

STATUS: Appears to be spreading. Has been known to reproduce by seed in Britain, but shows little sign of spreading to new sites without human introduction.
HABITAT: Grows in still water to 2m deep in lowland lakes and ponds.
IMPACT: Can overwhelm ponds and other small waterbodies.

Key differences between similar species

Similar to some other floating leafy plants.

	Cape Pondweed *Aponogeton distachyos* (non-native)	Pondweed *Potamogeton* species (native)	Floating Water-plantain *Luronium natans* (native)	Amphibious Bistort *Persicaria amphibia* (native)
Leaf shape and length	Oblong-elliptic, up to 25cm	Oval, oblong and/or elliptical. Variable, 2–10cm long	Elliptical, small, up to 2.5cm long	Oval to oblong, 5–15cm long
Leaf veins	*Parallel*	*Parallel*	*Three main parallel veins*	*Diverging*
Flowers	*White*, characteristic	*Inconspicuous, olive-green to brown-green*	*White to pale mauve with yellow blotch*	*Pink, characteristic*
Inflorescence	*Forked spike above water, 2–4cm across*	Short spike, can be *submerged or aerial, 1.5–6cm long*	Flowers *solitary* or in *groups of 2–5, each 1.2–1.8cm in diameter*	*Short spike, 2.5cm long*

Pondweed
Potamogeton species

Floating Water-plantain
Luronium natans

Amphibious Bistort
Persicaria amphibia

143

Water Primrose

Ludwigia grandiflora subspecies *hexapetala*

| J | F | M | A | M | J | J | A | S | O | N | D |

Native range:

South America

Introduced:

1998 (1812)

Spread:

Escape from horticulture

Other names:

Creeping Water Primrose, Uruguayan Hamsphire Purslane, Floating Primrose-willow, *Jussiaea grandiflora*. This species has had numerous incorrect names applied to it including *Ludwigia peploidezs* and *Ludwigia uruguayensis*. There is no evidence of these latter species occurring in Great Britain.

DESCRIPTION: Stoloniferous, perennial, aquatic herb, often forming floating mats. Stems ascending or prostrate, 20–80 (300)cm long, round, ridged, reddish, smooth or hairy. **Leaves**: Alternate along the stem, 4–8cm long, 1–2cm wide, widest above the middle and tapering to the base, occasionally ovate, with leaf stalk; *dark green with a lighter central vein*, rolled when young. *Vary considerably* due to having separate *emergent* and *floating* forms. Floating *round* or *egg-shaped*, emergent *long and slender*. Leaf stalk 2–3cm long **Flowers**: *Bright yellow on erect flowering stem, (1)1.5–2.5(3)cm long*, five petals, *anthers 2.5–3.5mm.* June–September. **Roots**: Adventitious above, thicker lower down; anchor into mud. **Fruit and seeds:** Capsule cylindrical, up to 25mm long and 3–4mm wide, contains small seeds, 1.5mm. June–July (September). **Identification year round:** Spring-summer. Dies back in winter leaving distinctive brown stems.

STATUS: Established and spreading rapidly in parts of mainland Europe. Only known from a limited number of sites in England and Wales partly due to efforts to eradicate the plant from Britain. Garden pond escape, subsequently spreads from fragments of stems, e.g. by birds.
HABITAT: Ponds, slow-flowing water.
IMPACT: Out-competes native vegetation and chokes waterways impeding flow.

Key differences between similar species

Similar to water forget-me-nots *Myosotis* species(natives), common species of margins of still and flowing waterbodies, the stems of which can root at nodes; leaves with marked midrib (no floating leaves); flowers small and sky-blue, sometimes pink; and Amphibious Bistort (native) with long, slender leaves in terrestrial/amphibious form and oval to oblong floating leaves up to 15cm long; flowers are pink, small, clustered in a spike, 2–4cm long (see similar species on page 143). **Hampshire Purslane** *Ludwigia palustris* (native, 15cm high) is known from only a few sites in Hampshire and Dorset (see table). **Hybrid Hampshire Purslane** *Ludwigia x kentiana* (*Ludwigia palustris* x *Ludwigia repens*) is the only non-native species of *Ludwigia* known from the wild in Britain, is probably the plant known to aquaria enthusiasts as *Ludwigia* x *mullerlii hort*. It is found from only one site in the wild. Its leaves are widest in uppermost third, whereas those of Hampshire Purslane are widest near its middle. It has tiny cream petals (0.5mm) whereas they are absent in the latter and the capsule is cylindrical, uniformly pale green and readily drops off compared to the more or less rotund capsule of Hampshire Purslane which remains on the plant and has four dark bands. Other species of similar appearance are apparently known from the continent and/or are used in aquaria.

	Water Primrose *Ludwigia grandiflora* (non-native)	Hampshire Purslane *Ludwigia palustris* (native)
Leaf shape and length	Floating form *round* or *egg shaped*, Emergent form *long and slender, 4–8cm long*	*Oval-elliptical, up to 3cm long, widest near middle*
Leaf	Alternate, distinctive light green midrib	Opposite with successive pairs at right angles to each other
Flowers	Large, yellow, 1.5–2.5cm in diameter, anthers 2.5–3.5mm	Very small, 0.2–0.5mm, greenish and inconspicuous. June
Stem	Ascending or prostrate, 20–80cm long, occasionally longer	30 to 60cm sometimes floating at ends
Capsule	Cylindrical, up to 25mm long and 3–4mm wide	Oblong–obovoid to subglobose2–5mm with 4 blunt green angles between yellow faces
Seeds	1.5mm	<1mm
Notes	Known only from a limited number of sites in England and Wales	Known from only a few sites in Hampshire and Dorset

Water Forget-me-not
Myosotis species

Water primrose species
Ludwigia peploides

Slender Sweet Flag

Acorus gramineus

J	F	M	A	M	J	J	A	S	O	N	D

Native range:

Eastern Asia

Introduced:

1986 (arrived in GB 1786)

Spread:

Escape from horticulture

Other names:

Japanese Rush,
Lesser Sweet-flag

DESCRIPTION: Rhizomatous perennial herb growing in shallow water or in the margins of water bodies. **Leaves:** Arching, dark, evergreen, *without obvious midrib*, (8) 15–25 (50)cm long and 2–8mm wide, *aromatic, sweet smell when crushed.* **Flowers:** Yellow, tiny and tightly packed in a stalkless spadix, 5–10cm long, 0.3–0.5cm wide, ascending to nearly erect. Often not flowering. **Roots:** Much branched creeping rhizomes; *aromatic, sweet smell if crushed.* **Identification year-round:** Small size and aromatic smell enable recognition spring to autumn.

STATUS: Only naturalised in a few locations. Discarded from garden ponds – it is a popular ornamental species, readily available from garden centres and occasionally seen as a house plant.
HABITAT: Grows in shallow water or in the margins of waterbodies.
IMPACT: No negative impacts reported.

Key differences between similar species

- **Sweet Flag** *Acorus calamus*. Non-native – archaeophyte. Leaves bright, shiny green, 50–100 (125)cm long, 0.7–2.5cm wide with well-defined and off-centre midrib, *often wrinkled down one edge; aromatic, sweet smell if crushed*. Stalkless spadix making a 45° angle to the stem; yellowish-green and tightly packed but often not flowering. Creeping rhizomes; aromatic, sweet smell if crushed.
- **Iris species**. Green-greyish leaves 25–80cm long, 4–10cm wide with central midrib. Rarely wrinkled. No aromatic sweet smell when crushed. Flowers *typically iris-like, yellow, blue or violet to dark violet*.

Pickerelweed

Native range:

North and South America

Introduced:

1949 (arrived in GB 1759)

Spread:

Escape from horticulture

Other names:

None.

DESCRIPTION: *Aquatic rhizomatous perennial herb*, 0.9–1.3m. *Semi-submerged, with creeping or floating stems.* **Leaves:** *Triangular/oval*, 5–25cm long, 0.5–21cm wide, *with heart-shaped base*, soft, pointed at tip, 20–30 main veins. *Long stalks, 40–60cm, no latex present.* **Flowers:** 6–10mm with 6 petals (tepals). *Violet-blue flowers in a dense emergent spike* 2–15cm. **Fruit:** Kidney-shaped capsule with 6 toothed ridges, 6–10mm. **Seeds:** Kidney-shaped, 3.5–4.5 x 2–2.5mm. **Identification year-round:** Spring–autumn. Usually dies off in winter as not frost-hardy.

STATUS: Mainly southern England, steadily increasing. Planted or occurs as a garden escape.
HABITAT: Still water up to 1m deep such as lowland ponds and gravel pits.
IMPACT: Potential to dominate marginal zone of water bodies.

Key differences between similar species

Only aquatic plant with oval/triangular leaves with heart-shaped bases and a spike of violet-blue flowers. The leaves could be confused with those of *Alisma* – also emergent, similar shape – and *Sagittaria*.

	Pickerelweed *Pontederia cordata* (non-native)	Water-plantain *Alisma plantago-aquatica* native)	American Skunk-cabbage *Lysichiton americanus* (non-native) (see page 77)	Docks *Rumex* species (native)	Arrowheads *Sagittaria* species (native and non-native) (see page 150)
Leaf shape	*Heart-shaped* at base	*Rounded* at base	*Flat or tapered* at base	*Tapered* at base	Emergent leaves *arrow-shaped*
Odour of leaves when crushed	None	None	Unpleasant, 'skunk'-like odour	None	None
Flowers	*6 violet-blue* petals (tepals), in *spike*	*3 pale white to mauve* petals with yellow blotch, in a *whorled panicle*	*1 large yellow hood* (spathe) partially enveloping a spike of greenish flowers (spadix)	*6 small green, red or brown* tepals, flowers *whorled in a spike or cluster*	*3 white* petals with *purple blotch* at base, in *whorls*
Rhizome	Yes	Yes	Yes	*None (taproot)*	Yes

Water-plantain
Alisma plantago-aquatica

American Skunk-cabbage
Lysichiton americanus

Docks
Rumex species

Arrowheads
Sagittaria species

Duck Potato

Sagittaria latifolia

J F M A M J J A S O N D

Native range:

North, Central and South America

Introduced:

1941 (arrived in GB 1818)

Spread:

Escape from horticulture

Other names:

Broadleaf Arrowhead, *Sagittaria obtusa*

DESCRIPTION: A tuberous and stoloniferous perennial emergent aquatic herb. **Stem:** 50 (100)cm long, smooth, angled. **Leaves:** Two leaf forms:

Emergent: Very variable emergent leaves: *large, ovate leaf with an arrow-shaped base up to 50cm long and 50cm wide* or any intermediate between this and *very finely arrow-shaped, up to 30cm long and less than 1cm wide*. The acute basal lobes are occasionally absent. Yellowish-medium green, hooded at tip, often with purplish margin. *Leaf stalk round or many sided with white latex (often sparse), with purple-black spotting at base*.

Submerged: Submerged parallel sided strap-shaped leaves, flat in cross-section, 5–20cm long and 1–2cm wide; translucent and yellowish green. 3 to many veins joining midrib before tip. Leaf stalk indistinct.

Flowers: Three, round, 30–40mm in diameter, *white petals with rounded ends, (no purple blotch at base), anthers yellow*. Flowers in whorls of 2–8, monoecious or with both sexes on same plant, male flowers on upper part and females on lower. **Roots**: White, thin, weakly septate producing white tubers covered with purplish skin, egg-shaped to round, 4–5cm long at end of slender stolons and 0.15–0.6m deep in bed of waterbody and some distance from parent plant. Pulling up the plant leaves tubers in the bed of waterbody as tops break off easily. **Fruit and seeds:** A spherical head made up of seeds (achenes) 2.5–4mm long, winged especially towards tip and with beak, 1–2mm long, almost at the tip. Ripe fruit rarely, if ever, produced in Britain. **Identification year-round:** Summer–autumn, dies down in autumn to tubers.

STATUS: Mainly lowland southern England, steadily increasing. Planted or occurs as a garden escape, can establish large stands. Reproduction is by vegetative spread from runners, tubers and possibly seeds, all enabling spread down rivers. Not frost tender.

HABITAT: Shallow water in lowland lakes, ponds, canals, ditches, streams and rivers.

IMPACT: No negative impacts observed.

Key differences between similar species

Can be very difficult to separate from Arrowhead *Sagittaria sagittifolia* (native), other non-native arrowheads, less so from Pickerelweed (non-native) (see page 147).

	Duck Potato *Sagittaria latifolia* (non-native)	Arrowhead *Sagittaria sagittifolia* (native)	Canadian Arrowhead *Sagittaria rigida* (non-native)	Narrow-leaved Arrowhead *Sagittaria subulata* (non-native)	Grass-leaved (or Chinese) Arrowhead *Sagittaria graminea* (non-native)
Emergent leaves	Arrow-shaped (very variable) with large, acute basal lobes which are occasionally absent), up to 30(50) cm long and can be <1cm wide	Arrow-shaped, 5–20cm long and always >4cm (up to 10cm) wide with apical lobe longer than basal lobes	*Narrowly to broadly elliptical or oval, rarely with two short basal lobes, 5–20cm long, 0.5–7cm wide*	Rarely, if ever, emergent	Linear to linear-lanceolate, long grass-like, consistently narrow
Leaf stalk (all exude white latex if broken – no odour)	Round-many sided; small air spaces, purple-black spotting at base	Sharply triangular with large air spaces; no purple-black spotting at base	Long, triangular with large air spaces; no purple-black spotting at base	Long, triangular to semi-cylindrical; no purple-black spotting at base	Triangular
Floating leaves	None at base	Elliptical-lanceolate, sometimes arrow-shaped	Similar to emergent leaves	Elliptical or ovate-oblong, 1.5–5cm, rarely with rounded lobes	None
Submerged leaves (all are flat in cross-section)	Strap shaped 5–20cm long and 1–2cm wide, 3 to many veins	Yellowish-green linear and strap-like, entire, up to 2m, translucent	Yellowish-green linear and strap-like	Elliptic-oblanc to strap shaped, 5cm long and 1cm wide, 3 veins	Extensions of the leaf stalk, flattened above and angled below
Flowers	Emergent, 3 white petals, in whorls; anthers yellow	Emergent, 3 white petals usually with purple blotch at base, in whorls; anthers purple	Emergent, 3 white petals, slightly yellowish at base, in whorls (very few), stalks of stamens with scale-like hairs (use hand lens)	Produced on water surface, a single flower at a time; 6 small green, red or brown petals, in whorls in a spike or cluster; stalks of stamens hairless (use hand lens)	In whorls on spindly flower stalk, shorter than surrounding stalks
Achene (one-seeded fruit)	2.4–4mm, with beak almost at the tip >1mm. Ripe fruit rarely, if ever, set in Britain	4–6mm, with beak at the tip, <1mm. Ripe fruit may or may not be set in Britain	2.5–4mm, with beak >1mm. Ripe fruit is set in Britain	1.5–2.5mm, with beak <1mm. Ripe fruit is set in Britain	1.5–2.8mm, with beak 0.2mm
Origin	North, Central and South America	Native	Eastern North America	South-eastern North America	North America
Distribution	Southern England and increasing	Scattered throughout England and Ireland	Very rare in England, Wales and Ireland	Extremely rare	Extremely rare

The identification of non-native arrowhead species is complicated by the variation in leaf form from the obvious arrow-shaped emergent leaf through oval-shaped leaves, emergent and floating, to submerged linear/strap-shaped translucent leaves. Identification of plants to the genus *Sagittaria* is relatively straightforward given the characteristic shape and nature of the leaves, the triangular cross-section of their leaf stalks and the fact that when the plant is damaged, it exudes white latex. In addition to those species summarised in the table, there could be other non-native arrowhead species, for example **Slender Arrowhead** *Sagittaria terres* and **Broad-leaved (or Delta) Arrowhead** *Sagittaria playphlla*, both planted in aquariums. Identification of these non-native species requires ripe fruits/seeds, but non-native species in Britain rarely produce ripe seed.

Slender Bulrush

Typha laxmanniii

J F M A M J J A S O N D

Not recorded in Britain

Native range:

Southern Europe, much of Asia

Introduced:

No records for outside horticulture

Spread:

Potential to spread from horticulture

Other names:

Laxmann's Bulrush, Dwarf or Graceful Cattail, Golden-headed or Slender Reedmace

DESCRIPTION: A small, slender, erect perennial, stem simple, (70)80–120(150)cm. **Leaves:** Blue-green, linear, narrow, 2–4(7)cm, not shiny; flattened U-shaped cross-section (use hand lens). No leaf stalk, leaf sheathing stem usually open at throat. **Flowers:** Small fox-brown spikes comprising minute flowers, 1–6cm between male and female parts (male on top) ; female part of inflorescence 4–7cm long, cylindrical. Wind-pollinated. **Seeds:** Tiny 1-seeded capsule, released as downy fluff, wind dispersed. **Root/rhizome:** Short rhizome, 5–8mm thick, up to 20cm deep in the soil or sediment. **Identification year-round:** Dead leaves with characteristic cross-section and seed heads enable recognition over winter.

STATUS: Rarely encountered outside cultivation. Vegetative propagation from sections of rhizome and seed (in Poland where non-native).
HABITAT: Potentially on periodically flooded banks of slow flowing, low-land water bodies, along lake margins, in marshes, ponds and swamps.
IMPACT: No negative impacts observed.

Key differences between similar species

	Slender Bulrush *Typha laxmannii* (non-native)	Least or Dwarf Japanese Bulrush *Typha minima* (non-native)	Lesser Bulrush *Typha angustifolia* (native)	Bulrush *Typha latifolia* (native)	*Typha latifolia* x *Typha angustifolia* (*Typha* x *glauca*) (native)
Leaf width and sheath	2–4 (7)mm. Sheath open at throat	1–3mm. Sheath open at throat	3–6 (10)mm. Sheath closed at throat	(7) 16–18 (24)mm. Sheath open at throat	Intermediate between Bulrush and Lesser Bulrus.
Flowers	Female part 4–7cm long separated from male part by 1–6cm. No bracts below inflorescences	Female part 1.5–4cm long and contiguous with male part or very nearly so. Leaf-like bracts below inflores-cences	Female part 8–20cm long and separated from male part by >30mm. No bracts below inflorescences	Female part 8–15 (20) cm long and usually contiguous with male part. No bracts below inflorescences	Female part sepa-rated from male part by <15mm. No bracts below inflorescences
Stem height	Up to 120 (150)cm	30–80 (140)cm	Up to 3m	Up to 2.75m	Up to 3m

Animals introduction

Although there are many more non-native plants than animals established in Britain, by proportion the animals are more likely to have an adverse impact (Roy *et al.* 2012). Most established non-native animals are terrestrial insects, with fewer other invertebrates and only a small proportion of vertebrates. Most terrestrial insects are associated with damage to crops and other plants, while the remaining animals cause a wide range of impacts from grazing damage to predation. In some cases invasive animals can even act as ecosystem engineers.

The majority of non-native vertebrates were intentionally brought into Britain, often as pets or livestock, and have then subsequently escaped or been released. Conversely the invertebrates were more commonly introduced as accidental contaminants of imported commodities or stowaways with goods, vehicles and equipment. There are some exceptions, for example the non-native crayfish were deliberately introduced for food and as ornamentals, while the House Mouse and rats were stowaways on ships.

Non-native deer have a significant impact on woodlands, forestry and timber production caused by browsing and tree damage (in this case bark stripping). In 2010 the cost of damage caused by non-native deer to the forestry sector was estimated to be just less than £18 million per annum.

In terms of identification, many of the established non-native animals are familiar, for example Rabbit, Grey Squirrel and Canada Goose, or unusual and distinctive in appearance, such as the Ring-necked Parakeet or the Pumpkinseed fish. In many cases the animals are so distinct that confusion with other non-native or native species is unlikely. However, in all groups there are species that require careful observation to confirm their identity. This is particularly true in the case of the invertebrates, where some groups, such as the flatworms and ants, can be particularly difficult to identify and are likely to require expert assistance.

Understanding an animal's life history and behaviour can greatly increase the chance of finding and identifying it in the field. Important aspects to consider include:

- **How common or rare is the species?** Use the distribution map and species account to give an indication of whether the species is likely to be present in your area. If it is not, double check your identification and consider other species with which it could be confused.

- **Time of year**. Some animals may reduce their activity or hibernate over winter, making them less likely to be encountered. Others may increase the frequency of their activity, or call at specific times. Use the 'identification throughout the year' guide to identify the best time to identify the species. This will be most relevant for the mammals, amphibians, reptiles and terrestrial invertebrates.

- **Time of day**. Animals can be nocturnal, diurnal or crepuscular. Use the guidance on animal behaviour to help ascertain the best time of day to look for the species.

A recent invader, the Quagga Mussel, causes ecological and economic impacts. As a biofouling organism it can encrust pipes in freshwater systems, causing expensive problems for water companies and others. It can also encrust native species, including the rare and protected Depressed River Mussel (*Pseudanodonta complanata*).

- **Habitat**. The chance of finding a species is greatly increased by searching in optimal habitat. Consider any climatic requirements of the species as well as specific conditions, such as the flow of water, the composition of woodland or in the case of some terrestrial invertebrates the presence of a host species.

- **Life-stage**. Particularly relevant for the amphibians and terrestrial invertebrates, some animal species can be distinctive at different life stages, for example as eggs, larvae and pupa. Consider which life-stage is likely to be present at a given time and where it is most likely to be found.

- **Field signs**. For many species the individual animals are less likely to be seen than the signs that they have left behind. Signs are many and varied, ranging from droppings to nests, and feeding signs to dead shell remains. These are particularly relevant for identifying mammals, terrestrial invertebrates and freshwater invertebrates such as mussels and crayfish.

- **Calls and sounds**. The call of some animals can be distinctive and is often heard well before seeing the animal. Listen carefully for deer rutting, parakeets screeching, the laughing call of Marsh Frog and the 'mooing' call of American Bullfrog. Animals may be noticeable by noises other than their calls, such as the scuttling noise made by Edible Dormice nesting in a wall cavity.

In many cases there are specialist survey techniques that can be used for non-native animals, including the use of camera traps, hair traps, bottle traps, artificial refugia, netting, lamping, pitfall trapping, mist netting and others. More on these can be found in many of the references to this field guide (see page 286).

Sacred Ibis are not yet established in Britain, but have established in a number of places in western France. They are predators of chicks and eggs and have been observed to push birds off the nest to consume their eggs. In 2004 two Sacred Ibises were reported to have consumed all the eggs in a Sandwich Tern (*Sterna sandvicensis*) colony (30 nests) inside four hours.

153

Mammals

There are 16 established non-native mammals in Britain, most of which are thought to cause negative impacts.

Impacts include:

- **Environmental** – predation on native species, including breeding birds on islands and the declining Water Vole population; grazing and browsing damage, for example by deer to native woodlands; spread of disease, in particular the spread of squirrel pox to native Red Squirrels.

- **Economic** – damage to crops and forestry by grazing and browsing, particularly Rabbit and deer; rats and House Mice are pests of stored products; impacts on livestock through predation such as American Mink on poultry or the spread of disease.

- **Human health** – road traffic accidents caused by deer and the spread of disease by rats and House Mice.

Non-native mammals have a long history of introduction to Britain, dating back to Neolithic times, when House Mice were introduced as stowaways on boats. Other key pathways have been deliberate introduction for food (e.g. Rabbits), fur (e.g. American Mink) and hunting (e.g. deer). Today pet and zoo escapes are more likely to introduce mammals, with records of escapes such as Siberian Chipmunk and Raccoon continuing to occur.

Unexpected introductions: the Black-tailed Prairie Dog has not yet established in Britain, but is becoming more frequently reported as an escapee of zoos and wildlife parks.

Identification tips

While some non-native mammals, such as Rabbit and Grey Squirrel, are easily seen, others are more secretive. Field signs, such as burrows, feeding signs, droppings, calls and other noises, are an important aid to determine the presence and identity of a non-native mammal.

Many mammals change their behaviour and sometimes appearance through the year, making them more or less easy to identify. For example, some reduce their activity or even hibernate over winter, making them unlikely to be seen; whereas others, such as many deer species, are more conspicuous during their rutting season when the males call loudly. Many non-native mammals are more active at dusk and dawn or are entirely nocturnal.

Different survey methods can be used to help confirm the presence of a non-native mammal. Further guidance should be sought if using any of these techniques (see References section, page 286).

This section covers the majority of non-native mammals likely to be considered invasive in GB. To keep the guide relevant and compact, some potential species have not been included such as feral cat, feral goat, Red-necked Wallaby and a number of mammals that have been occasionally recorded in Britain, but are not established.

House Mouse

Mus domesticus

J F M A M J J A S O N D

Native range:

Central Asia across to Iran

Introduced:

Since the Iron Age, hitchhiker on boats and ships

Spread:

Hitchhiker in boats, ships and transported goods

Other names:

Mus musculus, Grey Mouse

DESCRIPTION: Head and body 7–10cm. Tail approximately same length, sparsely haired with prominent rings and scales. Colour variable, commonly greyish-brown above and slightly lighter beneath. *Musky smell*. Female slightly larger than male.

BEHAVIOUR: Active night, dawn and dusk. Breeds throughout year. Diet extremely broad. May be heard scratching in wall, roof and floor spaces.

FIELD SIGNS: In buildings identified by faeces, runways, nest, smell and feeding signs.

DROPPINGS: Can be confused with droppings of other rodents and bats, although bat droppings are more friable. Cylindrical, approximately 7mm long. Pungent. Concentrated in favoured places.

NEST: Made from almost any material (e.g. grass, shredded newspaper).

STATUS: One of the earliest non-native species introduced to GB. Now widespread, extremely common.

HABITAT: Closely associated with man. Common in buildings of all sorts. Found in wide range of urban and rural areas.

IMPACT: Widely recognised pest of agriculture and in buildings.

Key differences between similar species

- **Wood Mouse** *Apodemus sylvaticus*. Native. Common. Present in broad range of habitat, including buildings and gardens, tends to *replace House Mouse in open countryside.* Nocturnal. Slightly larger (head and body to 11cm). *Dark yellow-brown above, pale grey below* with clear demarcation. Longer tail. *Larger ears and protruding eyes. Tail dark above, whitish below.* Orange or buff spot on chest. Droppings shorter and thicker. Juvenile similar in colour to House Mouse but with longer hindfeet, broader head, larger eyes and ears.

- **Yellow-necked Mouse** *Apodemus flavicollis*. Native. Restricted to central and southern Wales and England. Prefers woodland. Relatively *large* (head and body to 12cm, tail to 13.5cm). Similar to Wood Mouse. Colour more *golden-brown*. Collar more prominent yellow.

Brown Rat

Rattus norvegicus

J F M A M J J A S O N D

Native range:

Central Asia

Introduced:

1720s, hitchhiker on boats and ships

Spread:

Hitchhiker in boats, ships and transported goods

Other names:

Common Rat, Norway Rat, Sewer Rat

droppings actual size

DESCRIPTION: Large size and long, thin, virtually hairless tail separates rats from other rodents in GB. Brown Rat is 19–29cm from nose to base of tail. Tail 17–23cm (shorter than head and body), scaly, ringed, *dark above and lighter below.* Ears prominent, covered in hair. Typically *grey to dark brown*, lighter coloured below. Sexes alike, male slightly larger.

BEHAVIOUR: Nocturnal, most active at dusk and just before dawn. Present year-round in urban areas, population density fluctuates more in rural areas. Will climb. Good swimmer and can reach offshore islands.

FIELD SIGNS: In buildings *gnaw marks, droppings* and *dark greasy smears* along runs are distinctive.

DROPPINGS: *Large*, average 12mm long. Cylindrical, both ends *usually rounded*, may taper to slight point. Often deposited in *piles in dark corners. Unpleasant odour.*

FEEDING SIGNS: Gnaws many materials, from foam insulation to electric cables. Makes food piles of chewed tubers and snail shells.

NEST: Outdoors digs extensive burrow network. Entrance 6–9cm diameter with *characteristic fan-shaped spoil heap* at entrance. Well-trodden runs link burrows above ground.

TRACKS: Like most rodents, forefoot print star-shaped showing 4 toes while hind print elongate showing 5. Tail drag rarely present in tracks.

STATUS: Probably introduced as stowaways on ships. Now virtually ubiquitous and abundant in GB, only absent from a few small offshore islands.

HABITAT: Closely associated with habitation, particularly farms, warehouses and rubbish tips.

IMPACT: Many severe impacts including damage to crops and stored goods, spreading disease and competing with or preying upon native species, particularly breeding birds.

Key differences between similar species

Water Vole *Arvicola terrestris*

Native. Less common. Similar size, head and body 13–24cm. *Plump*. Muzzle much *blunter*. Ears *barely visible*. *Short furred tail*, about half length of body. Droppings *smaller* (8–12mm long), *blunt rounded ends*, smooth texture, *no odour*, usually piled prominently on riverbanks. Distinctive feeding stations made from grasses and reeds, always near water. Enters water with a 'plop'. More buoyant than rat, floating higher in water while swimming. Burrow entrance smaller, 4–8cm, without fan-shaped spoil, close to water margin, often below water line. Runs less obvious than those of rat, made very close to water's edge.

Black Rat *Rattus rattus*

Non-native from Asia, probably introduced in 3rd century by Romans. Formerly widespread in GB, displaced by the Brown Rat. Now only a few populations associated with seaports and an isolated population in the Hebrides. Smaller and *slimmer*, head and body 12–24cm. Unlike Brown Rat *tail always longer than head and body* (12–26cm) *thinner* and *uniformly dark. Larger, almost hairless ears. Larger eyes.* Fur colour variable, black common in urban areas, but may be grey or reddish-brown. Rarely enters water. Strong climber. Field signs very similar. Heavy tail drag sometimes present in tracks. Droppings shorter, 10mm long, thinner, more pointed at ends. Tend to be deposited singly.

	Brown Rat	Black Rat	Water Vole
Status	Ubiquitous	Highly localised	Widespread; less common
Habitat	Almost anywhere	Present on a few islands and seaports	Banks of water bodies
Muzzle	Pointed	Pointed	Blunt
Eye	Medium-sized	Large	Small
Ear	Medium-sized, covered in fine fur	Large, almost hairless	Inconspicuous
Body	Large and robust	Relatively small, less robust	Plump
Tail (length)	Shorter than head and body, hairless, thick, 2-tone (17–23cm)	Longer than head and body, hairless, relatively thin (12–26cm)	Very short, finely furred, thin
Fur	Grey-brown (may be black)	Black (may be grey-brown)	Light to dark brown
Droppings	12mm More rounded, may taper Strong odour May be piled or scattered	10mm More likely to be pointed Strong odour Usually scattered	8–12mm Rounded Lack odour Usually piled in distinctive latrines along water bodies
Track	Hind print 3–4.5cm. Lacks tail drag	Print same as Brown Rat Heavy tail drag may be distinctive	Print similar to rats. Lacks tail drag

Edible Dormouse

Glis glis

DESCRIPTION: Head and body 13–19cm, tail 11–15cm. *Dark rings around eyes. Dark stripes on legs. Bulging black eyes.* Tail bushy, but thin compared to Grey Squirrel, somewhat flattened, not usually held over head. Fur *uniform grey* above, white below.

BEHAVIOUR: *Nocturnal.* Hibernates (October to May) mostly underground, sometimes in roof spaces and building cavities. Makes noisy, scuttling, squeaking and snuffling sounds as well as aggressive *chirring.*

DROPPINGS: Oval, 5 x 10mm, sometimes deposited in large piles (50+).

FEEDING SIGNS: *Strips bark* in spring/early summer, forming patchy or spiral shapes.

NEST: Summer nest compact, high in canopy. Hibernation nest typically in old rabbit burrows, tree-holes, gaps among tree roots, nest boxes or in buildings (under floorboards, in wall cavities or roof space). In buildings nests loose and untidy, if material is used at all. May nest in large groups.

TRACKS: Not easily used for identification.

STATUS: Originally deliberately released in Tring Park. Now well established around Chiltern Hills.

HABITAT: Favours Beech but will use other woodland, also gardens, parks, orchards and buildings.

IMPACT: Damages trees by stripping bark. Pest in buildings.

Native range:
South and Central Europe across to Iraq

Introduced:
1902, deliberate release into the wild

Spread:
Deliberate movement by people is possible

Other names:
Fat Dormouse, Spanish Rat, Seven-sleeper, Squirrel-tailed Dormouse, Grey Dormouse

Key differences between similar species
Most likely to be confused with Grey Squirrel because of size, colour and bushy tail. Dissimilar to the native Hazel Dormouse which is much smaller.

- **Grey Squirrel** *Sciurus carolinensis.* Non-native. Common. *Diurnal.* Active year round. *Considerably larger*, head and body 23–30cm, tail 19.5–25cm. Fur, particularly tail, *not uniform colour*, mix of grey, brown and white. Tail *bushier*, fringed with white hairs, often held over head. *Lacks eye rings and stripes on legs*.

See page 160 for more similar species.

Grey Squirrel

Sciurus carolinensis

J F M A M J J A S O N D

Native range:

North America

Introduced:

1876, deliberate release; well established by early 1900s

Spread:

Unlikely to be spread by people

Other names:

Neosciurus carolinensis, Eastern Grey Squirrel

DESCRIPTION: *Large*, head and body 23–30cm, tail 19–25cm. Bushy tail, *fringed with white hairs*. Fur generally grey mixed with brown, white and black hairs, but may be reddish-brown or rarely black. White belly. *Lacks prominent ear tufts*.

BEHAVIOUR: Diurnal. Does not hibernate, but activity reduces over winter.

FEEDING SIGNS: *Strips bark* from trees in long spiral lengths. Splits nuts in two, leaving rough edges.

CALL: *Distinctive scolding 'chuck-chuck-chuck-quaaa'* when alarmed or agitated (particularly when defending territory).

NEST: Winter nest (drey) domed, made from twigs woven with bark, moss and leaves, usually positioned high in fork of tree.

STATUS: Widespread and very common, except in parts of Scotland.

HABITAT: Wide range of habitats. Requires tall trees. Prefers deciduous woodland, but will occupy coniferous woodland.

IMPACT: Significant forestry pest. Predator of native bird eggs and chicks. Vector of 'squirrel pox', which has helped it replace native Red Squirrel in most of its GB range.

Key differences between similar species

● **Red Squirrel** *Sciurus vulgaris*. Native. Extinct in much of England and Wales, though still present in Anglesey, parts of northern England and on some islands. More common in Scotland. Field signs and behaviour similar to Grey Squirrel. Smaller head and body 18–29cm, tail 14–23cm. *Ears with long tufts* in winter. Fur above *uniform* reddish to darker brown. Tail *lacks white fringe*.

See page 160 for more similar species.

	Grey Squirrel	Red Squirrel	Edible Dormouse	Siberian Chipmunk
Habitat	Broadleaved and coniferous woodland	Broadleaved and coniferous woodland (more often seen in the latter)	Prefers Beech, but also uses other broadleaved woodland	Ground-dwelling. Most likely in deciduous or mixed woodlands and parks
Status	*Widespread*, less so in Scotland	Mainly in *Scotland*, parts of *northern England* and *Anglesey*	Limited to the *Chilterns area*	*Not yet established*
Activity	Diurnal	Diurnal	*Nocturnal*	Diurnal
Colour	*Mix of colours*, mainly grey as well as brown and white	*More uniform – mainly red*	*Uniform grey*, white below	Brownish-grey with *5 stripes* along length of back
Body length	23–30cm	18–29cm	13–19cm	12–17cm
Tail	Bushy, *fringed with white hair*. Often held over head	Bushy, red or whitish. Often held over head	Less bushy, flattened, *uniform grey*. Not held over head	Less bushy, short, *striped*
Ears	No tufts	Tufted	No tufts	No tufts
Nest	Builds dreys in trees	Builds dreys in trees	*Often in buildings* or underground	Simple burrow

Grey Squirrel

Red Squirrel

Edible Dormouse

Siberian Chipmunk

Siberian Chipmunk

Tamias sibiricus

NP

Native range:

Northern Asia

Introduced:

Not established in the wild, but sightings have been reported since 1999

Spread:

Kept as a pet, in zoos and other collections, from which escapes may occur

DESCRIPTION: *Small squirrel*, head and body 12–17cm, tail 8–12cm. Five distinct *dark stripes* run length of back. Body brownish-grey to yellowish. Belly white. Tail bushy, grey with three dark stripes above. Ears without tufts, rather long, 13–18mm.

BEHAVIOUR: *Diurnal*, most active at dawn and dusk. Lives in family groups. *Mainly ground-dwelling* but agile and will climb trees. Hibernates November–March in natural range. Feeds mainly on seeds, nuts, berries and invertebrates.
CALL: Females make loud, repeated 'chip' call in spring to early summer to attract a mate.
NEST: Digs si*mple burrows*, usually under bushes and fallen trees.

STATUS: Not established, but escapes may occasionally be encountered. Established populations in parts of Europe have resulted from escaped pets.
HABITAT: Coniferous and deciduous forest with bushy understory, also in parks, gardens and cemeteries.
IMPACT: May compete with or prey upon native species, particularly low-nesting birds and small mammals. Potential garden and crop pest.

Key differences between similar species

- **Grey Squirrel** *Sciurus carolinensis* (page 159). Non-native. Common. *Almost twice the size*. Mottled grey fur *without dark stripes*. Large, bushy tail.
- **Edible Dormouse** *Glis glis* (page 158). Non-native. Localised. *Larger. Nocturnal.* Uniform grey colour. *No stripes* along back or tail.

Rabbit

Oryctolagus cuniculus

Native range:

Iberian Peninsula and southern France

Introduced:

12th century, deliberate release for fur and food

Spread:

Unlikely to be spread by people (but release/escape still possible)

Other names:

Lepus cuniculus

DESCRIPTION: 32–50cm long. *Ears roughly same length as head,* tips may be dark brown but not black. *Eyes brown.* Fur colour varies, commonly brownish-grey, sometimes black. Tail black above white below, held erect when alarmed creating a white flash. Limbs relatively short.

BEHAVIOUR: Mainly active at night, dawn and dusk but also in the day.
DROPPINGS: Small round pellets, hard to distinguish from those of hares.
FEEDING SIGNS: Close grazing typical. Browse line in hedgerows 50–60cm high.
NEST: Digs extensive burrows, unlike hares. Entrance 10–50cm wide, round or oval, almost always with droppings nearby. Could confuse with Fox den, which is larger, usually accompanied by musky odour and prey remains.

STATUS: Widespread and extremely common. Introduced for food and skins. Myxomatosis caused dramatic population decline in the 1950s.
HABITAT: Wide variety, including agricultural land, grassland, parks and gardens.
IMPACT: Significant agricultural, horticultural and forestry pest. Alters natural habitats.

Key differences between similar species

- **Brown Hare** *Lepus europaeus.* Probably non-native, thought to have been introduced in the Roman period. Much less common than Rabbit, primarily encountered in rural areas and farmland. Almost twice as *large* (42–68cm). *Long limbs. Leaping stride.* Does not burrow. *Longer ears* (9–10.5cm) with *black tips. Amber-coloured eyes.* Tail held down when alarmed showing *black top.*

- **Mountain Hare** *Lepus timidus.* Native. Present in heath and moorland in Scotland, parts of north Wales and Peak District. Larger, 41–68cm. Long limbs. Fur sandy or grey-brown but usually *distinct white in winter. Ears shorter than head* (6.7–8cm), with *black tips.*

Deer

There are six species of deer established in Great Britain. Red and Roe Deer are native, while Sika, Muntjac, Fallow and Chinese Water Deer are non-native. Other non-native species such as Père David's Deer sometimes escape, but are not established. Wild deer are more likely to be seen in early morning, but also dusk. The species described here are also found in deer parks.

When attempting to identify a deer species in GB, consider the following characteristics:

Antlers These become larger and more elaborate with age and so adult males with well developed antlers can be relatively easily identified. They are shed and regrown every year so less useful for identification early in the growth season. Antlers of young deer are usually relatively simple and more difficult to use for identification. Females do not have antlers.

Rump patch The white rump patch (or lack therefore) and size and colour of tail can be used to distinguish between deer species. When alarmed, some species will characteristically 'flare' their tails.

Vegetation damage Deer produce a characteristic browse line in shrubs and the lower tree canopy, although this can also be produced by other animals (e.g. farm animals). The height of the browse line reflects the size of the animal feeding and can help with species identification. Some species will leave other signs in vegetation such as chewed twigs, stripped bark and grooves caused by scraping antlers.

Tracks and droppings These can indicate the presence of deer, but are difficult to use for identification of specific deer species and may be confused with those of sheep. Sheep droppings tend to be more spherical and clumped together into sausage shapes. Deer droppings are typically more pointed at one end and indented at the other, and only loosely clumped, or dropped separately.

Shed antlers, skulls and bones These can also be used to identify the possible presence of different deer species. For more on skulls and bones see Harris and Yalden 2008.

The characteristic browse-line caused by deer in shrubs and the lower tree canopy. In this case caused by a mix of the non-native Sika and native Red deer.

Anatomy of a deer

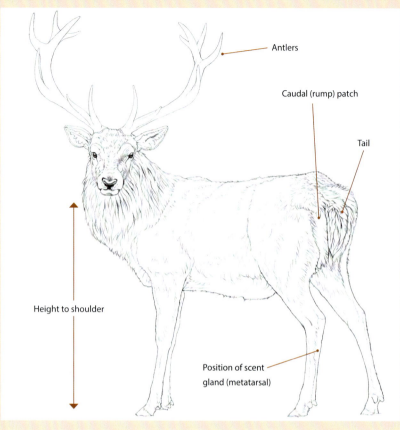

Antlers

Caudal (rump) patch

Tail

Height to shoulder

Position of scent
gland (metatarsal)

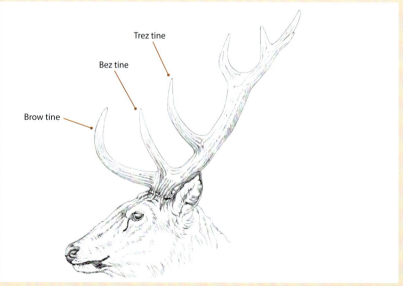

Trez tine

Bez tine

Brow tine

Antlers

Chinese Water	Muntjac	Roe (native)	Fallow	Sika	Red (native)
No antlers	Short, simple, <10cm. Prominent pedicle	Short, <30cm. Relatively simple, at most 3 points	Palmate, multiple points	Similar but smaller and less complex than Red Deer. More 'V'-shaped	Large, complex, multiple points (to 8). More 'U'-shaped than Sika

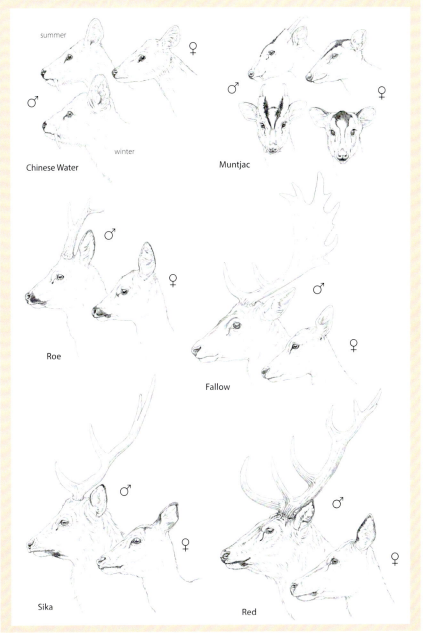

Chinese Water

Muntjac

Roe

Fallow

Sika

Red

Tail and rump markings

	Chinese Water	Muntjac	Roe (native)	Fallow	Sika	Red (native)
Tail	Short stump	Flashes rump in alarm Bushy Brown above, white below	No obvious tail	Long (to bottom of rump patch) Black above, white below Almost always in motion	Flashes rump in alarm Relatively short (approx half-way across rump patch) Less prominent black stripe	No stripe
Rump patch	Indistinct	White, no dark rim	White, no dark rim	Prominent white with dark rim.	Prominent white with defined black rim	Yellowy, without black rim

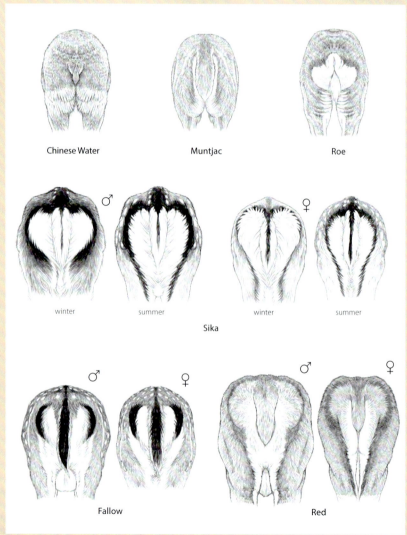

Chinese Water

Muntjac

Roe

♂   winter   summer   ♀   winter   summer

Sika

♂   ♀

Fallow

♂   ♀

Red

166

Optimal ID throughout the year

		J	F	M	A	M	J	J	A	S	O	N	D
Sika	Optimal ID				GOOD						BEST		
	Rut – whistling												
	Moult												
	Antlers shed												
Fallow	Optimal ID										BEST		
	Rut – groaning												
	Moult												
	Antlers shed												
Muntjac	Optimal ID												
	Rut – bark												
	Moult												
	Antlers shed												
Chinese Water	Optimal ID												
	Rut – squeak/whistle												
	Summer coat												
	Winter coat												
Roe (native)	Optimal ID						BEST						
	Rut – bark												
	Moult												
	Antlers shed												
Red (native)	Optimal ID									BEST			
	Rut – roaring												
	Moult												
	Antlers shed												

Comparison table of other features

	Muntjac	Chinese Water	Roe (native)	Fallow	Sika	Red (native)
Status	Common in England	Restricted to East Anglia	Common throughout GB	Common throughout GB (except Scotland)	More common in Scotland, restricted elsewhere	Common in Scotland, restricted elsewhere
Size	Small	Slightly larger than Muntjac	Medium sized	Between Roe and Red	Between Roe and Red	Largest
Pale spots on body	No	No	No	Yes (fade in winter)	Yes (fade in winter)	No
Face	*Dark lines* in 'v' or 'u' shape	*Beady eyes and black nose*, large erect ears	Large nose, often white chin, large erect ears	Long muzzle	*Short muzzle* with 'frowning' appearance	Long muzzle
Canine teeth protrude from top lip	*Yes* (small), more prominent in males	*Yes* (long), more prominent in males	No	No	No	No
Vocalisation	Loud short barks	Whistling and barking	Barking	Loud, deep belching	Loud, high-pitched whistling and screaming	Loud, deep roar

Chinese Water Deer

Hydropotes inermis

J F M A M J J A S O N D

Native range:

East China and Korea

Introduced:

19th century, into private collections; established in the wild by 1940s as a result of escapes and deliberate release

Spread:

Kept in zoos and collections, from which escapes may occur

DESCRIPTION: *Small*, 50–55cm to shoulder. *No antlers* in either sex. In males upper *canine teeth long* (to 7cm) and curved, protruding over bottom lip, smaller in females. Eyes *black and beady*. *Round black nose* prominent. *Large ears* usually held upright. *Rump higher than shoulder*. Uniform red-brown summer coat, paler in winter. Hair left on ground after bucks have fought is hollow, mainly whitish, but shade of brown at tip. *Tail short stump, no white rump markings*. Fawns have spotted coats.

BEHAVIOUR: Most activity at dusk and dawn. Usually *solitary* but may feed in groups.
CALL: During rut (mainly in December) male will make *bird-like whistling call or clicking calls*. Will bark throughout the year and scream if caught or trapped.

STATUS: Well established in parts of East Anglia into the East Midlands and southern England, occasionally sighted elsewhere. Absent in Scotland and Wales. Range expanding.
HABITAT: Densest populations in wetland and mixed vegetation, will use marshland, reedbeds, woodlands and arable farmland.
IMPACT: Potential impact on agriculture (diet includes root crops and cereals). If numbers increase may pose threat to conservation areas.

Key differences between similar species
Can be confused with Muntjac and Roe Deer because of small size.
- **Muntjac Deer** *Muntiacus reevesi*. (see opposite). Non-native. Much more common and widespread than Chinese Water Deer. Slightly smaller. Males have simple spike *antlers*. Dark face markings. *Tail longer*, with *white underside*. Canine teeth shorter. Eyes and nose less prominent.
- **Roe Deer** *Capreolus capreolus*. Native. Common. *Larger*, intermediate between Muntjac and Fallow, 65–70cm at shoulder. Ears held less erect. Males have short *antlers* with 3 points when mature. *Large nose*, often with distinctive white surround and chin. *White rump (no dark edge) with no obvious tail*, but may develop tuft of hairs.

Muntjac Deer

J F M A M J J A S O N D

Native range:

South-east China and Taiwan

Introduced:

1831, into private collections; established in the wild by 1930s as a result of escapes and deliberate release

Spread:

Kept in collections, from which escapes may occur; may be deliberately released

Other names:

Cervus reevesi, Barking Deer, Reeves' Muntjac

DESCRIPTION: *Smallest deer* in Britain, 40–52cm at shoulder. Ginger forehead. Tail 10–17cm long. When alarmed lifts tail to reveal *conspicuous white underside*. *Dark lines* on face form a 'V' (male) or 'U'-shape (female). Head relatively large, legs relatively short. *Hunched posture*, head low and back arched. Summer coat red-brown, winter coat duller. Belly buff. Front of forelegs can be almost black. **Male:** Antlers *short spikes* (to 10cm) emerging from prominent pedicles, may have small branch near base. Curved backwards, sometimes ending in hook. Upper *canine teeth*, to 2cm long, protrude over bottom lip. **Juvenile:** Tiny with white spots that quickly fade.

BEHAVIOUR: Usually *solitary*, may form small family groups. Mainly feeds dusk and dawn, can be active anytime. Breeds year round. **CALL:** Distinctive, *loud short barks* sometimes repeated many times. May shriek or scream when alarmed.

STATUS: England, well established south and midlands, less common north. Wales uncommon, not currently established in Scotland. **HABITAT:** Wide range, including deciduous and coniferous woodland as well as dense scrub. Prefers diverse understory. Not shy; uses urban and suburban areas including parks and gardens. **IMPACT:** Significant biodiversity and forestry impact. Garden nuisance. Frequently involved in collisions with vehicles.

Key differences between similar species

● Chinese Water Deer *Hydropotes inermis*, see opposite.

Fallow Deer

Dama dama

Native range:

Turkey and Iran

Introduced:

11th century, deliberate release for hunting

Spread:

Kept in collections, from which escapes may occur

Other names:

None.

Key differences between similar species

Could be confused with Sika Deer *Cervus nippon* (see opposite).

DESCRIPTION: Similar size to Sika Deer, 73–94cm at shoulder. Colour and pattern highly variable with white, brown and black forms. Summer coat typically reddish to yellowish-brown with *white spots*. Winter coat dull brown to grey with no or faded spots. Dark stripe along spine.
Rump: *White patch, with dark rim*. **Tail:** Dark above, white below, normally twitching from side to side. *Long* (14–24cm) usually *extending beyond rump patch*. **Male:** Antlers become branched and *palmate* with age, younger animals start with single spikes. Tuft of penis sheath usually visible.

BEHAVIOUR: Most active dusk and dawn. Forms stable groups (2–5 individuals) with larger transient groups at good feeding grounds (up to 200 individuals).
CALL: Generally silent except during rut, October–November, when male gives repeated *loud, deep belching sound*. Female issues short bark if alarmed.

STATUS: Common deer particularly of parks in England and Wales, less common in Scotland.
HABITAT: Mature woodland, prefers farmland and deciduous or mixed woodland with established understory.
IMPACT: Feeding damage to agriculture and forestry. Can significantly alter woodland habitat through grazing of tree shoots and undergrowth. Frequently involved in collisions with vehicles.

Sika

Cervus nippon

J F M A M J J A S O N D

Native range:

Japan, Taiwan and adjacent east Asia mainland

Introduced:

1860, into private collections; established in the wild by 1930s as a result of escapes and deliberate release

Spread:

Kept in collections, from which escapes may occur

Other names:

None.

DESCRIPTION: Medium-sized, height to shoulder varies but males typically 80–90cm, females 70–80cm. Relatively stocky with short neck and legs. Distinctive *small head with short stubby muzzle* and dark lines above eyes giving '*frowning*' expression. Lighter patch between eyes emphasises prominent brow and checks. *Small round ears* with 'thumb print' mark. Unusually prominent *white scent gland* often visible on lower hind leg. Summer coat chestnut with white spots on flanks, dark line along spine. Spots usually lost in winter when thicker, dark greyish-brown coat develops, males almost black. **Rump:** *Bright white outlined in black*. **Tail:** *Relatively short*, extends approximately halfway down rump patch, mostly white with black stripe. Distinctive *tail flash when alarmed*. **Male:** Mature antlers 41–46cm long, branched but relatively simple in comparison to Red Deer (see page 165). Mature males develop mane.

BEHAVIOUR: Most active dusk and dawn. Rarely in large groups except during and after rut.

CALL: During rut, September–December, male issues *piercing screams* and *high-pitched whistles*, sometimes a deeper moaning call. Outside rut may give squealing, barking and screaming sounds when alarmed.

STATUS: Only the Japanese subspecies is present in the wild, though other forms may be seen in parks. Not widely established in England, but strong populations in the New Forest, south-east Dorset, Lancashire and the Lake District. Well established in north-west Scotland, still spreading. One population in south-west Wales.

HABITAT: Found in a wide range of habitats, rarely far from woodland cover. Prefers coniferous woodland with adjacent heath and dense scrub.

IMPACT: Threatens native Red Deer population through hybridisation. Can cause serious damage to crops, forestry and sensitive habitats.

Key differences between similar species

- **Red Deer** *Cervus elaphas*. Native. Relatively common. *Largest* British deer, 100–130cm to shoulder, *less stocky*. *Longer face*. Antlers *larger* and *more complex* with more branches. *Large pointed ears*. Adult coat lacks spots, though juveniles are spotted. Summer coat reddish-brown, winter coat darker. Tail short and stubby, caudal patch indistinct. During rut male gives *bellowing roars*.
- **Fallow Deer** *Dama dama*. Non-native (see opposite). Similar size (73–94cm). Mature males with *palmate antlers*. Tail considerably *longer with more prominent black stripe*. *Lacks obvious white gland* on lower leg. Summer coat may be similarly spotted. Females and juveniles are easier to confuse with Sika females and juveniles.

171

American Mink

Neovison vison

J F M A M J J A S O N D

Native range:

North America

Introduced:

1929, into fur farms; established in the wild by 1950s as a result of escapes and release

Spread:

Now unlikely to be spread by people

Otter

DESCRIPTION: Head and body 32–47cm, tail 13–23cm approximately half length of body. Dark brown, sometimes verging on black. *White patch on chin*, rarely extends to top lip or above. Tail slightly bushy. Ear tips same colour as head and body. **Female:** smaller (average weight 0.7 kg) than male (average weight 1.2 kg).

BEHAVIOUR: Crepuscular and nocturnal, but often seen in the day.
DROPPINGS: 5–8cm long, 1cm diameter, usually found at dens or on prominent objects such as rocks. Cylindrical with *twisted ends*. Solid to very loose and liquid. Colour varies, usually from dark green to brown. *Unpleasant fetid odour*. Often contains fur.
FEEDING SIGNS: Opportunistic predator. Often kills and stores prey, including fish, invertebrates, amphibians and small mammals. Larger prey often stored in hollow trees or beneath rocks by the waterside.
NEST: Dens usually close to water's edge, often among roots of riverside tree or boulders. Also in coastal areas. May use old Rabbit burrows. Rarely digs own den.
TRACKS: Print 2–4cm wide, *splayed star shape* often with claw marks. Only 4 of 5 toes usually imprint. Typically found close to watercourse.

STATUS: Introduced for fur farming, subsequently escaped or deliberately released. Widespread and well established across GB, but absent from most offshore islands. Mainland population may be decreasing slightly, linked to recent increase in native Otter population.
HABITAT: Generally associated with aquatic habitat. Lake shores, river banks, estuary and coastal areas.
IMPACT: Significant predator, linked to decline of native Water Vole and threat to ground-nesting birds.

Key differences between similar species

- **Polecat** *Mustela putorius*. Native. Relatively scarce. Similar in size and shape. Footprints and scat indistinguishable. Melanistic and other coloured forms do occur. *Lighter fur not uniformly coloured* but brown on back, with long dark hairs and yellowish underfur visible on flanks. Additional *white markings on muzzle and around eyes forming mask. White ear tips.*
- **Otter** *Lutra lutra*. Native. Becoming more common. Easily distinguishable. Much *larger*, almost twice the size of American Mink. Tracks *larger* (5–7cm wide) with pronounced *webbing* between toes. Droppings (spraints) *larger,* 10cm long, cylindrical *without twisted ends, sweeter odour* and often contain *fish bones*. Mid-brown. Muzzle blunt. Tail long and smoothly tapering to a point.

Feral Ferret

Mustela putorius furo

Native range:

Domesticated

Introduced:

11th century, for ferreting; established in the wild by the 1930s as a result of escapes

Spread:

Kept as a pet and for ferreting, from which escapes occur

Other names:

Polecat Ferret

DESCRIPTION: Domesticated descendent of European Polecat. Often *albino or with very light fur*, particularly on throat and face and easily identified. Albinos also have pink eyes. Feral populations and some other dark forms closely resemble or are indistinguishable from native Polecat. Deliberate cross-breeding has also created difficult to identify Polecat-Ferret **hybrids** with intermediate characteristics. *Paler fur, particularly on throat*, can be used to identify some hybrids, but identification often requires expert assistance.

STATUS: Widely kept pet and escapes occur. Used for ferreting (hunting mainly Rabbits) although this became less common when the Rabbit population declined in the 1950s. Viable populations known from some Scottish islands, Isle of Man and Jersey. Some mainland populations in Scotland and northern England may be sustained by continual release.
HABITAT: Can utilise a wide range of lowland habitat, but not very successfully. More likely to form sustained populations on islands.
IMPACT: Potentially significant impact on native ground-nesting birds (especially on islands). May take poultry. Hybridises with native Polecat.

Key differences between similar species

Polecat *Mustela putorius*. See opposite page.

Black-tailed Prairie Dog

Cynomys ludovicianus

NP

Native range:

North America

Introduced:

Not established in the wild. Colonies have been reported since 1976, though not thought to be persistent and self-sustaining.

Spread:

Kept as a pet, in zoos and other collections, from which escapes may occur

Other names:

None.

GENERAL: *Large ground-dwelling* rodent of squirrel family, head and body 25–40cm. Tail 6–10cm with black tip. Fur yellowish to brown. *Pear-shaped body* apparent when adults *stand on hind legs* in 'lookout' position. Head short and broad. Small ears. Large *dark brown eyes*, with black line over eye.

BEHAVIOUR: Diurnal. Herbivorous, may take insects. *Colonial*.
CALL: May make chirring, yipping or barking calls.
NEST: Builds extensive burrow networks. Burrows are interconnected tunnels, with one or more entrances. Entrance diameter 10–30cm. Made *vertically* straight down in fields. Dirt mound often present at entrance, sometimes built up forming *conspicuous large crater*.

STATUS: Not established in GB, but escapes from wildlife collections have been known to breed and persist for a number of years, including in Cornwall, Cambridge, Isle of Wight, Norfolk, Staffordshire and at least one site in Scotland.
HABITAT: In native range usually forms large colonies in flat landscapes such as grassland, prairie and desert. In GB escaped individuals are generally found in farmland near to wildlife parks.
IMPACT: Negative impacts uncertain, could cause agricultural damage through burrowing and herbivory.

Key differences between similar species

Unlike any other species likely to be encountered in GB.

Raccoon

Procyon lotor

NP

Native range:

North and Central America

Introduced:

Not established in the wild, but sightings have been reported since 1970s

Spread:

Kept as a pet, in zoos and other collections, from which escapes may occur

Other names:

None.

DESCRIPTION: *Size of large cat*, head and body 45–70cm. Tail short 20–26cm, bushy with 4–6 *black rings*. Face with distinctive dark *'bandit' mask*. Muzzle pointed. Ears large, 4–6cm. Body plump with *hunched back*. Short legs. Fur grey-brown. Highly dextrous.

BEHAVIOUR: *Nocturnal*. Solitary or small family groups. Opportunistic feeder with broad diet, mainly carnivorous but will take fruit and other plants. Prefers to feed in water or douses food with water. Agile climber.
DROPPINGS: Droppings similar to that of medium-sized dog, often contain seeds or insect parts. *Not strongly musky* (unlike Fox).
FEEDING SIGNS: May *turn out rubbish bins or dig up gardens*.
NEST: Lives in den or hollow tree.
TRACKS: Distinctive showing long toes with relatively small pad. Forefoot print approximately 7 x 7cm, *star-shaped*, usually showing 5 toes with claws. Hind print more elongated.

STATUS: Not yet established in Great Britain. Invasive in parts of Europe where introduced for fur farming. Clever and highly dextrous, occasionally escapes from captivity. Significant risk of future establishment.
HABITAT: Wide range, most likely to be associated with human habitation. Prefers woodlands near water.
IMPACT: Nuisance in urban areas. Agricultural pest. Potential competitor and predator of native species.

Key differences between similar species

Unlikely to be confused if seen (but see Racoon Dog, page 176).

Raccoon Dog

Nyctereutes procyonoides

J F M A M J J A S O N D

NP

Native range:
East Asia

Introduced:
Not established in the wild, but sightings have been reported since 2005

Spread:
Kept as a pet, in zoos and other collections, from which escapes may occur

Other names:
Racoon-like Dog

DESCRIPTION: Similar in size to a small dog or fox (head and body 50–70cm) but *heavily built* with *short legs*. *Distinctive Raccoon-like face*, light-coloured with black patches around eyes. Tail short (13–25cm) and bushy. Ears short and rounded. Brownish-grey or yellowish fur on back, flanks and head with some black hairs. Legs, feet, throat and chest black or brown.

BEHAVIOUR: *Nocturnal*. Generally solitary or in small family groups. Does not hibernate, but may spend cold winter days in torpor. Omnivorous, taking small animals (fish, insects, amphibians) and fruit and scavenging in refuse. Mates February to March, cubs born April to June.

DROPPINGS AND TRACKS: Digs *communal latrines*, similar to Badgers. Droppings usually twisted, containing hard fragments. Tracks and droppings difficult to distinguish from those of domestic dogs. Tracks 50 x 40mm, with 4 toes, claw marks usually present.

NEST: Uses dens of other animals, outside of which it may leave bones and other prey remains.

STATUS: Introduced for fur to Russia and eastern Europe in the first half of the 20th century. Now well established in many eastern and northern European countries as well as Germany. Not established in GB, but occasionally kept as pet or in wildlife collections, from which escapes sometimes occur.

HABITAT: Favours deciduous forests, damp areas and river banks.

IMPACT: In Europe has had a negative impact on native species as a predator of birds and amphibians and competitor with other carnivores such as Fox and Badger. May spread disease.

Key differences between similar species
- **Raccoon** *Procyon lotor* (see page 175). Not established in GB. Similar in size and colour, sharing dark face mask. Has *flexible prehensile hands*, can climb and uses hands to feed. Has less *dog-like build and posture, has a banded tail and more pronounced ears*.

Coatimundi

Nasua nasua

NP

Native range:
South America

Introduced:
Not established in the wild, but sightings have been reported since 2003

Spread:
Kept as a pet, in zoos and other collections, from which escapes may occur

Other names:
Brown-nosed Coati, Ring-tailed Coati

DESCRIPTION: Characteristic *long prehensile snout* used for foraging. Small ears. Long, thick, bushy tail with *prominent rings*. yellowish to red-brown and black coat which lightens to yellow-brown on the underside. Darker feet and face markings.

BEHAVIOUR: Diurnal. Omnivorous, feeding on fruit, invertebrates and sometimes other small animals. Males generally solitary, but females and juveniles in groups. Frequently climbs and *rests in trees*. Walks on soles of feet with a bear-like gait, will travel long distances. Strong *digger*. Roots in soil with snout.
CALL: Makes chirping and grunting sounds.

STATUS: Kept in wildlife collections in GB, occasionally as a pet. Approximately 10 individuals had been seen in the wild up to 2006, notably in the Cumbria area. Not established and no signs of breeding.
HABITAT: Most likely to be associated with woodland near wildlife parks. In native range uses a wide variety of woodland.
IMPACT: Sometimes a pest of orchards and poultry farms in native range. Could potentially impact on ground-nesting birds.

Key differences between similar species
Closely related to Raccoon (page 175) but easily distinguished by coloration and long snout.

Striped Skunk

Mephitis mephitis

J F M A M J J A S O N D

Native range:

North America

Introduced:

Not established in the wild, but sightings have been reported since 2001

Spread:

Kept as a pet, in zoos and other collections, from which escapes may occur

Other names:

None.

DESCRIPTION: Cat-sized (head and body 52–77cm; tail 17–40cm). Black fur with single narrow *white stripe* from nose to forehead, wider on crown, dividing into two wide stripes along flanks. Fur coarse, long and oily. Tail long, wide and bushy. Head with pointed muzzle. Short stocky legs. Front paws with long claws for digging. *Strong, unpleasant, musky odour.* Males slightly larger than females.

BEHAVIOUR: *Nocturnal.* Lives in rock crevices or underground burrows. Solitary or small family groups over winter. Keen sense of smell and hearing, poor eyesight. Omnivorous. If cornered may assume defensive arched posture, growl or hiss, stamp feet and in some cases discharge musk. Generally quite sedentary, but capable of travelling long distances. Does not usually climb or swim.

STATUS: Introduced to parts of Europe for fur farming, but unsuccessful and has not established. In GB occasionally kept as pet or in wildlife collections, from which escapes sometimes occur. Experience from Europe suggests establishment in GB unlikely.

HABITAT: Wide range including woodlands, farmland and suburban areas.

IMPACT: May disrupt or prey upon ground-nesting birds and eggs. Nuisance in urban areas, also takes poultry. Major vector of disease in the USA.

Key differences between similar species
Unlikely to be confused with other species.

Crested and Himalayan Porcupines

Hystrix cristata (Crested Porcupine); *Hystrix brachyura* (Himalayan Porcupine)

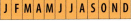

Native range:

Crested Porcupine – parts of Europe and Africa; Himalayan Porcupine – parts of Asia

Introduced:

Not established in the wild, but sightings have been reported since 1969.

Spread:

Kept as a pet, in zoos and other collections, from which escapes may occur

Other names:

European Porcupine (Crested Porcupine); Hodgson's Porcupine (Himalayan Porcupine)

Key differences between similar species

Unlike any other species in GB.

Crested Porcupine

DESCRIPTION: Distinctive, but unlikely to be seen due to nocturnal burrowing nature. *Large*, head and body 60–90cm, easily recognisable with thick black and white *quills covering back*. Head with crest of long hairs.

BEHAVIOUR: Mates in spring, young born late spring to early summer.

STATUS: A pair of Himalayan Porcupines escaped from a farm in Okehampton, Devon, in 1969. Several individuals were recorded over the following years, suggesting a population may have established. In 1973 the animals were trapped and removed, following concerns about their potential impact on nearby plantations and agricultural land. A pair of Crested Porcupines escaped from the botanical gardens at Alton Towers, Staffordshire, in 1972; however these did not persist after the late 1970s. Both species may continue to escape from collections and additional sightings of individuals have been recorded.

HABITAT: Able to disperse long distances; in GB have been found in woodland, farms and gardens.

IMPACT: Agricultural and forestry pests in parts of Europe. Potentially dangerous to humans and pets if cornered.

Himalayan Porcupine

Coypu

J F M A M J J A S O N D

Native range:

South America

Introduced:

1932, introduced for fur farming; subsequently eradicated

Spread:

Now unlikely to be spread by people (keeping is prohibited)

Other names:

Nutria

Coypu droppings

DESCRIPTION: Very *large* distinctive rodent (head to tail length 60–110cm). Head broad and sturdy. Ears small and indistinct. Tail long, almost hairless, cylindrical and scaly. Fur dark or reddish brown, glossy and thick, white on tip of muzzle. *Hind feet webbed*. Large *bright orange incisor teeth* usually visible.

BEHAVIOUR: Most active at dusk, dawn and at night, sometimes seen during the day. Breeds all year round.

FIELD SIGNS: Runs bare of vegetation when well used, to 15cm wide.

DROPPINGS: Distinctive. *Large*, 2 x 7mm to 11 x 70mm. *Lozenge-shaped*, may be slightly curved with *longitudinal ridges*. Dark brown or green. Deposited in water or randomly on bank.

FEEDING SIGNS: Digs out roots and rhizomes. Piles of cut and chewed vegetation, including reeds, grass and roots, with large bite marks (up to 17mm) may be found in or near water.

NEST: Digs complex burrow networks in river banks with multiple entrances above and below water level on banks. Occasionally builds shallow nests from leaves in reeds.

TRACKS: Large. Hind footprint to 15cm long. Imprint of web often visible. Up to 5 claw marks in hind and fore print. Shallow tail scrape up to 2cm wide sometimes present.

STATUS: Well established in East Anglia by 1960s following introduction for fur farming. Eradication was undertaken successfully from 1981–1989. Keeping of Coypus is now prohibited in GB.

HABITAT: Aquatic, living by rivers, streams, ponds and marshes.

IMPACT: Was a significant crop pest in East Anglia. Burrows can cause bank erosion and impact on waterways and flood defences. Damages sensitive native habitat through grazing.

Key differences between similar species

- **European Beaver** *Castor fiber*. Native, reintroduced. Only a few small populations in GB, around the River Tay and in Argyll. Unlikely to be confused. *Much larger* (head and body 75–100cm, tail 28–38cm). Broad, *horizontally flattened tail* unlike round tail of Coypu.

Muskrat

Ondatra zibethicus

DESCRIPTION: Large *vole-like animal* (head to tail length 41–62cm). Tail long, hairless and *vertically flattened*. Small ears. Thick fur dark or chestnut-brown, no clear demarcation between dorsal and slightly lighter belly fur.

BEHAVIOUR: Most active early morning and at night.
DROPPINGS: Cylindrical with blunt ends, similar to those of Water Vole but *larger* (to 15mm) and more *elongate*.
NEST: Built in 'lodges' above ground made from aquatic vegetation, or burrows in river banks with entrances underwater.
TRACKS: Up to 5 claw marks. Fore 35 x 35mm, hind 60 x 65mm. Strong tail drag.
OTHER: Musky odour.

STATUS: Previously established in 1930s, following introduction in 1920s for fur farming. Eradicated by 1937. Keeping of Muskrats is now prohibited in GB.
HABITAT: Aquatic, living by rivers, streams, ponds and marshes.
IMPACT: Burrowing and grazing can cause significant damage to agriculture, waterways, flood defence and natural habitats. Competes with native species. Vector of Weil's disease.

Native range:

North America

Introduced:

1920s, introduced for fur farming; subsequently eradicated

Spread:

Now unlikely to be spread by people (keeping is prohibited)

Other names:

None.

Key differences between similar species

Size makes this species dissimilar to any others in Great Britain.

Birds

There are 11 established non-native birds in Britain, most of which are thought to cause negative impacts.

Impacts include:

- **Environmental** – competing with, preying on or displacing native species (Egyptian Goose, Ring-necked Parakeet); increasing the eutrophication of water bodies (Canada Goose); and threatening the genetic integrity of some native species (Ruddy Duck which is threatening the genetic integrity of the White-headed Duck in Spain).

- **Economic** – damage done by non-native birds through damage to crops (Canada Goose, Monk Parakeet);

- **Human health / social** – a number of non-native birds can be a general nuisance, making noise and fouling; some birds, particularly the larger geese, pose a risk to aircraft by colliding with them in flight.

Most non-native birds established in GB were deliberately introduced as ornamentals into wildfowl collections, but also as pets and for display and have subsequently formed self-sustaining populations in the wild. A number of quarry species have also been introduced for sport and hunting. Other pathways that could pose a future risk include stowaways on boats (Indian House Crow) and escapees from zoos (Sacred Ibis).

This section covers the majority of non-native bird species established in GB that could be considered invasive as well as a number of horizon species. We have not covered quarry species, such as Common Pheasant and Red-legged Partridge, or less likely horizon species such as the Alexandrine Parakeet.

Monk Parakeet nests can cause problems on structures including pylons and phone masts

Identification tips

Many of the non-native species can still often be found associated with wildfowl collections at lakes across GB.

Many are distinctive and unlikely to be confused with native species. However, in some cases identification is more difficult, particularly for females which can be less distinctly coloured than the males.

Time of year can be important in terms of both appearance and behaviour. For example, during the winter Ruddy Ducks congregate at water bodies making them easier to spot, but disperse during summer months. The males also lose their distinctive colouration during winter months.

Many have distinctive calls, which is often the first indication that the birds are present. Other field signs can also be useful, such as nests and feeding damage.

Case study: The impact of Ruddy Duck and its eradication in Britain

The Ruddy Duck (*Oxyura jamaicensis*), from North America, was introduced to Britain in the 1940s for captive waterfowl collections. Subsequent escapes led to the first breeding population in the wild by 1960s, which had grown to a peak of 6,000 individuals by 2000.

As the number of Ruddy Ducks in Britain increased they began to migrate to continental Europe and reached Spain in the 1980s.

Spain has one of the last remaining populations of the White-headed Duck (*Oxyura leucocephala*), the only stiff-tail duck species native to Europe. The White-headed Duck is globally threatened with extinction and in the last century its numbers have reduced from 100,000 birds to fewer than 10,000. The Spanish population represents a quarter of the total world population and is the result of a substantial conservation effort to restore the population after it dwindled to just 22 individuals in the 1970s.

The globally threatened White-headed Duck

The Ruddy Ducks in Spain interbreed and hybridise with White-headed Ducks producing fertile offspring. This hybridisation with the Ruddy Duck became the biggest threat to survival of the White-headed Duck as a distinct species. In response, an agreement was made under the auspices of the Bern Convention to eradicate Ruddy Duck from Europe by 2015. Acknowledging that the UK had the largest feral population in Europe (95% of all individuals), the UK government and European Commission funded control trials that started in 1999, with full-scale eradication commencing in 2005.

The programme has achieved considerable success and by 2014 had reduced the numbers of Ruddy Duck from 6,000 to just 40 individuals. Ongoing work aims to remove the final individuals by the end of 2015. Combined with work to remove smaller populations in France, Belgium and the Netherlands this effort should help safeguard the future of the White-headed Duck worldwide.

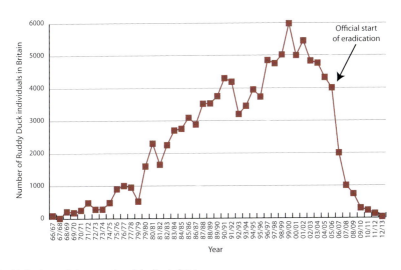

Ruddy Duck population growth and decline in Britain

Parakeets

There are two established parakeet species in Great Britain. Ring-necked Parakeet is well established in much of London, while Monk Parakeet is established in only a few locations in London. They are unlike any native species and hard to miss, being brightly coloured and noisy. Other parrot species occasionally escape, but have not become established.

Ring-necked Parakeet

Psittacula krameri

Native range:

South Asia and central Africa

Introduced:

1855 first record in wild, established since 1969; escaped or deliberately released pet

Spread:

Kept as a pet and in collections, from which escapes or deliberate release may occur

Other names:

Rose-ringed Parakeet

Similar species
See page 186.

DESCRIPTION: *Bright, emerald green,* other colours possible. 39–43cm long, wing-span 42–48cm, weight approximately 125g. Short, *bright red bill*. Eyes with orange-red surround. Tail tapering and long, about half total length of bird, characteristic in flight. **Male:** Distinguished by *black ring around neck*, bordered by pinkish-red on nape, may have bluish sheen particularly on rear of crown and tail. **Female:** *Lacks distinct neck ring*, instead neck ring is indistinct pale green.

BEHAVIOUR: Highly social, often forming large flocks.
NEST: In tree holes, not usually visible.
CALL: *Highly vocal; very loud* squawking 'kyik kyik kyiek'.

STATUS: Well established in much of London, particularly west and south-east, and spreading to surrounding areas. Escapes may be seen elsewhere.
HABITAT: Urban and suburban parks, gardens and cultivated land with some mature trees. Will use large nestboxes.
IMPACT: Strips fruit from trees. Pest of orchards. Potential threat to native birds through competition for nest sites. Can be a noisy nuisance.

Monk Parakeet

Myiopsitta monachus

J F M A M J J A S O N D

Native range:

South America

Introduced:

1936 first record in the wild, established since 1990s; escaped or deliberately released pet

Spread:

Kept as a pet and in collections, from which escapes or deliberate release may occur

Other names:

Quaker Parrot, Grey-breasted Parakeet

NB Defra have recently undertaken a programme to eradicate Monk Parakeets. As of September 2014 there were estimated to be 50 birds remaining.

Similar species
See page 186

DESCRIPTION: 28–31cm long, weight approximately 125g. Bright green back and wings, yellow-green belly, *grey face, throat and breast*. Long bright green tail. Blue flight feathers. *Pale bill.* Sexes alike.

NEST: Distinctive, *very large, communal and constructed from sticks* in trees or on man-made structures.
CALL: Ranges from incessant *chattering* to loud screeches.

STATUS: Currently there are only two colonies in suburban London (Borehamwood and the Isle of Dogs), likely to expand range. Escapees may be encountered elsewhere.
HABITAT: In GB most likely to be found in urban and suburban parks and gardens.
IMPACT: Feed in large flocks and have become an agricultural pest elsewhere in the world. Large nests cause problems on electricity pylons and mobile phone masts.

Differences between similar species

Unlikely to be confused with any native bird species. Ring-necked Parakeet distinguished from Monk Parakeet by larger size, colour (look for the grey breast of the Monk Parakeet), call and nesting behaviour. Other species of parrots occasionally escape from captivity.

Alexandrine Parakeet *Psittacula eupatria*

Considerably larger (to 62cm). Very large red bill. Can interbreed with Ring-necked Parakeet producing hybrid with intermediate characteristics.

Blue-crowned Parakeet *Aratinga acuticaudata*

Blue forehead makes this parakeet particularly distinctive.

Rosy-faced Lovebird *Agapornis roseicollis*

Much *smaller*. Short-tailed. Green with a pink face and upper breast.

Eurasian Eagle Owl

Bubo bubo

Native range:

Parts of Europe and Asia

Introduced:

1984 first breeding attempt in the wild, several breeding pairs recorded by 1990s; escaped from collections and falconry displays

Spread:

Kept in collections and for falconry, from which escapes may occur

DESCRIPTION: *Largest owl in Europe*. Strongly built, 59–73cm long, wingspan 138–175cm, weighing 2.3–4.2 kg. Dark brown plumage on back with many black streaks and marks. Underside paler with fewer dark streaks, mainly on chest. Head large with obvious *ear tufts*. Large, *piercing orange eyes* circled black. Feet large and feathered with substantial talons. **Female:** Usually larger than male.

BEHAVIOUR: Highly secretive. Nocturnal, sometimes crepuscular. Carnivorous hunter.
NEST: In tree cavity, cliff crevice or ledge.
CALL: Can be very vocal during breeding season. Male call is monotonous 'buho', female gives higher-pitched 'u-hu'. Alarm call is croaking 'grack'.

STATUS: Non-native, although there is some debate (see Melling *et al* 2008). Only a few (c. 10) breeding pairs known in Great Britain. Commonly kept for falconry displays and private collections, regularly escapes.
HABITAT: In Great Britain found mainly in forest and woodland, also favours mountainous areas and cliffs.
IMPACT: Has potential to compete with and prey on native raptors as well as other native species.

Key differences between similar species

Unlikely to be confused with native owls as much larger.

● **Common Buzzard** *Buteo buteo*. Native. Common. Unlikely to be confused, but may appear similar in flight at distance. Quickly distinguished by much *smaller head.*.

Greater Canada Goose

Branta canadensis

Native range:

North America

Introduced:

<1665 introduced as an ornamental; breeding in the wild since 1700s

Spread:

Escapes from collections and deliberate release/translocation

Other names:

Canada Goose

DESCRIPTION: Largest wild goose in Great Britain. 90–100cm long, wingspan 160–175cm and adult weight 4.3–5 kg. *Long black neck.* Head black with *white chin strap* and *black bill*. Legs and feet black. Strong regular wingbeats in flight with white tail-base clearly visible. Sexes similar. **Juvenile:** Duller coloration.

BEHAVIOUR: Highly social. Flocks adopt typical 'V' formation in flight. Grazing creates typical closely cropped grass areas around water bodies.
NEST: Down-lined scrape, often on small islands or hidden beside water bodies.
EGGS: 5.8–8.6cm, white or cream-coloured. Laid March–June in clutches of 5–6.
CALL: Deep, *loud honking.*

STATUS: Introduced as an ornamental. Expanded range considerably in the 1950s and 60s due to translocation. Widely established by 1970s.
HABITAT: Common in parklands, pastures, cereal fields and on water bodies.
IMPACT: Large flocks cause grazing damage, add to the eutrophication of freshwaters and increase risk of aircraft bird strike. Trampling of vegetation can disrupt nesting of other birds.

Key differences between similar species

Barnacle Goose *Branta leucopsis*

Native. Winter visitor, but escapes may be seen year round. Relatively easy to distinguish by *smaller* size, 58–70cm long, and coloration. *Breast black*, unlike white breast of Canada Goose. *Face white*, not just chin strap. Body grey. In flight, contrast between black breast and white belly is distinct.

Brent Goose *Branta bernicla*

Native. Winter visitor. Unlikely to be confused. *Strictly maritime* in Great Britain, found along coastline and in adjacent fields. Much *smaller*, 56–61cm. *Darker*. Head, neck and breast dull black with *small white crescent on upper neck*.

Greylag x Canada hybrid

Intermediate characteristics. *Head and face usually duller* with *orange bill. Legs and bill often pink*.

Egyptian Goose

Alopochen aegyptiacus

J F M A M J J A S O N D

Native range:

Sub-Saharan Africa

Introduced:

17th century introduced as an ornamental, breeding in the wild by early 1800s; population relatively small until rapid increase in the 1980s

Spread:

Escapes from collections and deliberate release/translocation

Other names:

None.

DESCRIPTION: *Small stocky goose.* 63–73cm long, approximately 1.5–2kg. Considerable variation between individuals. *Distinctive colouring.* Front of body buff with chestnut-brown breast patch and brown collar. Head and underside pale, upperparts grey to brown. Large white panels on wing. *Usually has brown 'spectacles' around eyes.* Bill dull pinky-red with dark outline. Long dull pinkish legs. Females smaller than males with lighter coloration. **Juvenile:** Duller coloration.

NEST: Usually a mound of grass or reeds lined with down.
EGGS: 6.9 x 5cm, laid March–April in a clutch of 8–9. Creamy-white.
CALL: Generally silent, though male may make husky, wheezing sounds and female a harsh quacking or trumpeting.

STATUS: Well established in Norfolk and Suffolk. Expanding westwards. Also in ornamental parks across GB.
HABITAT: Lakes, marshes and rivers. In GB often found in parkland around freshwater bodies.
IMPACT: Causes crop damage and eutrophication of water bodies. Highly territorial and may compete with or disrupt native birds. Potential aircraft strike risk.

190

Egyptian Goose in flight.

Key differences between similar species

● Unlike any native species.

Ruddy Shelduck
Tadorna ferruginea

Non-native. Uncommon. Quite dissimilar, but may be confused in flight because of large white wing markings. *Smaller. Brighter orange body. Buff-coloured head. Dark bill* and *legs*.

Ruddy Duck

Oxyura jamaicensis

Native range:

North America

Introduced:

1930s introduced into wildfowl collections, established in the wild by 1960s

Spread:

Now unlikely to be spread by people

Other names:

None.

♂ summer

DESCRIPTION: Small, *compact duck*. 35–43cm long, wingspan 53–62cm, weight 350–800g. Long, stiff tail held flat or cocked upwards. Rounded back, large head and strong bill. **Male:** Summer – deep *chestnut-brown* body with striking *blue bill, bright white cheeks*, black cap and dark nape. Winter – much duller grey-brown colour with black-grey bill. Dark cap and white cheeks retained. **Female:** Similar to winter male with grey-brown body and grey-black bill, has paler cheeks with broad dark stripe.

BEHAVIOUR: *Sits low in the water*. Dives often. Weak flier, lacking agility, rarely leaves water.
NEST: April–June in thick vegetation and reeds, building floating platform often covered by meshed stems.
EGGS: One brood per year, 6–10 dull or creamy-white eggs.
CALL: Mostly silent, occasionally makes grunting sounds. Males make *tapping noise* during display by vibrating bill against breast.

STATUS: Formerly well established, now significantly reduced as result of a coordinated eradication campaign.
HABITAT: Pools and smaller water bodies in spring and summer, flocking to large lakes and reservoirs in autumn and winter.
IMPACT: Hybridises with the White-headed Duck in Spain, threatening the survival of this species.

♂ winter

Female. Ruddy Duck can be confused with females of other species.

♀ year round

Key differences between similar species

Smew *Mergus albellus*

Native. *Uncommon* winter visitor. Female similar to male Ruddy Duck in winter, male quite different. Female Smew has *smaller head* and tail. *White chin and throat. Chestnut head and neck.*

Common Scoter
Melanitta nigra

Native. Resident in parts of Scotland, winter visitor in rest of GB. A seaduck, usually found *offshore or on coastal waters*. Male pure black and unlikely to be confused. Female is more brown with a paler face, similar to Ruddy Duck female. *Bulbous bill with yellow markings. Has pale face but lacks the dark cheek stripe* of female Ruddy Duck.

Mandarin Duck

Aix galericulata

J F M A M J J A S O N D

Native range:

East Asia

Introduced:

1745 introduced as an ornamental, breeding in the wild by 1950s; population rapidly increased after 1980s

Spread:

Escapes from collections

Other names:

None.

♂

DESCRIPTION: Small. *Male:* distinctly *exotic*-looking. *Brightly coloured* in winter and spring, dark breast, orange 'whiskers' on cheeks and orange 'sails' on wings. Wide white streak on head. Bill bright red. **Female:** More difficult to identify. Body dull grey. Pale rounded spots on breast and flanks. Bill pale. *Narrow white eye ring and stripe behind eye*. Chin white.

NEST: Perches in trees and nests in tree holes. Will use nestboxes.
EGGS: 5.1 x 3.7mm, buff to ivory colour. Clutch 9–12 eggs, usually laid March–May.
CALL: Generally silent, but male may make a short rising call and shrill whistle in alarm. Female makes low clucking noise.

STATUS: Common ornamental duck in waterfowl collections. Has spread quickly in latter half of 20th century. More frequent in southern England.
HABITAT: Most likely to be found at parks, lakes and rivers with surrounding trees and vegetation.
IMPACT: May compete with other hole-nesting birds.

♀

Key differences between similar species

Unlikely to be confused with any native species.
● **Wood Duck** *Aix sponsa*. Non-native. Not established, but sporadically encountered in parks or as escaped ornamentals. Adult males very different. Females and juveniles difficult to distinguish from female Mandarin. Somewhat darker body, head and tip to bill. White marking around eye is *wider, shorter and somewhat untidy*, compared to neat eye ring and long, thin stripe of female Mandarin. Light spots on breast and body of Mandarin *rounder and more prominent*. Mandarin has green on rear of crown.

Black Swan

Cygnus atratus

J F M A M J J A S O N D

Native range:

Southern Australia and New Zealand

Introduced:

1791 introduced as an ornamental, first breeding record in wild 1851

Spread:

Escapes from collections and deliberate release

Other names:

None.

DESCRIPTION: The *only black swan*. 111–140cm long. *Bright red bill* with white band near tip. Bright white primaries and outer secondaries partly visible when at rest, but striking when wings are raised or in flight. Neck very long, in flight obviously over half length of body. Inner flight feathers twisted. Black legs and feet. Sexes alike.

BEHAVIOUR: Highly social compared to other swans.
NEST: Usually made of reeds and grass, near water.
CALL: High-pitched bugling.

STATUS: Pairs and individuals recorded widely across Great Britain, but breeding is rare. Probably not currently forming self-sustaining populations.
HABITAT: Found on freshwater or brackish water bodies with nearby grassland.
IMPACT: Competes with native waterfowl, also known to damage crops.

Key differences between similar species

Unlikely to be confused with any other species. Note: hybrids with Mute Swan occur in Europe with intermediate characteristics.

Sacred Ibis

Threskiornis aethiopicus

J F M A M J J A S O N D

NP

Native range:

Sub-Saharan Africa

Introduced:

Not established in the wild, but sightings have been reported since 1995. Escapes from zoos and collections

Spread:

Escapes from collections

Other names:

None.

DESCRIPTION: Highly distinctive. 60–85cm long, wingspan 110–125cm, weight 1.5 kg. Bright white body. *Black featherless head. Long, black, down-curved bill.* Long black legs and black plumes in tail. In flight broad white wings and black head characteristic, as well as black tips and trailing edge of wings. Sexes alike. **Juvenile:** Head and neck with black, grey and white feathers.

BEHAVIOUR: Generalist feeder, including on birds' eggs and chicks.
NEST: In trees, bushes or on the ground. Built March to May, usually from sticks and branches. Gregarious, breeding in large colonies of up to hundreds of pairs.
CALL: Generally silent, sometimes a harsh croak in flight.

STATUS: Not established in Great Britain, but could become invasive in the future. Invasive on west coast of France where several non-native populations have established. May arrive in GB from populations in Europe or as an escape from captive birds kept in GB.
HABITAT: Thrives around human settlements. Mainly found on shallow wetland, such as wet grassland, as well as landfill sites, arable fields and intertidal areas.
IMPACT: Considered a general nuisance where invasive, may out-compete or prey upon native species. Has had a significant impact on native tern colonies in France where they disturb nests and prey upon eggs and chicks.

Nesting colony of Sacred Ibis.

Juvenile Sacred Ibis.

Key differences between similar species

Unmistakable if clearly seen. If not, possibly confused with other black-and-white or white medium to large wading birds (such as Spoonbill or Avocet).

Spoonbill *Platalea leucorodia*

Native, rare. Large, 80–93cm. White-bodied wading bird with straight *spoon-shaped bill*. Head and neck white, feathered.

Avocet *Recurvirostra avosetta*

Native, becoming more common. Small, 42–46cm. Distinct black-and-white patterning on body and neck. Thin *upturned* black bill. Feathered head and neck.

Indian House Crow

Corvus splendens

J F M A M J J A S O N D

Not recorded in Britain

NP

Native range:

Indian subcontinent

Introduced:

Has not been recorded in GB. Most likely to arrive as a stowaway on ships from non-native population in the Netherlands.

Spread:

Stowaway on ships

Other names:

House Crow

DESCRIPTION: Slightly smaller than native Carrion Crow, 37–42cm long with wingspan of 68–80cm and weight 245–370 g. *Slender*, almost lanky, with long legs, tail, and wings. Legs and feet black. Back, wings, throat and most of head glossy black. Underside of body dark grey, nape, breast, upper back and sides of head *grey*. Black on head extends from bill to just behind the eye, unlike almost entirely black head of Hooded Crow. *Head relatively small* with *large black bill*.

NEST: In trees or manmade structures April–May. Untidy mess made from natural and manmade items.

CALL: Quite quiet, with muffled Hooded Crow like 'kraar'. Mobs raptors with harder 'krao krao'.

STATUS: Not present in Great Britain, a potential future invader. Has been recorded in Ireland though is not established. Introduced to Europe (the Netherlands) as a ship stowaway

HABITAT: Closely connected with human populations, particularly ports.

IMPACT: A pest in many countries where it damages crops, aggressively competes with native species and is a significant predator.

Key differences between similar species

Carrion Crow *Corvus corone*

Native. Common, except north and west Scotland.
Larger, 44–51cm. Plumage *all black*. Smaller bill. Shorter legs.

Hooded Crow *Corvus cornix*

Native. In Britain *rarely found outside of north and west Scotland*. *Larger*, 44–51cm. *Clearly demarcated light grey nape* and belly, unlike less demarked and darker grey of House Crow. *Almost entirely black head. More black* on breast than Indian House Crow. Smaller bill. Shorter legs.

Forms hybrid zone with Carrion Crow along southern boundary of distribution.

Jackdaw *Corvus monedula*

Native. Common except in Scottish Highlands. *Small*, 30–34cm long. Head, back and wings glossy black. Rest of body greyish sheen, but *lacks distinct grey colouring except on nape*. *Pale eye,* unlike dark eye of Indian House Crow.

Amphibians

There are six established non-native amphibian species in Britain, most of which are thought to cause negative impacts. Marsh Frog is very well established in south-east England and Alpine Newt is found in a number of scattered localities, but the other non-native species are relatively rare. The African Clawed Frog was established, but is now thought to have been eradicated. A number of other species have been incidentally recorded, but are not thought to be established.

An important concern with non-native amphibians is their potential to introduce and spread disease to native species (see chytrid fungus below). Other environmental impacts include competition with and predation on native species as well as genetic introgressive hybridisation in the case of the Italian Crested Newt. There are no economic or social impacts, although the loud calling of some species can be a nuisance.

Most species have either escaped from ornamental collections, have been deliberately released or in some cases were imported with contaminated aquatic stock (for example with water plants).

Identification tip:

- Generally easiest to identify during their breeding seasons, when they are returning to water bodies to spawn. Male newts develop more distinctive crests and colouration during this time, whereas the frogs and toads often have a distinctive breeding call.

- More active at night than by day, often hiding among vegetation or under stones during daylight hours. Inspecting a water body at night with a torch is often the best way to see them; however, care should be taken not to disturb protected native species.

- On sunny days non-native frogs may be seen basking on the banks of a pond or stream or heard jumping back into the water with a 'plop'.

- It is often possible to identify the non-native species as spawn and tadpoles as well as at the adult stage.

Chytrid fungus

A type of chytrid fungus, *Batrachochytrium dendrobatidis*, is a disease seriously threatening amphibians around the world and in Britain. First recorded in Britain in 2004, it appears to be associated with the movement of non-native species, including African Clawed Frog, American Bullfrog and Alpine Newt. As with other diseases, biosecurity protocols should be carefully followed to avoid accidentally transferring this disease between water bodies.

Newts

There are two established non-native newts in Great Britain: the Alpine Newt, which is quite distinct from other species and the Italian Crested Newt, which is very similar to the native Great Crested Newt. Both are unlikely to be encountered, given their currently limited distribution, although Alpine Newt is more common.

	Alpine Newt	Italian Crested Newt	Great Crested Newt	Smooth Newt/Palmate Newt
Status	40 or so populations scattered across GB	Two sites: Surrey and Birmingham	Widespread, relatively common	Widespread, common
Size	9–11cm	10–18cm	12–16cm	Up to 10cm
Colour	Males dark blue-black, females mottled grey. Velvety skin	Dark black or brown. Flanks with large dark spots, no white speckles. Face with white spots	Very similar to Italian Crested Newt but with white speckles and less obvious large dark spots on flanks	Usually lighter brown to grey
Belly	Bright orange-red, no spots	Bright orange with large dark spots	Yellowy-orange with large dark spots	Whitish edges, yellowy-orange in middle with dark spots
Crest (breeding males)	Low, light yellow stripe with black spots	Tall dark crest	Tall dark crest	Tall dark crest

Newtpoles

Newt and spawn

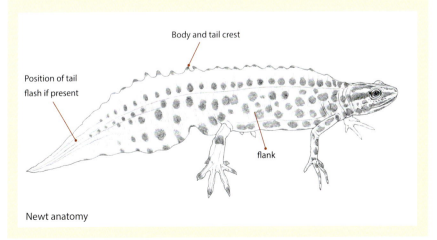

Body and tail crest

Position of tail flash if present

flank

Newt anatomy

Alpine Newt

Ichthyosaura alpestris

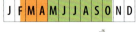

Native range:

Continental Europe

Introduced:

1903, deliberately stocked in the ponds of an aquatic nursery in Surrey

Spread:

Deliberately stocked in garden and ornamental ponds

Other names:

formerly *Mesotriton alpestris* and *Trituris alpestris*

♂

DESCRIPTION: Distinctive, medium-sized newt. Bright orange-red belly *without spots*. On land skin velvety but granular. **Male:** 9–11cm generally dark blue-black, with *spotted flanks* and pale blue tail flash. When breeding develops *low, yellow crest*, usually darkly spotted or barred. **Female:** Up to 12cm, duller brown colour with grey marbling on flanks. **Tadpole:** Intermediate in appearance between those of Smooth and Great Crested Newts. **Eggs:** Females attach eggs singly to water plants.

STATUS: More than 40 populations have established in Great Britain, including Scotland, following release into garden ponds. Capable of relatively wide dispersal, but has spread little so far.
HABITAT: In Britain, mostly garden ponds and surrounding habitat. Highly aquatic, unlikely to be found far from water.
IMPACT: A vector of amphibian disease. May compete with native newt species.

Key differences between similar species

Quickly distinguished from Smooth Newt *Lissotriton vulgaris* (below) and Palmate Newt *L. helveticus*, which are smaller, to 10cm long, not as brightly coloured (usually a light grey brown), have orange bellies with dark spots (reduced or absent in Palmate Newt) and males have large crests along their backs. Unlikely to be confused with Italian Crested Newt (opposite).

Smooth Newt

♀

♂

Italian Crested Newt

Triturus carnifex

J	F	M	A	M	J	J	A	S	O	N	D

Native range:

Central southern Europe, including Italy and western Balkans

Introduced:

1903, deliberately stocked in the ponds of an aquatic nursery in Surrey

Spread:

Deliberately stocked in garden and ornamental ponds

Other names:

None.

♂

♀

DESCRIPTION: Easily confused with the native Great Crested Newt. Large (male 10–15cm, female 12–18cm). Dark-coloured, black, brown, grey or sometimes yellowish body. *Flanks with large dark spots* and usually *without white speckles*. Belly bright orange with large black/brown spots. Throat and sides of head dark with small white spots. **Male:** Develops crest along body and tail in breeding season (March–June). **Female and juvenile:** Often with *orange or yellow stripe along the back*. **Eggs:** Female lays single eggs wrapped in leaf of aquatic plant.

STATUS: Introduced for pet trade and subsequently escaped. Established at only two sites – in Surrey and Birmingham.
HABITAT: Prefers open, unvegetated ponds. Most likely to be found in garden ponds.
IMPACT: Closely related to and can interbreed with native Great Crested Newt, potentially threatening the genetic integrity of this species. Also a vector of amphibian disease.

♂

Key differences between similar species

- **Great Crested Newt** *Triturus cristatus*. Native. Widespread in lowland Britain. Adult 12–16cm long. Great Crested Newt is very similar to Italian Crested Newt; expert identification likely to be required. *Slimmer* than Italian Crested Newt. Has *wartier* skin. Flanks often with less obvious *dark spots*. *Has white stippling*. Belly less yellow.

Frogs

	Common Frog	Marsh Frog	American Bullfrog	African Clawed Frog
Status	Widespread	Mainly in south-east England and Somerset levels	Previously established in south-east England, possibly still present	Previously established in Lincolnshire and South Wales
Size	6–9cm	10–13cm	Up to 15cm	Up to 11cm
Colour	Highly variable, often brown, green or yellowish	Variable, usually all or some bright green	Variable, often greens, browns and yellows	Albino forms quite common, also dark greys and browns
Ear drum	Ear drum same size as eye but with prominent dark mask next to eye	Ear drum same size as eye	Ear drum same size as eye in females, larger in males	Ear drum indistinct
Two parallel ridges on back?	Yes	Yes	No	No
Call	Low, rattiing croak	Laughing 'brek-ek-ek'	Deep cow-like 'br-wum'	Rarely makes audible call
Tadpole	Small (4cm)	Large (to 8cm)	Very large (to 15cm)	Very small (to 2cm)
Other features	Single vocal sac	Two vocal sacs (at cheek)	Single vocal sac	Body very flattened, eyes on top of head, highly aquatic

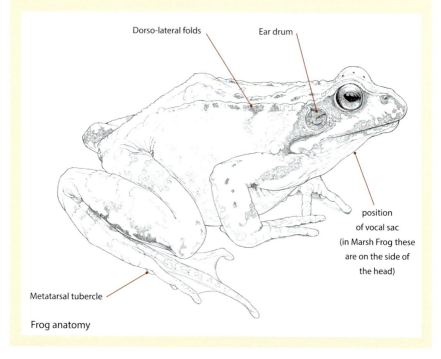

Dorso-lateral folds

Ear drum

position
of vocal sac
(in Marsh Frog these
are on the side of
the head)

Metatarsal tubercle

Frog anatomy

Frog and toad spawn

Spawn of Common Frog

Spawn of Common Toad

Spawn of Marsh Frog and other pool frogs

Spawn of American Bullfrog

Frog and toad tadpoles

Midwife Toad tadpole: to 7cm

Common Toad tadpole: to 2.5cm

Marsh Frog and other green frog tadpole: to 8cm

Common Frog tadpole: to 4cm

African Clawed Frog tadpole: to 2cm

American Bullfrog tadpole: to 15cm

African Clawed Frog

Xenopus laevis

J F M A M J J A S O N D

NP

Native range:

Sub-Saharan Africa

Introduced:

<1930s, introduced for use in laboratories, breeding in the wild by 1960s

Spread:

Escape from laboratories or re-lease of unwanted pets, in some cases deliberately introduced

Other names:

None.

DESCRIPTION: Up to 11cm long. Highly distinctive and unlikely to be confused. Hind limbs powerful. Feet fully webbed, with distinctive *sharp black claws* ❶. Front limbs small with *long splayed fingers* and no claws. Head and body distinctly *flattened*. Skin smooth and very slimy. *Eyes on top of head*. Lacks external ear-drum. Colour from white (albino) to dark brown with blotchy or mottled grey-brown back and uniform white underneath. Sometimes has white, stitch-like marks on flanks ❷. **Tadpole:** *Small*, 1–2cm long. Unusual with *2 long barbels*, giving catfish-like appearance, and little pigmentation. Head flattened and wedge-shaped. **Eggs:** Approximately 1mm diameter. Deposited singly into water in clutches of 500–2,000.

BEHAVIOUR: Secretive. Will hide in mud and vegetation at bottom of pond.

CALL: Rarely above water and generally silent. Males lack vocal sac but may make trill-like call from underwater, rarely heard. Breeds year-round, more often in spring and early summer.

STATUS: Introduced as a laboratory animal for research and pregnancy testing. Also common in pet trade. Has subsequently escaped into the wild. In some cases deliberately released to establish a population. Localised populations were established in south Wales, Lincolnshire and the Isle of Wight, though now thought to be extinct. Breeding only partially successful in Great Britain.

HABITAT: Almost entirely aquatic, but will move across land to find new ponds. Tolerates wide variety of permanent and temporary freshwater habitat. Prefers stagnant and still waters such as ponds.

IMPACT: A predator of native species. Vector of amphibian disease.

Key differences between similar species

Unlikely to be confused with any other species, particularly because of flattened appearance, clawed limbs and eyes on top of head.

American Bullfrog

Lithobates catesbeianus

| J | F | M | A | M | J | J | A | S | O | N | D |

♀

Native range:

Eastern North America

Introduced:

1970s, introduced for pet trade from which escapes or deliberate releases occurred; established in the wild by 1999

Spread:

Escape from garden ponds; may also be spread as a contaminant of plants or pond water

Other names:

Rana catesbeiana, North American Bullfrog

DESCRIPTION: *Very large*, 9–15 (20)cm long. Olive-green to brown with dark mottled blotches on back. Belly pale. Skin smooth but with warts. *Large eardrum* ❶ with conspicuous dark outer ring. Hind limbs large, powerful ❷, usually with dark banding. *No prominent ridges on back* (unlike native frogs). **Male:** Single yellow *vocal sac under the chin*. Eardrum larger than eye ❸ **Female:** White throat. Eardrum same size as eye ❹. **Tadpole:** Distinctly *large*, up to 15cm long. Takes 1–2 years to develop. May be found year round. **Eggs:** About 1.5–2mm diameter. Thousands are laid in a large *floating mat* across water surface.

BEHAVIOUR: Highly aquatic. Timid, but will bask in sun on margins of a watercourse. *More likely to be heard than seen*. Active day and night, but usually calls after dark.

CALL: A deep repeated 'br-wum', which can be distinctly cow-like. Heard during breeding season, June to July.

STATUS: Several populations have established in south-east England and have been subsequently eradicated. New populations occasionally occur and eradication efforts continue to remove them.

HABITAT: Survives in a variety of freshwater habitat, but prefers ponds, lakes and slow-flowing streams. May be present in garden ponds.

IMPACT: Highly invasive, significant threat to native wildlife. Competes with native amphibians and is a voracious predator, even taking small Grass Snakes and waterfowl chicks. Vector of amphibian disease.

♂ ❸

❹
♀

Key differences between similar species

See page 209.

Marsh Frog

Pelophylax ridibundus

Native range:

Central and eastern Europe

Introduced:

Deliberately introduced towards the end of 19th century. Established in the wild by the 1930s

Spread:

May be spread through deliberate releases, escapes from ponds and as a contaminant (tadpoles and eggs) of fish or aquatic plant stocks

Other names:

Lake Frog, Laughing Frog

DESCRIPTION: *Large*, 10–13cm long. Variable in colour but usually *green*, rarely brown. May have a *lighter yellow-green stripe* along middle of back ❶. Skin rough. Back with dark spots and *two prominent parallel ridges* (dorsal-lateral folds). Dark banding on back legs. *Snout usually more pointed* than that of Common Frog *Rana temporaria* and eyes slightly closer together. Males with *two grey vocal sacs* ❷, visible when calling. **Tadpole:** *Solitary*. Grows to *80mm*. Olive-green colour, often lighter mauve underneath. Usually found among vegetation. **Eggs:** Laid in small clumps a few centimetres beneath the water's surface, often attached to vegetation.

BEHAVIOUR: Frequently basks in sun on sides of waterbodies, but timid and dives back into water if approached, making a *distinctive 'plopping' sound*. Likely to be heard before being seen.
CALL: Distinctive *loud, laughing or quacking 'bre-kek-kek'*, made day or night during breeding season, May–June.

STATUS: Well established in parts of south-east England, particularly in Kent around Romney Marsh, but also the Somerset Levels and Tamworth area. Small populations found elsewhere and becoming more common.
HABITAT: Highly aquatic. Found in marshland, drainage ditches, ponds, lakes and other water bodies with plenty of vegetation.
IMPACT: Voracious predator of native species. Vector of disease. Loud calling can be a nuisance.

Key differences between similar species

American Bullfrog *Lithobates catesbeianus*

Can be confused with large Marsh Frog but usually larger, to 15cm long. Lacks long parallel ridges on back. Males have a single yellow vocal sac and ear drum larger than the eye Ⓐ . Often less bright green in colour. Calls distinctly different, American Bullfrog is lower pitched 'br-wum' compared to higher-pitched laughing call of Marsh Frog.

Common Frog *Rana temporaria*

Native and widespread. Relatively easy to distinguish. Small, 6–9cm long. Dark mask next to eye Ⓑ. Male with single vocal sac under chin.

Other 'water frogs'

Marsh Frog is part of a species complex called the water frogs. They are characterised by their colour, noisy call and aquatic nature. Other water frogs in GB include the Pool Frog, the northern race of which is native, and Edible Frog, a non-native hybrid between the Marsh and Pool Frog.

It is very difficult to distinguish between the water frogs and specialist examination of morphological features and/or call is likely to be required. A brief summary of identification features is provided below but note expert assistance should be sought. For more information refer to Inns (2009).

	Marsh Frog	Edible Frog (intermediate characteristics)	Pool Frog
Distribution	Widespread in south-east England, becoming more common elsewhere.	Established populations mainly in southern England, but could be found elsewhere.	One population of native northern subspecies (Norfolk). Non-native southern form highly localised in parts of England.
Colour	Green, sometimes with dark green spots (occasionally with yellow green dorsal stripe)	Green to brown (often with green dorsal stripe). Upper lip often white.	Brown with some green and black, usually without dorsal stripe
Leg length in relation to head and body	Long	Medium	Short
Metatarsal tubercle	Small	Medium	Large
Vocal sac colour	Grey	Light grey	Pure white

Midwife Toad

J	F	M	A	M	J	J	A	S	O	N	D

Native range:

Parts of Europe

Introduced:

Turn of the 19th century, introduced accidentally to an aquatic nursery as a contaminant of plant stock, subsequently deliberately stocked in garden ponds; well established in a few localities by the 1950s

Spread:

Deliberate releases and as a contaminant with fish or aquatic plant stocks

Other names:

Common Midwife Toad

DESCRIPTION: *Small, plump* toad, 3–5cm. Skin is rough with warts, which are usually more prominent in two lines along back. Usually grey-brown, with dark blotches, lighter underneath. Warts are frequently red or yellow. *Snout pointed* with prominent eyes. *Distinctive cat-like vertical pupils* ❶. Short legs with powerful forelimbs used for digging. **Male:** Males smaller than females. **Tadpole:** Highly distinctive, very large, *up to 70mm*, with distinctive *black spots on tail*. Unlike native species, large numbers of tadpoles may still be found in ponds over winter.

BEHAVIOUR: *Nocturnal*, hiding under debris and in crevices during day. When threatened inflates body and draws limbs close to body. Occasionally assumes a 'fright posture' with rump raised and head down between forelimbs. Secretive, more likely to be identified by call than sight.
CALL: Breeding call is loud, sonar-like, *high-pitched 'peep'* repeated at frequent intervals. Made usually at night, May–June.
EGGS: Following breeding in summer males carry 10–15 large, creamy yellow eggs in strings *wound around back legs*. Deposited in water when ready to hatch.

STATUS: Originally introduced to a nursery in Bedford, probably by accident on water plants from France. Stronghold still in Bedfordshire. Established in few locations, but range expansion possible.
HABITAT: Found mainly around original establishment sites, gardens and nurseries. Adults mostly terrestrial, but usually found near water. Prefers habitat with light or sandy soil in which to burrow.
IMPACT: Not known to cause significant impacts, though may be a vector of amphibian disease.

Key differences between similar species

Common Toad *Bufo bufo*

Native, widespread. *Larger,* up to 9cm long. Never carries eggs. Call is *croaky squeak* which does not carry. *Large glands behind eye.* Ⓐ *Pupils horizontal* Ⓑ.

Natterjack Toad *Epidalea calamita*

Native, highly restricted to certain areas of sand dune and sandy heath mainly in Merseyside, Cumbria and the Solway Firth in Scotland, scattered elsewhere in England and Wales. Small, 5–7.5cm, but still larger than Midwife Toad. Call is long, carrying, high-pitched rattle. Distinct, thin *yellow stripe along middle of back. Pupils horizontal.*

	Common Toad	Natterjack Toad	Midwife Toad
Status	Common, widespread	Main population around Merseyside, Cumbria and Solway Firth in Scotland	Main population around Bedford
Size	Up to 9cm	Up to 7.5cm	Up to 5cm
Pupil	Horizontal	Horizontal	Vertical
Spawn	Long strings of eggs laid in ponds	Long strings of eggs laid in ponds	Long strings of eggs wrapped around legs of males
Call	Croaky squeak	Long, high pitched rattle	High pitched sonar-like 'peep … peep'
Tadpole	Small (to 2.5cm)	Small (to 2.5cm)	Very large (to 7cm)
Other features	Large gland behind ear	Stripe along middle of back	Pointed snout

Reptiles

There are three established non-native reptile species in Britain, all of which have the potential to cause negative impacts. Green Lizard and Aesculapian Snake are only in a few well-separated locations, whereas Wall Lizard is well established in parts of southern England and south Wales. Red-eared Terrapin is relatively widespread, but cannot reproduce successfully in our climate and is therefore not considered established. Other species, including Snapping Turtle, European Pond Turtle and Rat Snake, have been recorded, but are not thought to be established.

The impacts of non-native reptiles in Britain are not well studied or understood. The non-native lizards could compete with and potentially displace native species including the rare native Sand Lizard. Non-native species may also harbour diseases that could be a risk to native species. Red-eared Terrapin is a voracious predator; however its impact is limited by its inability to establish.

Some non-native reptile populations, such as Red-eared Terrapin, were introduced to Britain as pets which escaped or were released into the wild. Others escaped from zoos or were deliberately introduced into the wild by individuals keen to add them to the British fauna.

Reptiles should be approached carefully and quietly, binoculars can be useful to help keep distance.

Identification tips for snakes and lizards

Usually hard to spot so avoid disturbance. They are unlikely to be seen over winter, but are usually active for the rest of the year. As cold-blooded animals they are most likely to be seen basking in the morning or late afternoon sun, but not when the weather is overcast, windy, wet, or during the midday summer sun.

- Prefer habitat with suitable open spots in which to bask near to areas of vegetation to flee to for cover. Fallen logs and rocks often provide good basking sites.
- The first sign may be a quiet rustling as animal flees, however they often return to the same basking site.
- Sloughed skins indicate their presence and if in good condition can sometimes be used for identification.
- Shelter under logs, rocks and other debris.
- Outside of the winter months, Red-eared Terrapins may be seen basking in the sun on rocks or logs in or at the edges of lakes and ponds.

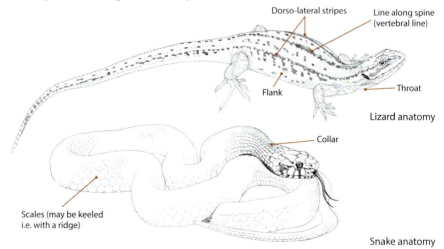

Dorso-lateral stripes

Line along spine (vertebral line)

Flank

Throat

Lizard anatomy

Collar

Scales (may be keeled i.e. with a ridge)

Snake anatomy

Red-eared Terrapin

Trachemys scripta elegans

Native range:

North America

Introduced:

1980s, introduced for pet trade; recorded in the wild shortly after, though not established

Spread:

Pet escapes or deliberate releases

Other names:

Red-eared Turtle,
Red-eared Slider

DESCRIPTION: To 20–30cm long, hatchlings much smaller (2–3cm). Distinctive *red markings behind eyes* (may be yellow indicating subspecies *T. s. scripta*). Body, neck and legs *dark with distinct yellow stripes*. Shell smooth, dark olive-green to brown with lighter bar, stripe and spot markings. Underside dull yellow with dark markings. Feet bear long, curved claws. **Juvenile:** Smaller, more brightly coloured, fading and turning darker with age. **Eggs:** White, oval, approximately 3–4cm long and 2–3cm wide. Successful breeding very rare in GB. Courtship underwater starts in May. If mating is successful multiple clutches of up to 30 eggs, usually fewer, are laid in loose substrate. GB climate is thought not consistently warm enough for eggs to hatch.

BEHAVIOUR: Active April–October. May be seen *basking on banks* of water body, or on logs and boulders. Timid and slips back into water if disturbed.

STATUS: Large numbers of hatchlings imported for pet trade in mid 1980s. Subsequently introduced to wild, either as escapes or deliberate releases. Breeding is unsuccessful in British climate, but with long lifespan (up to 30 years) individuals are able to persist.

HABITAT: Prefers still or slow-flowing water. Mostly seen in urban parks.

IMPACT: Predator of native species.

Key differences between similar species

There are no native terrapins, tortoises or freshwater turtles in Great Britain, although other non-native species occasionally escape.

European Pond Terrapin
Emys orbicularis
Non-native. No known populations in Britain but may be seen as an escape. Relatively easy to distinguish. *Lacks red marks behind eye*. Legs, neck and body dark, may have light speckles but *lacks stripes*.

Wall Lizard

Podarcis muralis

| J | F | M | A | M | J | J | A | S | O | N | D |

Native range:

Continental Europe and Jersey

Introduced:

1932 deliberately released; current populations mainly relate to introductions in the latter half of the 20th century.

Spread:

Escape from collections and deliberate release

Other names:

None.

DESCRIPTION: Medium-sized. Up to 18cm including *long tail*, which is approximately twice as long as head and body. Limbs long, with *distinctly long hind toes*. Head large in relation to body, and flattened. Belly has black and cream chequered pattern. **Male:** Markings highly variable. Back strikingly mottled, usually either *brown or green*, reflecting different colours of various subspecies that have been introduced. Flanks usually dark, spotted with white. **Female and juvenile:** Duller colour, usually with dark flanks and a dark stripe along the spine. Female has narrower head than male. Juveniles present from September. **Eggs:** Laid May–July in sandy soil, gravel or rock crevices in multiple clutches of up to 8.

BEHAVIOUR: *Readily runs up vertical surfaces* such as walls, unlike other lizards.

STATUS: Well established and spreading in parts of southern England and Wales, with strongholds including Bournemouth, Isle of Wight and Shoreham Beach. Warming climate may allow for more northerly spread.

HABITAT: Sunny, south-facing rocky habitat such as cliffs or quarries. Often seen clinging to garden walls or buildings with cracks and crevices.

IMPACT: May out-compete native lizards. May be a vector of disease.

Key differences between similar species

Sand Lizard *Lacerta agilis*

Native, rare and restricted to a few dry lowland heaths and coastal dunes, mainly in southern England but also parts of north Wales, Merseyside and one population in Scotland. Range overlaps with Wall Lizard in some places and could be confused. 6–19cm long. Males develop a striking green face and flanks during the breeding season (April to June) fading to lighter green yellow afterwards. Females generally brown or grey colour. Both sexes have **brown spots with lighter centres** typically dotted along the back which are quite characteristic. Usually larger and more robust than Wall Lizards with short tail in proportion to body. Head shorter and deeper than Wall Lizard.

Common Lizard *Zootoca vivipara*

Native. Common. 13–15cm long. Usually brown but may be grey or olive-green, never bright green like some Wall Lizards. Patterning highly variable, but usually less distinct than Wall Lizards. Females of both species are most difficult to distinguish because they are relatively dull in colour. Shorter tail (1.3 to 2 times the length of head and body). Somewhat stockier, with shorter legs and smaller, narrower head. Eyes set lower on head. Body not flattened.

Western Green Lizard

Lacerta bilineata

J F M A M J J A S O N D

Native range:

Central Europe

Introduced:

19th century, deliberate release; current populations originate from deliberate release in around 2000

Spread:

Deliberate release and escape from collections

Other names:

Lacerta viridus

Juveniles

DESCRIPTION: *Large*, 30–40cm long (including tail). *Distinctive bright green* with white or pale yellow underside and darker green head. **Male:** Black bead-like spots. *Blue throat during breeding season* (April–May). **Female:** Occasionally with dark spots or parallel stripes running along the back. **Juvenile:** Hatch from eggs August–September, 7–8cm long. Usually light brown with pale stripes running along body, developing green colour in second year. **Eggs:** Oval, 15–20mm long, with white, parchment-like skin. Buried in clutches of 5–20 in open sand or vegetation from late May. Hatching occurs August–September.

STATUS: Deliberately introduced by those keen to establish a population in Great Britain. Very *restricted range*, only one small population known, in Boscombe, Bournemouth area. Unlikely to spread far in current climate, but could expand range with climate change. **HABITAT:** In Great Britain found on south-facing cliffs with scrub. **IMPACT:** May compete with other lizards. Possible vector of reptile disease.

Key differences between similar species

Sand Lizard *Lacerta agilis*

Considerably **smaller** (16–19cm). May have bright green flanks, but always has **brown back**. Males do not develop blue face during breeding season. Females may be confused with juvenile Green Lizard, which can be more brown in colour, but proportionately larger and still usually with some green.

Wall Lizard (see also page 214).
Podarcis muralis

Non-native. Up to 18cm long. Much **smaller** than Green Lizard **without bright green coloration**.

Western Green Lizard

Wall Lizard

	Common Lizard (native)	Wall Lizard	Sand Lizard (native)	Green Lizard
Status	Widespread, relatively common	Well established in some part of southern England	Rare	Only one population on south coast
Length (including tail)	13–15cm	17–18cm	16–19cm	30–40cm
Tail length	Moderate (1.3–2 times length of head and body)	Long (approx. twice length of head and body)	Short (1.3–1.7 times length of head and body)	Long (2 times body length or more)
Colour	Usually brown, rarely green	Green or brown forms, usually highly mottled	Brown on back, adult males with green flanks	Bright green

Aesculapian Snake

Zamenis longissimus

Native range:

Central Europe

Introduced:

1960s, established in the wild; escape from local zoo

Spread:

Escapes from collections or deliberate release

Other names:

Elaphe longissima

DESCRIPTION: Slender and agile. Grows to 1.75m, usually much smaller. Scales *unkeeled* giving smooth appearance. *Body colour generally uniform* dark brown, bronze, grey or olive, usually flecked with white. Belly yellowish. **Juvenile:** Yellow marking around collar, fading to indistinct light patches in adult. Dark stripe on cheek behind eye is distinctive.

BEHAVIOUR: Good swimmer, like Grass Snake, but unlike other British snakes regularly climbs. May be seen in bushes and trees.
EGGS: Large and grooved. Laid in clutches of up to 18 in piles of decaying vegetation, loose soil or holes.

STATUS: Only two established populations, in north Wales and London, escapes from local zoos. Other escapes may occasionally occur from specimens kept as pets or in wildlife collections. Able to disperse long distances, but little sign of spreading in Great Britain.
HABITAT: Tolerates wide variety of habitats in native range, in Great Britain generally limited to sheltered south-facing slopes on light soils.
IMPACT: No impact yet recorded, but could be a significant predator if establishes more widely. Potential vector of disease.

Key differences between similar species

Smooth Snake *Coronella austriaca*

Native, only a few locations in GB. Grows to 60–70cm long. Slender and with smooth unkeeled scales. Grey or dull brown colour. Black markings arranged in bars or dots on back. Black *mark* on top of head (may be heart-shaped), with *dark stripes* on either side running through the eye.

Adder *Vipera berus*

Native, declining, usually found on heathland, chalk downland and other habitats with free-draining soils. Quite different from Aesculapian Snake. *Zigzag pattern* on head and body and *wider body. Keeled scales*.

Slow-worm *Anguis fragilis*

Native, widespread. A legless lizard (not a snake). May be similar bronze colour, but otherwise very different to Aesculapian Snake. *Small*, 25–45cm, body relatively wide and *worm-like*, tail blunt. Head barely broader than body, with *no distinct 'neck'*. Underside black, may have dark stripe along back but few other markings. Has eyelids, unlike snakes.

Grass Snake *Natrix natrix*

Native, widespread and relatively common in England and Wales. *Scales keeled. Yellow collar* behind head can lead to confusion between Grass Snakes and juvenile Aesculapian Snake. Grass Snake has an additional black collar behind yellow collar and lacks the dark stripe on the cheek.

Fish

There are 12 species of non-native fish recorded as established in Britain, most of which have the potential to cause negative impacts. They cause a range of environmental impacts, often through competition with and displacement of native species, but also through predation and the spread of disease. The feeding behaviour of some invasive non-native fish can increase the turbidity (silt in the water) of water bodies, with knock-on impacts for plants and invertebrates. Invasive non-native fish can also have economic impacts, for example reducing desirable fish stocks and interfering with angling.

The most common pathways of non-native fish introduction have been deliberate stocking, as ornamentals, for angling or for food, and as accidental contaminants usually in stocks of other fish.

Anatomical features that can be useful for identification are:

- **Body shape**, for example slender and streamlined or round and deep. Consider whether the fish is flattened or rounded in cross section.

- **Fin shape and arrangement**. Fins can be straight, convex or concave. The number of rays (structures that support the fin) in the fin can be important, as can whether the rays are spiny or soft as well as singular or branched (when counting the number of rays, branched rays count as one).

- **The lateral line**, a sensory system visible on the surface of the fish as a series of pores in the scales, usually running in a line from head to the base of the tail. The number of scales with pores and the shape of the lateral line can be important for identification.

- **Mouth shape**. Bottom-dwelling fish often have mouths that are turned downwards, whereas surface feeders have turned-up mouths.

- **Colour** can be a useful indication for some fish, but can also be highly variable and so should be used with caution.

This section covers the majority of non-native fish likely to be considered invasive in GB. To keep the guide relevant and compact, some potential species have not been included such as Grass Carp.

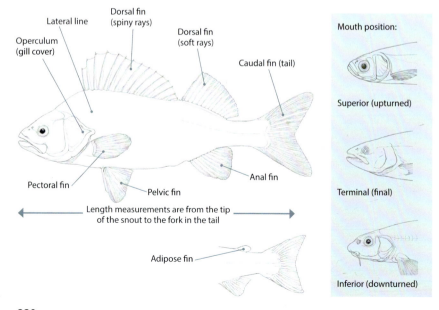

Lateral line · Dorsal fin (spiny rays) · Operculum (gill cover) · Dorsal fin (soft rays) · Caudal fin (tail) · Pectoral fin · Pelvic fin · Anal fin · Adipose fin

Length measurements are from the tip of the snout to the fork in the tail

Mouth position:
Superior (upturned)
Terminal (final)
Inferior (downturned)

Sunbleak

Leucaspius delineatus

Native range:

Continental Europe

Introduced:

Imported as an ornamental fish in 1987, subsequently escaped with wild records from the 1990s

Spread:

Escape or deliberate release from ponds, also a contaminant of stocked fish

DESCRIPTION: *Slender* and *small*, 5–9 (12)cm long. Distinguished from most other small cyprinids by distinctive, *short dark incomplete lateral line* (over the first 2–13 scales). Scales large, thin and *easily dislodged*. Relatively *large eyes*. *Upturned mouth*, with protruding lower jaw. Back olive-green colour, belly white, flanks silver, with iridescent silvery blue sheen. *Pelvic fin has 10 rays*. Anal fin has 3 spines and 10–13 branched rays and a longer base than dorsal fin.

BEHAVIOUR: Feeds predominantly on zooplankton and invertebrates.
REPRODUCTION: Spawns April–August, when temperature is between 16–18°C. Females spawn multiple times in one season. Territorial male cleans nest site and guards eggs. Eggs small (approx 1mm diameter) attached in strings to roots, aquatic vegetation or material on water's surface.
STATUS: Established in a few sites in southern England (Somerset), likely to continue spreading.
HABITAT: Slow-flowing lowland rivers. Often in ponds and small water bodies not connected to main rivers. Tolerant of high water temperatures and low levels of dissolved oxygen.
IMPACT: Can attain very high densities. Competes with native fish species and preys upon their eggs and fry. May act as a vector of disease.

Other names:

Belica, Motherless Minnow, Sundace, Moderlieschen

Key differences between similar species

- **Bleak** *Alburnus alburnus*. Native. Locally common in south-east England. Quite similar to Sunbleak. Adult *larger* (12–15cm). *Anal fin with more rays* (20–23). *Complete lateral line* (55 scales) which lacks dark pigment.
- **Topmouth Gudgeon** *Pseudorasbora parva*. Non-native (see page 226). Only a few populations in GB. *Complete lateral line* (34–38). *Iridescent dark blue/ purple band* along flank. *Dorsal and anal fins strongly convex*.

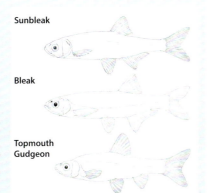

Sunbleak

Bleak

Topmouth Gudgeon

Orfe

Leuciscus idus

Native range:

Parts of continental Europe and Asia

Introduced:

1874, stocked in Woburn Abbey estate

Spread:

Escape or deliberate release from ponds, also introduced for angling

Other names:

Ide

DESCRIPTION: Relatively deep, thickset body. Small head, blunt snout and small mouth. 25–50cm (100)cm long, weight up to 3.5 kg, usually much less. *55–61 scales in lateral line*. *Anal fin concave* (9–10 rays). Dorsal fin with *8 rays*, convex with short base. Origin just behind base of pelvic fins. Colour variable, usually darkish grey-brown on back, shading to silvery grey on sides and silver belly. Golden or blue varieties commonly stocked for ornamental purposes. *All fins except dorsal have reddish hue*, tail fin somewhat darker.

BEHAVIOUR: Diet mainly invertebrates and plants, adults will take small fish.

REPRODUCTION: Spawns March–April when temperatures exceed 10°C. Adults often undertake long spawning migrations. Males assemble at spawning grounds and follow ripe females. Eggs pale yellow. Up to 2mm in diameter. Female attaches sticky eggs to gravel or submerged plant material.

STATUS: Scattered sites in England, rare in Wales and Scotland. A popular ornamental fish, also used for angling. Rarely establishes self-sustaining populations in GB.

HABITAT: Slow-flowing middle and lower reaches of large rivers and lakes. Preferred temperature range of 4–20°C. Migrates to tributaries to spawn in moderate current on gravel or submerged vegetation. Golden form common in ornamental lakes.

IMPACT: Impacts not well understood. Can hybridise with other cyprinid species, producing infertile hybrids.

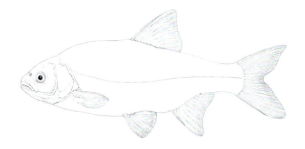

Key differences between similar species

Rudd
Scardinius erythropthalmus

Native and common in England, non-native in Wales and Scotland. 15–30 (45)cm long. Deep body with large scales. Silvery yellowish flanks, dark on back. **Large eye**. Upturned mouth. All fins, **including dorsal fin**, have a **reddish hue**. Pectoral, pelvic and anal fins can be **bright red**. Dorsal fin with 3 spines and 8–9 soft rays, set well back from pelvic fins. Anal fin has long base. *40–43 lateral line scales*.

15–30cm

Roach *Rutilus rutilus*

Native. Common. 20–35 (44)cm long. Silvery with greenish back. Pectoral, pelvic and anal fins may be red. Dorsal fin origin inline with pelvic fin, *9–12 branched rays. Scales somewhat larger. 42-45 lateral line scales*.

20–35cm

Chub *Leuciscus cephalus*

Native. Common. 30–50 (80) cm long. Thickset. Large silvery scales. *Anal fin of Chub is convex* compared to concave anal fin of Orfe. *44-46 lateral line scales*.

30–50cm

Goldfish

Carassius auratus

DESCRIPTION: 15–35 (45)cm long, maximum weight about 3kg. Pet fish highly variable in colour, often gold, but feral populations revert to dull green-brown. *Deep body*, somewhat *rounded in cross-section*, gently curved dorsal profile. *27–31 lateral line scales*. *No barbels at mouth*. *Dorsal fin concave*, with long base, 15–19 branched rays. First ray strong and coarsely serrated. Anal fin with 5–6 branched rays. Large head and eyes. Large scales.

BEHAVIOUR: Omnivorous benthic feeder, eating plants and invertebrates.

REPRODUCTION: Breeds May–June when water temperature exceeds 20°C. Spawns over weeds, producing small, sticky, yellow eggs, which are attached to plants. In absence of males, females can reproduce via gynogenesis (utilising the sperm of other carp species to initiate egg division).

STATUS: Common pet. Unwanted animals regularly released in the wild. Sometimes stocked as a sport fish. Populations scattered across GB.

HABITAT: Slow-flowing, well-vegetated lakes, ponds and lowland rivers.

IMPACT: Hybridises with native Crucian Carp. Vector of disease. Predator of native fish eggs. Competes with native species.

Other names:

Golden Carp, Ryukin, Comet, Shubunkin, Veiltail, Gibel Carp

Native range:

Central and eastern Asia, China, Korea and Japan

Introduced:

Probably in 17th century, widely kept as pets from the 1750s

Spread:

Escape or deliberate release from ponds and aquaria, sometimes stocked for angling

Key differences between similar species

- **Crucian Carp** *Carassius carassius*. Native in parts of south-east England, non-native elsewhere. Declining. 20-45 (50cm), maximum weight 5kg, usually much less. Deep body with rounded head. *31–36 scales* (normally 32–34) in lateral line. *Convex dorsal fin. Dark pigmentation on bottom of ventral fin*. Tail *less noticeably forked*. Front spine of dorsal and anal fins *not or barely serrated*. Flanks more *brassy*, with dark greenish back and lighter, brownish belly. Scales usually smaller. Tail fin less noticeably forked.

- **Common Carp** *Cyprinus carpio*. Larger with barbels around mouth, which are absent in Goldfish.
- **Hybrids:** Goldfish, Common Carp and Crucian Carp can interbreed, forming intermediate hybrids that are difficult to identify.

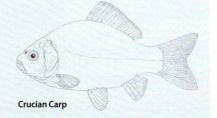

Crucian Carp

Common Carp

Cyprinus carpio

Native range:

Eastern Europe and Asia

Introduced:

Before 1496 as a food fish

Spread:

Stocked for angling and aqua-culture, escape or deliberate release may occur

Other names:

Mirror Carp, Leather Carp, Koi Carp

Mirror

Koi

Leather

Similar species

- **Crucian Carp** and **Feral Goldfish** (see opposite).

DESCRIPTION: Highly variable. Various forms have been bred including Common Carp (with even spread of *large scales*), Mirror Carp (from fully scaled to lightly covered in uneven oversized scales), Leather Carp (without or with very few scales) and Koi Carp (highly coloured ornamental form). 25–75 (up to 102)cm long, maximum weight about 30 kg. Body thick to rounded. Upper jaw with *two long and two short barbels*. Large, protruding *rubbery lips*. 33–40 scales in lateral line. Back and upper sides of feral carp brown-green, sides silvery to golden brown, belly white (colour varies with seasons). Dorsal fin concave with long base and strongly serrated spine at front. Powerful tail.

BEHAVIOUR: Omnivorous, mainly bottom-feeder. Forms small shoals in spring. Most active at dusk and dawn.
REPRODUCTION: Spawns June–July, requiring water temperatures of at least 18°C, not achieved in most British waters. Spawning energetic with splashing, usually takes place around dusk in shallow margins of a lake or river. Eggs 1–1.5mm, pale to yellowish, sticky and deposited on weeds, submerged roots or other substrates. Hatch within 5–8 days depending on temperature. Young sexually mature within 3–5 years.

STATUS: Originally introduced in medieval times for food, now one of the most popular angling fish. Sustained by continual stocking. Widespread in England and Wales, limited to few populations in Scotland. Likely to establish more widely with climate warming.
HABITAT: Tolerates wide range of freshwater conditions including rivers, streams, lakes and ponds. Prefers slow or stagnant water with muddy bottom and thick vegetation.
IMPACT: Alters habitats by consuming plants and invertebrates and increasing turbidity. Also hybridises with native Crucian Carp.

Mirror Carp

Topmouth Gudgeon

Pseudorasbora parva

Native range:

East Asia (China, Japan, Amur River Basin)

Introduced:

In the ornamental trade from 1986, recorded in the wild from 1996

Spread:

Contaminant of stocked fish, also present in the ornamental trade

Other names:

False Harlequin, Stone Moroko, Clicker Barb, Japanese Minnow

DESCRIPTION: *Small slender fish*, usually 4–8cm long. *Full straight lateral line* with 34–38 scales with thin dark purple/blue stripe. *Scales quite large and thin* with dark edges. Small high-set mouth with upturned lower jaws. *No barbels.* Generally iridescent silvery blue. All fins rounded. Anal fin has 3 spines and 6 branched rays. Dorsal fin has 7 branched rays, originates directly above pelvic fin. Tail fin large and deeply forked. No ventral keel present. **Male:** Larger than female. During spawning season becomes darker and develop *white tubercles on snout*. **Female:** Develops yellow colour ventrally.

BEHAVIOUR: Short-lived. Omnivorous, feeding on small aquatic invertebrates, crustaceans and the eggs and young of native fish. Emits audible 'click' when feeding (hence its other name 'Clicker Barb').

REPRODUCTION: Generally late March–September. Batch spawner, with females laying up to 4 batches a year. Eggs laid on flat surfaces, prepared by males. Sexually mature at 1 year old. Males guard eggs until hatching.

STATUS: Introduced as a contaminant of other stocked fish. Also present in the ornamental trade. Established in scattered self-contained lakes in England. Three populations known to exist in Wales. Absent from Scotland.

HABITAT: Bentho-pelagic, generally found in and around marginal and emergent macrophytes. Prefers still/slow-moving waters, can be found in rivers, canals, drains and ditches.

IMPACT: Can attain very high densities, out-competing native fish for food, habitat and spawning areas. Vector of disease. Pest species for recreational anglers.

Key differences between similar species

See page 228.

Fathead Minnow

Pimephales promelas

J F M A M J J A S O N D

X ▢ 🔍 ❗

Native range:

North America

Introduced:

2003 stocked in a private pond, first wild record 2008

Spread:

Escape or deliberate release from ponds, also used for research in laboratories

Other names:

Rosy Red, Blackhead Minnow, Tuffy

DESCRIPTION: Small, 4–8 (to 10)cm long, minnow- like fish with *rounded head*. Olive/brown colour, cream belly. Sometimes golden or pink colour, hence other name 'Rosy Red'. Somewhat indistinct *dusky stripe along flank*, usually more prominent towards base of tail. Fins rounded. Dorsal fin (8 soft rays), with *dark blotch*, located immediately above pelvic fin (7–8 soft rays). Anal fin has 7 branched rays. Lateral line incomplete (41–54 + 2 midlateral row) usually not reaching dorsal fin. **Male:** Develops multiple *white tubercles* on snout and *prominent pad of spongy tissue on nape* during spawning period.

BEHAVIOUR: Feeds on plants, detritus and benthic invertebrates. Male uses spongy nape pad and dorsal fin to clean the nest site.
REPRODUCTION: Females spawn repeatedly in a season (every 2–26 days). Up to 700 eggs laid over submerged objects. Males defend territories and eggs.

STATUS: Only one known population in the wild, though this was eradicated in 2010. Present in many private ponds. Introduced as a pond and aquarium fish, also used for research in laboratories. Sometimes an accidental contaminant of other stocked fish.
HABITAT: Stocked in garden ponds. Favours streams and muddy ponds, tolerates turbid, poorly oxygenated water. Can be found in small rivers.
IMPACT: No impacts yet recorded in GB, if established in large densities may compete with native species and disrupt food webs. Has been associated with the spread of disease to native species.

Male in breeding season with spongy pad on nape and white tubercles

Key differences between similar species
See page 228.

Key differences between similar species

Topmouth Gudgeon
Pseudorasbora parva

Full straight lateral line.

4–8cm

Common Minnow *Phoxinus phoxinus*

Native, very common across most of GB. 80–100 scales in lateral line. Numerous brown and black blotches along sides, may also have distinctive black and gold stripe along side. 6–10cm long. Dark spot on wrist of tail is distinctive. Small scales.

6–10cm

Gudgeon *Gobio gobio*

Native to Europe and England. Gudgeon have a small barbel at the edge of the mouth. Can reach greater lengths than Topmouth Gudgeon.

10–15cm

Fathead Minnow *Pimephales promelas*

Lacks a complete lateral line, which ends at dorsal fin. Males have spongy pad on nape.

4–8cm

Wels Catfish

Silurus glanis

Native range:

Central and eastern Europe (east of River Rhine), western Asia

Introduced:

First wild record from 1864, introduced as a food fish. Did not become well established until 1950s

Spread:

Stocked for angling; escape or deliberate release may occur

Other names:

Wels Catfish, European Catfish, Som Catfish, Sheat Fish, Danube Catfish

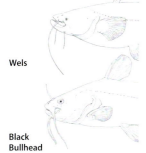

Wels

Black Bullhead

DESCRIPTION: *Elongated body and broad head. Large* 2 (5)m and 80 (300)kg. Unlike any other British freshwater fish. *Small eyes compared to body size. 2 long barbels* ('whiskers') protrude from upper lip, 2 smaller pairs on lower jaw. Body smooth and scaleless. Coloration *mottled cream, green, brown, olive and bronze* providing camouflage. *Anal fin very long* with 4–5 spines and 83–95 soft rays. Dorsal fin with 2–5 rays. Caudal fin *truncate* (rounded) with 17 rays. No adipose fin.

BEHAVIOUR: Largely nocturnal, usually spends daylight hours hidden amongst tree roots, weed beds and similar substrate.

REPRODUCTION: Spawns May to July, eggs laid in shallow depression on bottom or among submerged tree roots. Males build and defend nests until fry emerge. Eggs 3mm in diameter. Stick together in large mound. Hatch 2–3 days after fertilisation. Fry remain in nest until yolk sack absorbed (2–4 days).

STATUS: Originally introduced as a food fish, subsequently a popular angling fish. Scattered in England, more likely to be established in the south. Few records from Wales. Absent in Scotland.

HABITAT: Managed stillwaters for fishery purposes. Limited numbers in slow flowing deep lowland rivers.

IMPACT: Voracious predator with broad diet. Competes with and preys upon other fish, invertebrates, waterfowl, small mammals and amphibians.

Key differences between similar species

Unlike any native species. Distinguished from **Black Bullhead** *Ameiurus melas* by barbel formation (Wels has 6 barbels whereas Black Bullhead has 8 (1), larger size and long anal fin (see page 230).

Black Bullhead

Ameiurus melas

J F M A M J J A S O N D

Native range:

Central and eastern North America, from southern Canada to northern Mexico

Introduced:

Introduced 1885, probably for angling. First established in the wild in the late 20th century

Spread:

Escape or deliberate release from ponds

Other names:

Black Catfish, Small Catfish, Poisson Chat

DESCRIPTION: *Small catfish*, 20–30 (up to 45)cm long to 3 kg. Broad and flattened head. *Eight barbels in total,* four on upper jaw, including two long whiskers at the sides of the mouth and four on lower jaw. Dark brownish-black back with greenish-gold on flanks and muddy white belly. Tail fin 'squared off' *not forked. No scales.* Lacks serrae on pectoral spine. 7 dorsal fin rays, with 17–21 anal fin rays. Adipose fin present.

BEHAVIOUR: Omnivorous, taking mainly plant material, invertebrates and fish.

REPRODUCTION: Spawns June–July when temperatures are 18–30°C. Eggs laid in nest on stones, logs or other cover. Remain in ball, guarded/tended to by both parents. Fry form shoals after hatching.

STATUS: Popular angling and food fish in America, but mainly sold in GB as an aquarium or pond fish. One known population, eradicated in Essex in 2014 although others are suspected. May be present in private ponds and lakes. Considered likely to spread.

HABITAT: Primarily found in still to slow-moving waters, such as drainage ditches, canals, lakes and ponds.

IMPACT: Predation and competition with native species. Viewed as a pest species where it occurs in large numbers in Europe as a result of competition with native fish and disrupting angling effort.

Key differences between similar species

Black Bullhead *Ameiurus melas*

Non-native. One possible population. Distinguished from other species
by relatively small size (20–30cm), 8 barbels around
mouth and relatively short anal fin.

20–30cm

Brown Bullhead *Ameiurus nebulosus*

Non-native. Not present in GB; easily confused with Black Bullhead.
Large barbs on pectoral spine. 21–41 anal rays. 13–15 gill rakers.
Darker dorsal fin membrane. Refer to Wheeler 1978
for more guidance.

20–30cm

Channel Catfish *Ictalurus punctatus*

Non-native. Not established. Max length 127cm, usually less than
100cm. Distinguished from other species by deeply forked tail fin.

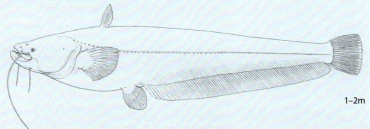

Up to 127cm,
usually much less

Wels Catfish *Silurus glanis* (see page 229)

Non-native. Quite different. Established populations scattered in south
of England, some records for Wales, none in Scotland. Large 1–2 (5)m
long and 80 (300)kg in weight. Elongated anal fin. Only one pair of long
barbels (whiskers) on upper jaw, two pairs of small barbels on lower jaw.

1–2m

Rainbow Trout

Oncorhynchus mykiss

J F M A M J J A S O N D

Native range:

Coastal pacific basin, including north-west North America and far east Asia

Introduced:

1880s, as a farmed fish

Spread:

Escapes from fish farms, also stocked for angling

Other names:

Salmo gairdneri

DESCRIPTION: Streamlined. Highly variable size and colour. In GB usually 25–45 (up to 70)cm long, weighing up to about 10kg. Black *spots on fins* are distinctive, particularly on tail and adipose fin. Back and flanks also with black spots. Body silvery to olive-brown, gradually lightening on sides to silvery white belly. Flanks with *iridescent pink band*. Upper jaw extends back to beneath rear edge of the eye. Dorsal fin with 11–12 main rays. Anal fin with 9–12 rays. Adipose fin often edged in black. Tail fin slightly forked. Very small scales, 135–150 in lateral line. 15–16 scales from adipose fin to lateral line.

BEHAVIOUR: Diet of insects, crustaceans, other fish and sometimes fish eggs.

REPRODUCTION: Breeds October–March. Eggs are pink or yellowish-orange, 4–6mm diameter, laid in stream or still water in nests dug into gravel beds. Juveniles rarely survive in GB waters.

STATUS: Widespread, but not well established. Popular sport and table fish, commonly farmed in GB. Widely stocked, but very few established populations due to unsuccessful breeding. Reasons for inability to reproduce successfully are unclear, but may be linked to competition with native Brown Trout and/or suboptimal environmental conditions.

HABITAT: Stocked in lakes and reservoirs, occasionally escapes into rivers. Tolerates higher temperatures and slightly poorer water quality than Brown Trout.

IMPACT: May alter habitat through direct and indirect competition with native species.

Juvenile Rainbow Trout may have parr marks on their flanks (grey thumbprint-like marks that fade as the fish grow). These are also present in juvenile Brown Trout and in Salmon.

Rainbow Trout

Key differences between similar species

Brown Trout *Salmo trutta*

Native. Very common. Similar to Rainbow Trout, occupying similar habitats. 15–50 (70)cm long, to about 14 kg in weight. 110–120 scales in lateral line. Variable colour, *no pink band on flanks*. Wide variety of spots on body, mostly black but *some red* (unlike Rainbow Trout). Tail and adipose fin *lack prominent black spots*.

15–50cm

Atlantic Salmon *Salmo salar*

Native, anadromous, found in clear, stony unpolluted rivers and lakes. *Larger*, 40–100 (120) cm to about 30 kg in weight. 120–130 scales in lateral line. Variable colour, silvery to multicoloured, *no pink band on flanks*. *Tail and adipose fin lack prominent black spots*. Young fish are spotted with parr marks on each side.

40–100cm

Zander

Sander lucioperca

Native range:

Central and eastern Europe

Introduced:

1878 as an angling fish, became well established after the 1960s

Spread:

Stocked for angling

DESCRIPTION: *Large predatory fish*, 30–70 (up to 130)cm long, maximum weight to 18 kg but usually smaller. Grey-green on back, lighter along flanks, white underbelly. *Streamlined*, like Pike. *Two dorsal fins*, the first with 13–14 *obvious spines*, the second with 2 spines and 17–19 branched rays. Mouth with many small sharp teeth and distinctly *large canine teeth*. Large, dark eyes with glassy appearance. Anal fin has 2–3 spines and 11–13 branched rays. 80–95 lateral scales. Juveniles with *dark bands* on flanks, almost absent in adults.

BEHAVIOUR: Piscivorous. Adapted to nocturnal feeding. Gregarious 'pack hunter', when small, though large adults become solitary.

REPRODUCTION: Spawns in shallow water April–June, in sand or gravel depressions excavated by the male, or exposed roots. Male defends nest and eggs until hatching.

STATUS: First introduced to lakes in Woburn by 9th Duke of Bedford. Later introductions include The Great Ouse River Authority in 1959–60. A popular sporting fish. Now widely established in East Anglia, the rivers Avon, Severn and Thames and the Midlands. Not recorded in Scotland.

HABITAT: Prefers large, turbid or slow-flowing rivers. Tolerates brackish coastal lakes and estuaries.

IMPACTS: Preys upon native fish, particularly Roach.

Other names:

Stizostedion lucioperca, Lucioperca lucioperca, Pike-perch

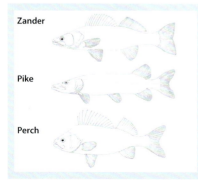

Zander

Pike

Perch

Key differences between similar species

- **Pike** *Esox lucius*. Native. Common. Can be longer, 30–120 (150)cm, with similar streamlined body. Large head and snout with *very large mouth* and teeth. *Lacks distinctive canine teeth* of Zander. Only *one dorsal fin*, close to of tail end, with short base.
- **Perch** *Perca fluviatilis*. Native (England and Wales only). Common. 20–35 (51)cm long. Deep-bodied. 5 or 7 *dark vertical bars along flanks. Red pelvic and anal fins. Red tip to ventral side of tail fin*. Lacks fangs of Zander.

Pumpkinseed

Lepomis gibbosus

J F M A M J J A S O N D

Native range:

Eastern North America

Introduced:

Introduced as an ornamental fish in the early 1900s

Spread:

Escape or deliberate release from ponds and aquaria, also a contaminant of stocked fish

Other names:

Pond-perch, Common Sunfish, Yellow Sunfish, Sun Bass, Sun Perch

DESCRIPTION: *Distinctive and colourful*, unlikely to be confused with any other northern European freshwater fish. 10–15 (up to 22)cm long, maximum weight about 300 g. Large scales. *Deep and laterally compressed body*. Colour variable, *green-bronze back, gold to turquoise-blue sides mottled with darker patches*, and yellowish belly. Small black and red spot on operculum, which is approximately the same size as the eye. Mouth small. *Single long dorsal fin* divided into two parts with 10–11 spines and 10 soft rays. 36–47 lateral line scales. Anal fin with 3 spines and 10 –11 branched rays.

BEHAVIOUR: Feeds on wide variety of insects and aquatic invertebrates, fish eggs and larvae. Larger specimens become piscivorous, even cannibalistic.
REPRODUCTION: Spawns early summer, when water temps are high (>16°C). Males zealously guard eggs in nest (a depression in sand or gravel) until eggs hatch. Can live to 8–9 years.

STATUS: Ornamental fish of ponds and aquaria, from where it has escaped or been released. May also have spread as a contaminant in fish stocks. There are a few well established populations in still waters in southern England, but not yet in rivers. A population in Scotland has since become extinct. Not established in Wales.
HABITAT: Wide variety of slow-moving vegetated water bodies, large rivers, lakes, ponds, canals, backwaters and estuaries.
IMPACT: Highly territorial, will compete with and prey upon native species, including fish eggs and fry.

Key differences between similar species
Unlike other species likely to be encountered in Britain.

235

Sturgeon species

Acipenser spp.

Sturgeons are generally anadromous, spending most of their time in coastal waters and returning to rivers to breed. Common Sturgeon (*Acipenser sturio*) is native to GB but extremely rare. Other non-native sturgeons have been introduced for ornamental purposes and angling. The Siberian Sturgeon (*A. baerii*), Sterlet (*A. ruthenus*), Russian Sturgeon (*A. gueldenstaedtii*) and hybrids have been recorded in a number of still-water fisheries in England and Wales.

| J | F | M | A | M | J | J | A | S | O | N | D |

Not present in the wild

Native range:

A. baerii, Serbia. *A. gueldenstaedtii*, Black, Azov and Caspian Seas. *A. ruthenus*, Black and Caspian Seas

Introduced:

Not yet established. Stocked in ornamental ponds and occasionally stocked illegally for angling

Spread:

May escape or be released from ponds or for angling

Siberian Sturgeon *Acipenser baerii*

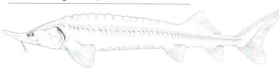

Sterlet *Acipenser ruthenus*

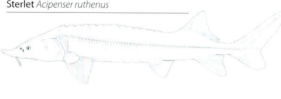

Common Sturgeon *Acipenser sturio*

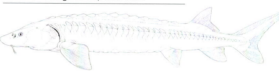

DESCRIPTION: *Primitive* appearance. *No scales. Four barbels. Long pointed snout.* Body partially covered with *bony plates* or 'scutes' in five longitudinal rows: one on dorsal midline, one either side along midlateral line and one ventrally on each side from pectoral fin base to anal fin origin.

BEHAVIOUR: Diet predominantly benthic invertebrates, molluscs and fish. Anadromous populations usually migrate to sea after 2–4 years, where they stay until mature. Long-lived (up to 50 years).

STATUS: Introduced to ornamental ponds and illegally for angling. Scattered records from England and Wales, but no breeding populations.

HABITAT: Bottom-dweller, migrating to rivers to spawn. Prefers coastal and estuarine waters with soft bottoms while at sea, and estuaries and large rivers when migrating.

IMPACT: Uncertain but potential impacts from competition with other species for food and through predation. May act as a vector of disease.

Key differences between similar species

Distinguished from native fish, except the Common Sturgeon, by *primitive* appearance with bony plates instead of scales and long snout.

- **Common Sturgeon** *Acipenser sturio*. Native, very rare. Lateral scutes 24–36, unlike Siberian Sturgeon (42–47), Sterlet (more than 50) and Russian Sturgeon (24–50).

236

Eastern Mosquitofish

Gambusia holbrooki

Native range:

East and south USA

Introduced:

Not yet present in GB

Other names:

Gambusia affinis

DESCRIPTION: Male to 30mm long, female to 60mm. Body slightly compressed, translucent brownish-grey with silver belly and sometimes a bluish sheen on the sides. Large eyes and small, terminal mouth. *Dorsal and tail fins translucent with rows of black spots*. The anal fin of males has long modified anal rays that form a gonopodium (a structure used to inseminate females). Females have a large dark blotch just above the vent.

STATUS: Not yet present in GB. Introduced to Spain in a failed attempt to control mosquitos in 1921, now present in many European countries as far north as the Loire estuary in France. Most likely to reach GB from continental Europe as an accidental introduction by anglers or aquarists.

HABITAT: Prefers warmer waters (around 25°C), but able to tolerate and establish in GB temperatures. Prefers still or slow-flowing water with lots of aquatic vegetation. Tolerates wide range of salinities, low oxygen levels and pollution.

IMPACT: Rapidly reaches high population densities. Competes with similar-sized fish and preys upon fish fry and eggs. Highly aggressive, attacking other fish and fin nipping which can lead to disease.

Ponto-Caspian gobies

Neogobius melanostomus, Proterorhinus marmoratus

Native range:

Ponto-Caspian region: Black, Caspian and Azov sea basins

Introduced:

Not yet present in GB

Other names:

None.

DESCRIPTION: Species illustrated is Round Goby (*Neogobius melanostomus*). A relatively large goby, up to about 25cm long. Large head. Key feature is the *fused pelvic fins* that form a suction disk on the underside of the fish, providing anchorage in fast currents. Brownish or yellowish grey, with blotches along flanks and *large oval black spot, usually at the end of the dorsal fin*.

STATUS: Not yet present in GB. A number of goby species from the Ponto-Caspian region (principally Round Goby and Tubenose Goby *Proterorhinus marmoratus*) have become invasive in continental Europe. Spread as a hull foulant on boats and in ballast water.

HABITAT: Bottom-dwelling fish of freshwater to brackish water, considerable tolerance of salinity and temperature.

IMPACT: Aggressive and territorial. Predator of young fish and fish eggs. May out-compete native species. Known host of native parasites.

Freshwater invertebrates

There are about 40 established freshwater non-native invertebrate species in Britain, including the brackish and estuarine environments. More than half of these are thought to have a negative impact. The large majority are non-insect invertebrates that cause wide ranging environmental impacts including predation on and competition with native species, disrupting nutrient cycling and ecosystems, damage to the physical environment and spread of diseases. Other impacts include interfering with angling and fisheries, and biofouling, which can be a costly problem for the water industry and a nuisance for boat owners.

Freshwater non-native invertebrates have been introduced by a range of both intentional and unintentional pathways. Many of the molluscs and shrimps have been introduced as stowaways on vessels, goods and equipment. Species of crayfish were deliberately introduced for aquaculture and the pet trade. Of particular concern is the increasing trend in species arriving from the Ponto-Caspian region. Three of the species covered in this guide have arrived from this region, probably as stowaways on vessels or contaminated equipment, but there are many more likely to arrive in the future.

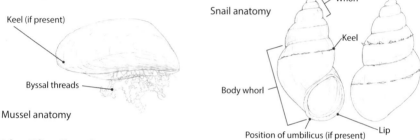

Snail anatomy

Whorl

Keel

Body whorl

Position of umbilicus (if present)

Lip

Keel (if present)

Byssal threads

Mussel anatomy

Identification tips

There are two main groups: molluscs (mussels and snails) and crustaceans (shrimp-like species, crayfish and a crab).

Both groups can often be detected from remains of the organisms, e.g. shells or shell fragments and limbs, claws and other parts of crustacean exoskeleton, and in the case of the crab and some of the crayfish their burrowing activity. These apart it is necessary to search carefully for living organisms, for example attached to solid structures in the case of mussels or living in the sediment or amongst aquatic plants.

The figure below provides a summary of the key features of a crayfish. An amphipod shrimp can be found on page 257.

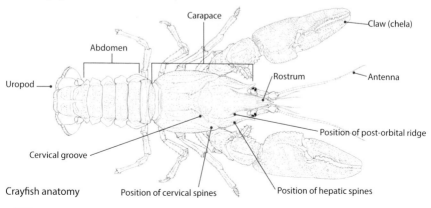

Carapace

Claw (chela)

Abdomen

Rostrum

Antenna

Uropod

Position of post-orbital ridge

Cervical groove

Crayfish anatomy

Position of cervical spines

Position of hepatic spines

Non-native mussels

Zebra Mussel is widespread and relatively common in Britain. Quagga Mussel, a closely related species, was discovered in Britain in 2014 and is much less widespread. The two species are difficult to distinguish from each other, but easily separated from other freshwater species. Both are highly invasive.

Zebra Mussel

Dreissena polymorpha

J F M A M J J A S O N D

Native range:

Ponto-Caspian region (drainage basins of the Black, Caspian and Aral Sea).

Introduced:

1824, probably introduced on timber imported from the Baltic

Spread:

Most likely with boats and other equipment moved between water bodies

Other names:

None.

DESCRIPTION: *Freshwater mussel*. Triangular shape, similar to marine mussels but much smaller; *2–5cm long*. Distinctly keeled so that hinge edge is almost flat or concave, creating a *D-shaped cross section*. Shells usually with alternating dark and light zigzag stripes (hence 'zebra'), but variable in pattern and colour. Shells are swollen, strong, thick-walled and smooth or shallowly ridged. Attaches firmly to hard surfaces by tufts of sticky threads (byssal threads), usually in groups.

STATUS: Common in much of England and Wales, limited distribution in Scotland. Easily spread either as adults attached to boats and other equipment or as veligers in water moved between water bodies.
HABITAT: Fresh and weakly brackish water. Prefers clean and well-oxygenated water such as slow rivers, canals, docks, reservoirs and lakes. Attaches to almost any hard surface underwater.
IMPACT: Filters large amounts of nutrients and other particles from water, altering whole ecosystems and reducing nutrients available to other species. Major biofouling species, blocks pipes and smothers hard surfaces including boat hulls and screens. Causes significant problems for water industry.

Key differences between similar species
- See Quagga Mussel (see pages 240–241).

Quagga Mussel

Dreissena rosteriformis bugensis

J F M A M J J A S O N D

Native range:

Ponto-Caspian region (drainage basins of the Black, Caspian and Aral Sea)

Introduced:

Unknown, but possibly ballast water, hulls of boats or angling gear

Spread:

Likely to spread in or attached to boats and trailers or other equipment used in freshwater

Other names:

None.

DESCRIPTION: Similar size and shell pattern to Zebra Mussel (page 239) but lacks strong keel and is therefore more *rounded in cross section. Tends to roll on side* when placed on front (hinge edge). *Sinuous midventral line* (the line formed where the 2 shells of the mussel meet). Byssal groove (small notch in shell associated with byssal threads) *closer to hinge and relatively inconspicuous.* Fewer byssal threads than Zebra Mussel and is usually *easier to detach from surfaces*.

STATUS: Established in the Wraysbury River and surrounding waterbodies in West London. Spreads as veligers, for example in bilge and ballast water, or as adults attached to boats or trailers and other equipment. Introduced to Europe via canals connecting major rivers with those in the Ponto-caspian area and has spread rapidly in recent decades.

HABITAT: Fresh and weakly brackish waters. Survives in both hard and muddy substrates, unlike Zebra Mussel, including silty or sandy lake bottoms. Tolerates waters ranging from warm and shallow to deep and cold. Attaches to anything solid underwater, such as masonry, stones, wooden posts, tree roots or shells.

IMPACT: Similar to Zebra Mussel, causing significant alteration to whole ecosystems and considerable problems from biofouling. Potentially more invasive than Zebra Mussel and has replaced this species in much of its range.

Key differences between similar species

Distinguishing Zebra and Quagga Mussel

The mid ventral line of Zebra Mussel is straight with a large byssal grove towards the middle ❶. In Quagga Mussel the line is sinuous with less obvious groove close to the hinge ❷. Zebra Mussel has a strong keel ❸, making it D-shaped in cross-section whereas Quagga Mussel is more rounded and wider ❹. As a result Zebra Mussel may lie face down on a surface ❺ whereas Quagga Mussel rolls to one side ❻.

Zebra Mussel   Quagga Mussel

Native freshwater mussels

Not found fixed to surfaces and do not grow in colonies but are free-living in the sediment, with smaller species found amongst water plants. Larger species (Swan, Painter's, Duck and Pearl Mussels) could only be confused with Zebra and Quagga Mussels as juveniles but their shells are much thinner and lack the distinctive stripes. Orb cockles (*Sphaerium* species) and pea cockles (*Pisidium* species) are much smaller (less than 20mm) and are unlikely to be confused.

Should not be confused with marine mussels, which are usually much larger (5–10cm) and found only in marine and estuarine habitats.

Swan Mussel

Painter's Mussel

Zebra Mussel

Orb cockle

Pea cockle

Jenkins' Spire Shell

Potamopyrgus antipodarum

J F M A M J J A S O N D

Native range:
New Zealand

Introduced:
1852 in the Thames, originally introduced in drinking barrels

Spread:
Most likely on boats and trailers and by fish

Other names:
New Zealand Mud Snail, *Hydrobia jenkinsi*, *Potamopyrgus jenkinsii*, *Paludestrina jenkins*

DESCRIPTION: *Tiny* snail of fresh and brackish waters, 3–6 (up to 11)mm long, 3mm wide. Last whorl (body whorl) large, more than half shell height. *Possesses operculum* (horny plate which closes the mouth of the shell when snail is retracted – use hand lens) unlike other freshwater species. Spiral-shaped, pointed shell (5–6 whorls in an adult), sometimes with spiral keel or row of minute spines (use hand lens). Ranges from grey or horn-coloured to dark brown, sometimes slightly translucent. When encrusted, shells vary widely in colour. Body pale grey to white with dark patches or bands; tentacles slightly tapering and uniformly pale. Mouth pear-shaped, lip raised, umbilicus (hollow cone-shaped space within the whorls of the shell) cleft and closed. Populations consist almost entirely of females. Reproduction is slower at higher salinities.

STATUS: One of the commonest freshwater snails, still extending distribution in parts of northern England, Scotland and Wales. Reproduces parthenogenetically (females bear young that have developed from unfertilised eggs). Spread on boat hulls and trailers, to which it easily attaches, and can pass intact through the guts of many fish species.

HABITAT: Common in flowing freshwater of all kinds, also found in caves, springs, roadside trickles, brackish ditches and lagoons. Scarce in still waters but can be found in lakes, ponds, water tanks and reservoirs. Feeds on detritus and occurs on a wide range of substrates including mud, stones and submerged aquatic plants. Modest requirements in terms of water quality, coping with both turbid and clear water. Tolerant of pollution and can live in sewage. Very hardy, coping with wide range of temperatures, and can withstand some desiccation.

IMPACT: Can occur at very high densities (several 100,000 snails per square metre), altering ecosystems and displacing native species through competition. Potential to block drains, water mains and other pipes.

Key differences between similar species

Easily distinguished from adults of truly freshwater snails by much smaller size, but may be confused with juveniles, although the presence of an operculum in Jenkin's Spire Snail is distinctive.

There are several similar mud snails of similar size and with opercula in brackish water, usually restricted to the coast (none is found on rocky shores). Laver Spire Shell is the only common mud snail that might be confused.

	Jenkins' Spire Shell *Potamopyrgus antipodarum* (non-native)	Laver Spire Shell *Hydrobia ulvae* (native)	Spire Snail *Hydrobia ventrosa* (native)	*Hydrobia neglecta* (native)
Status	Common	Common	Rare	Rare
Habitat	Wide range of *freshwater* habitats to brackish lagoons	*Coastal*, brackish lagoons, estuarine muds through to fully marine	*Coastal*, lagoons without direct communication with sea, estuaries and mudflats	*Estuaries* and coastal mudflats
Shell	Somewhat thick-set, up to 6mm long, 5–6 whorls, last whorl (body-whorl) large, more than half shell height; may be keeled with or without bristles; curvature pronounced	Slender, up to 6mm long, blunt apex, flat-sided spire, 6–7 whorls, never with a keel in middle of whorls; curvature pronounced. Body-whorl half shell height or less	Slender, up to 5mm long, often with sharp apex, 6–7 whorls. More rounded and swollen than in *H. ulvae*, last whorl not proportionately large, never with a keel in middle of whorls; curvature slight	Slender, up to 4mm long. Whorls less rounded than in *H. ventrosa*, never with a keel in middle of whorls
Tentacles	Slightly tapering with pale line down centre*	Pale with dark pigment patch at a distance greater than its own length from the tip*	Pale, occasionally with a faint terminal black streak*	Pale with a dark pigment patch at a distance less than its own length from tip
Reproduction	Parthenogenesis, rarely viviparous	Eggs hatch as planktonic larvae	Eggs hatch as crawling juveniles	Eggs hatch as crawling juveniles

* = Use hand lens

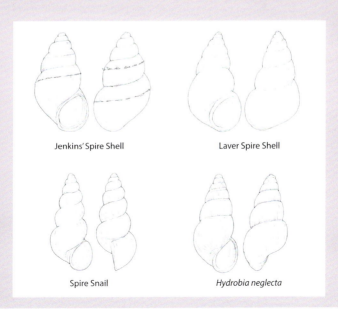

Jenkins' Spire Shell

Laver Spire Shell

Spire Snail

Hydrobia neglecta

Asian Clam

Corbicula fluminea

| J | F | M | A | M | J | J | A | S | O | N | D |

Native range:

Southern and eastern Asia

Introduced:

1998, River Chet on the Norfolk Broads, probably in ballast water

Spread:

Potentially spread by ornamental use in ponds and aquaria, as bait and on boats

Other names:

Asiatic Clam, Golden Clam

DESCRIPTION: Small, usually less than 25mm in diameter, rarely longer (40mm). Distinctive **thick** shell with **prominent, evenly spaced concentric ridges**. Yellow-green to brown colour outside shell, inside glossy light purple nacre.

STATUS: Well established in Norfolk Broads and rivers in the area, also present in the Thames and Great Ouse system. Continuing to spread in GB. Widespread in Europe.

HABITAT: Wide range of rivers, lakes, canals and channels, but requires well-oxygenated water. Prefers sand and gravel substrate to mud.

IMPACT: Highly invasive, can occur in vast densities. Significantly alters ecosystems by filtering nutrients, altering substrate and potentially increasing sedimentation through pseudofaeces production. May compete with native species. Large accumulations of shells can restrict water flow, blocking drainage and intake pipes.

Key differences between similar species

Orb cockles (*Sphaerium* spp.) **and pea cockles** (*Pisidium* spp.)

Native, common. **Much smaller**, usually less than 15mm and unlikely to be confused. Shells very thin and lack prominent ridges

Orb cockle

Pea cockle

Chinese Mitten Crab

Eriocheir sinensis

Native range:

Between eastern Russia, China and Japan

Introduced:

1935, in ballast water

Spread:

Likely to continue to be spread in ballast water, potentially deliberately spread for food

Burrows in river banks dug by Chinese Mitten Crabs.

DESCRIPTION: Adults and juveniles highly distinctive with *claws covered in dense mitten-like fur*, more prominent in males. *Carapace squarish*, 5–7 (up to 10)cm across, with 4 spines on each side and 4 spines at the front. Brownish-orange or green. Notch between eyes. Legs long and hairy. **Male:** Identified by bell-shaped abdominal flap. **Female:** Wider, dome-shaped abdominal flap.

BEHAVIOUR: Digs multiple burrows in soft river banks. Omnivorous, mainly taking gastropods and bivalves.

STATUS: Main populations in the rivers of southeast England (particularly the Thames and Medway) but also in parts of northern England (including the Mersey, Tyne, Humber and Ouse) and Wales (the Dee). Absent in Scotland.

HABITAT: Partly marine, but primarily freshwater. Marine larval stages float freely in water column. Once larvae settle they make their way to estuaries where they develop into juveniles and migrate long distances (sometimes 100s of km) upstream in rivers. Tolerates a wide variety of habitats and conditions.

IMPACT: Significant environmental pest, burrowing into river banks causing destabilisation and erosion. Predator of and competitor with native species. Gathers in large numbers when migrating and can block equipment such as pipes and screens.

Similar species

There are no other freshwater crabs in Great Britain. Quickly distinguished from marine crabs (e.g. *Carcinus maenus* right) which lack the hairy claws and squarish carapace of Chinese Mitten Crab.

Non-native crayfish

There is only one native crayfish in Great Britain, the White-clawed Crayfish (*Austropotamobius pallipes*). It is in significant decline at least in part because of competition with, and spread of disease by, non-native crayfish species. Of the non-natives, Signal Crayfish is by far the most widespread and well established with small populations of five other species. Two further non-native crayfish that are not yet present, but have the potential to arrive and become invasive, are described in these pages.

Crayfish are mainly active at dusk and dawn, rarely coming out in the open during daylight hours. They are more active during warmer months, often with periods of inactivity during winter. They are normally found hiding under rocks, boulders and other debris in a river, stream or lake and are omnivorous, feeding on a wide variety of food types including vegetation, invertebrates as well as fish and their eggs.

Care should be taken when looking for crayfish as the native species is protected by legislation and should not be disturbed. Because of the risk of spreading crayfish plague, the disease threatening the native crayfish, particular attention should be paid to biosecurity when moving between water bodies. It is an offence to return any non-native crayfish to the wild once it has been removed. There are also strict laws governing the keeping of crayfish in Great Britain.

	Status	Average Total length (max)	Carapace	Claws	Body colour	Plague carrier
White-clawed Crayfish	Widespread, declining	10 (12)cm	Smooth, pitted appearance, row of spines on shoulders	Rough above, *underside dirty white to pink*	Brown to olive colour	No (highly susceptible)
Signal Crayfish	Widespread	16 (22)cm	Smooth, pitted	Large, *turquoise/ white spot on hinge*, underside red	Bluish or reddish-brown	Yes
Marbled Crayfish	Not present	<10(13)cm	Smooth with spines on sides	Small (approx. 5cm)	*Marbled brown/ silver*	Yes
Noble Crayfish	Only a few populations in Somerset	<15 (18)cm	Rough with spines on shoulders	Large and robust	Dark brown to beige	No (highly susceptible)
Narrow-clawed Crayfish	Mainly around London	15 (20)cm	Rough with spines on shoulders	*Long and narrow*	Dark green to light green/yellow	No (highly susceptible)
Red Swamp Crayfish	A few locations around London	10 (15)cm	Rough	Thin, 'S' shaped, covered with *bright red spines*	Red to dark red	Yes
Spiny-cheek Crayfish	A few scattered locations	12cm	Somewhat smooth, prominent hepatic spines. Prominent long rostrum	Tips orange with black band below, rows of pits	Pale to dark brown/green, *abdomen with dark red bands*	Yes
Virile Crayfish	One population north of London	10 (12)cm	Smooth, spines at sides but lacks hepatic spines. Less prominent rostrum	*Flattened with yellow/orange warts in two rows*	Dark brown with wine glass-shaped pattern on back	Yes
Rusty Crayfish	Not present	9cm	Large dark *rusty spots on either side*	Rusty colour above, dirty white underside	Brown/green with rusty spots	Yes

White-clawed Crayfish

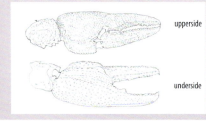

upperside

underside

Signal Crayfish

Noble Crayfish

Narrow-clawed Crayfish

Red Swamp Crayfish

Marbled Crayfish

Spiny-cheek Crayfish

Virile Crayfish

Rusty Crayfish

Signal Crayfish

Pacifastacus leniusculus

J F M A M J J A S O N D

Native range:

North-west USA and south-west Canada

Introduced:

1970s for aquaculture

Spread:

Further spread for food and accidentally on equipment used in water

Other names:

American, Pacific or Californian crayfish

DESCRIPTION: Male up to 16cm long, female 12cm, but larger individuals have been found (22cm). Bluish or reddish-brown, to light or dark brown. **Carapace:** Smooth, slightly pitted. No spines on shoulder. **Claws:** Large and robust. *White or turquoise spot* at junction of claws (hence 'signal'), *underside often reddish-brown*. Smooth, slightly pitted.

STATUS: Well established in much of southern England, with significant advancement into northern England and Scotland.

HABITAT: Wide range, from small streams to large rivers, ponds, lakes and reservoirs. Can move some distance overland.

IMPACT: Considered largely responsible for the rapid decline in native White-clawed Crayfish numbers through competition and spread of crayfish plague. Burrows into banks of water bodies, causing them to collapse and mobilising silt. Highly competitive, out-competing other species for resources. Negatively affects fish populations through predation of eggs and competition with young.

upperside

underside

Key differences between similar species

- **White-clawed Crayfish** *Austropotamobius pallipes*.
  Native, widespread but being displaced by Signal Crayfish across most of range. Smaller (10cm) less robust and less aggressive. Lacks bright red underside to claw and white/turquoise spot on hinge. Has spines on shoulder of carapace.
- **Noble Crayfish** *Astacus astacus*. Non-native (see page 249). Only a few populations in Somerset. Underside of claw may be red, like Signal Crayfish, but lacks the distinctive white/turquoise spot on hinge of claw. Has spines on shoulder of carapace.

Noble Crayfish

Astacus astacus

J F M A M J J A S O N D

DESCRIPTION: Less than 15 (18)cm long. Usually dark brown to beige, although blue or orange colour variations found. **Rostrum:** Parallel sides culminating into a sharp point, similar to a fountain pen. **Carapace:** Often *rough* to touch, with spines on the shoulders. **Claws:** Rough. Large and robust (smaller in females). *Underside often red*.

STATUS: Has not spread far since introduction to River Chew in Somerset. Limited to a few ponds and streams in the area.
HABITAT: Small streams to large rivers, ponds, lakes and reservoirs, but absent from muddy ponds. In GB only found in two still water sites.
IMPACT: Not considered highly invasive. Highly susceptible to crayfish plague. Could have some impact through feeding and burrowing if present in high densities.

Native range:

Central and Eastern Europe

Introduced:

Mid-1980s, for aquaculture

Spread:

Has not spread much since introduced, could potentially be spread by anglers or others that find it in a water body

Other names:

Red-footed or Red-clawed Crayfish

upperside

underside

Key differences between similar species

- **White-clawed Crayfish** *Austropotamobius pallipes*. Native. *Smoother claws and carapace.*
- **Signal Crayfish** *Pacifastacus leniusculus*. Non-native (see page 248). Very common and widespread. Has red undersides to the claw but *distinctive turquoise/white spot* on the top of the claws. *Lacks row of spines on the shoulder of the carapace*, which is present in Noble Crayfish.

Narrow-clawed Crayfish

Astacus leptodactylus

Native range:

Ponto-Caspian region (drainage basins of the Black, Caspian and Aral Sea).

Introduced:

1970s, imported for food

Spread:

Possibly by human action as angling bait and food or accidentally as a contaminant of fish stock or aquatic vegetation

Other names:

Turkish Crayfish, Long-clawed Crayfish, Pond Crayfish

DESCRIPTION: 15 (up to 20)cm long. Colour variable, normally dark olive green to yellow-brown or pale green, occasionally blue. May be mottled. Leg joints often dark orange. **Rostrum:** Borders more or less parallel. With or without spines, ending in a very pointed tip. **Carapace:** Variable in size and shape. Slightly *rough* to touch. Spines present at shoulders. **Claws:** Distinctly *long and narrow*. Often pale underneath. Rough on top, smooth underside. Smaller in females than males. **Behaviour:** More active during day light hours than other crayfish species.

STATUS: Originally introduced for food and either escaped or was deliberately introduced to water bodies. Now well established in parts of south-east England around London, with isolated populations elsewhere. Highly susceptible to crayfish plague, which is likely to keep populations in check.

HABITAT: Tolerates a wide range of environmental conditions, including brackish waters. Tends to prefer still water.

IMPACT: Can be a nuisance to anglers. Likely to out-compete native White-clawed Crayfish where ranges overlap, but does not pass on crayfish plague. Could have a negative impact on the wider ecosystem through feeding behaviour if present in large numbers.

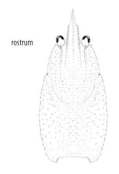

rostrum

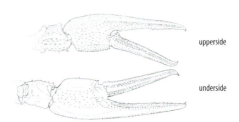

upperside

underside

Key differences between similar species

● Can be confused with other *Astacus* species. Distinguished by elongated claws and rough carapace.

Red Swamp Crayfish

Procambarus clarkii

| J | F | M | A | M | J | J | A | S | O | N | D |

DESCRIPTION: Usually 10 (up to 15)cm long. Normally red to dark red in colour, but light brown to green when young. Other colour variations such as white or blue also known. **Rostrum:** Prominent and triangular. **Carapace:** Rough. **Claws:** Often *thin and S-shaped*. Red on both surfaces, with many *bright red spines on top*. **Behaviour:** Aggressive. More suited to warmer climates; breeding in GB is limited to warmer summers.

STATUS: Limited to a few locations around London, but with the potential to expand rapidly. Can travel considerable distances over land. **HABITAT:** Tolerates a wide range of environmental conditions, including saline waters.

IMPACT: Carrier of crayfish plague. Will out-compete native crayfish. Feeding may impact on ecosystems. Burrowing likely to cause bank destabilisation and turbidity.

Native range:

South east USA and northern Mexico

Introduced:

1980s, probably for food; first wild record from 1990

Spread:

Unlikely to be spread by people, though may escape or be released if kept in aquaria

Other names:

Louisiana Crayfish

upperside   underside

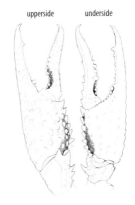

Key differences between similar species

- Coloration and heavy spines on the claws distinguishes this species from others found in Britain.

Spiny-cheek Crayfish

Orconectes limosus

DESCRIPTION: Up to 12cm long. Body smooth, colour pale or dark brown-green. Abdomen with *dark red bands*, though may not be visible as often covered in mud. Tips of legs orange. **Carapace:** Has *prominent hepatic spines on sides* (hence 'spiny cheek'). **Claws:** Upper surface has parallel lines of pits. Tips are often orange with a black band below. **Behaviour:** In addition to raising the claws in a fighting stance, this species will also cross its claws to make itself harder for predators to swallow.

STATUS: Found in at least five separate locations in GB including north London, Warwickshire, Lincolnshire and Nottinghamshire. Spreading quickly.

HABITAT: Can withstand relatively unfavourable conditions, including pollution, habitat drying out for short periods and brackish water. Found in a wide variety of lowland waters including rivers, streams, canals, ponds and lakes. Unlike other species it will live on soft-bottomed, silty, turbid and muddy waters.

IMPACT: Carrier of crayfish plague. May burrow, causing erosion to river banks and siltation. Potential pest of angling.

Native range:

Atlantic seaboard of the USA

Introduced:

1990s, probably escaped or released from an aquarium

Spread:

Could spread via aquarium escapes or as fishing bait

Other names:

Striped Crayfish

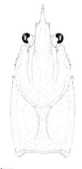

rostrum

upperside

underside

Key differences between similar species

- **Rusty Crayfish** *Orconectes rusticus*. Non-native (see page 254). Not yet present in GB. *Lacks hepatic spines on sides of carapace* and *bands on abdomen*. Lacks distinctive spots on the side of the carapace.
- **Virile Crayfish** *Orconectes virilis*. Non-native (see page 253). Limited to a single population in GB. *Lacks hepatic spines on sides of carapace* and *bands on abdomen*. Rostrum less pronounced than that of Spiny-cheek Crayfish.

Virile Crayfish

Orconectes virilis

| J | F | M | A | M | J | J | A | S | O | N | D |

Native range:

North America

Introduced:

2004, probably escaped or released from an aquarium

Spread:

Potentially by further aquarium escapees

Other names:

Northern Crayfish

rostrum

DESCRIPTION: 10 (up to 12)cm. Body smooth and dark rich brown colour, with a clear *'wine glass'-shaped pattern* in lighter brown on the back. **Carapace:** Smooth, with spines on sides. **Claws:** Flattened, with many *yellow/orange tipped 'warts',* often in two lines along the inside margin. Upper surface with parallel lines of pits. Tips yellow-orange.

STATUS: Established in the River Lee, east London. Likely to spread. Elsewhere in the world presence in aquarium trade and use as fishing bait have facilitated spread, though this is unlikely in GB as it is illegal to possess.

HABITAT: Tolerant of a wide variety of conditions including extreme winters, but is sensitive to deoxygenation. Can be found in rivers, streams, ponds and lakes. Most often found on rocky substrate.

IMPACTS: Can reach very high densities. Carrier of crayfish plague. Aggressive and highly fecund, will out-compete native species. Burrows extensively, causing river bank erosion and sedimentation.

upperside

underside

Key differences between similar species

- **Rusty Crayfish** *Orconectes rusticus.* Non-native (see page 254). Not yet present in GB. Claws and legs *lack orange tipped 'warts'.* Also *lacks 'wine glass' shape* on back. *Has rusty spots on either side of carapace,* unlike Virile Crayfish.
- **Spiny-cheek Crayfish** *Orconectes limosus.* Non-native (see page 252).Lacks orange 'warts' on claws. Also lacks the wine glass shape on the back. Has a striped abdomen.

Rusty Crayfish

Orconectes rusticus

Not recorded in Britain

NP

Native range:

North America: Southern Ontario, Michigan, Kentucky and Tennessee

Introduced:

Not yet present in GB

Spread:

Unlikely to be spread by people, though may escape or be released if kept in aquaria

Other names:

None.

DESCRIPTION: Approximately 9cm long. Body generally brown-green, with small rusty spots on carapace, abdomen and claws. Abdomen may also have darker spots. **Rostrum:** Narrow with parallel sides terminating in a sharp point. **Carapace:** Smooth with small spines on sides. Prominent *large dark rusty spots on each side*. **Claws:** Large and robust. Upperside dark rusty colour, underside dirty white. Tips orange followed by a black band. *Moveable 'S' shaped finger*.

STATUS: Not yet present in GB, but likely to quickly establish if introduced. Has a very limited distribution in Europe. Could potentially be introduced for food, or as a contaminant of equipment used in freshwater.

HABITAT: Wide range of freshwater, including ponds, lakes, rivers and streams. Prefers substrates that offer hiding places, with rocks and logs, but can also be found on softer substrates such as silt and mud. Generally does not dig burrows.

IMPACT: One of the most invasive crayfish worldwide. Establishes quickly and rapidly dominates, displacing other crayfish. May have an impact on native species diversity. Carrier of crayfish plague.

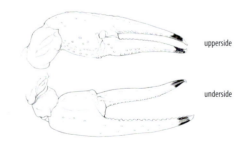

upperside

underside

Key differences between similar species

- **Spiny-cheek Crayfish** *Orconectes limosus*. Non-native (see page 252). Dark bands on abdomen and sharp, hepatic spines. Has dark spots on either side of the carapace. Lacks 'S' shaped moveable finger and large rusty spots on side of carapace.
- **Virile Crayfish** *Orconectes virilis*. Non-native (see page 253). Lacks the rusty spots on either side of the carapace. Has very distinct orange 'warts' on the claws. Lacks 'S' shaped moveable finger.

Marbled Crayfish

Not recorded in Britain

NP

Native range:

Probably south-eastern North America

Introduced:

Not yet present in GB. Has been found in ornamental trade

Spread:

Unlikely to be spread by people, though may escape or be released if kept in aquaria

Other names:

Marmokrebs

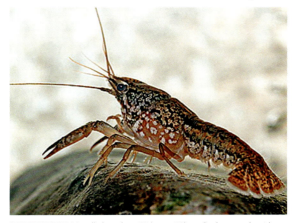

DESCRIPTION: Usually less than 10 (up to 13)cm. Body smooth with spines on side of carapace. Distinctive *'marbled' silvery coloration* on a brownish, dark brown, green or blue background. **Claws:** *Small* (half length of carapace). **Rostrum:** Triangular-shaped with broad base.

BEHAVIOUR: All individuals are female. Parthenogenetic (reproduces asexually without males), unlike other crayfish, meaning only one individual is required to start a new population. Subsequent reproduction can be rapid (every 4–8 weeks).

STATUS: Not yet known in the wild in GB. Unusual species only from aquarium trade, no native population has been found. First found in the German aquarium trade in the mid-1990s, where it was popular because of ornamental coloration. Genetic analysis shows it is closely related to the North American species *Procambarus fallax*. Present in GB aquarium trade in mid-2000, but now illegal to possess.

HABITAT: Unknown, but probably wide-ranging including small streams to large rivers, ponds, lakes, reservoirs as well as drainage ditches and marshland.

IMPACT: Likely to colonise and dominate rapidly due to rapid replication. Voracious feeders, possibly out-competing native species. Carrier of crayfish plague.

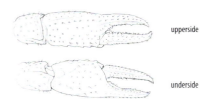

upperside

underside

Key differences between similar species

● Unlike other species. Easily recognised by marbled coloration and small claws.

Killer Shrimp

Dikerogammarus villosus

DESCRIPTION: 10–20 (30)mm from tip of tail to tip of head, *somewhat larger than native freshwater shrimps*. Usually with striped back, rarely uniform in colour. *Two cone-shaped protrusions* on urosome are characteristic.

BEHAVIOUR: Found in large densities where invasive. Nocturnal, hiding underneath stones, rocks and pebbles during daylight hours. Omnivorous. Strong swimmer.

Native range:

Ponto-Caspian region of south-west Russia

Introduced:

2010, pathway unknown, possibly on boats or in angling gear

Spread:

Could be spread by any equipment used in water such as boats and angling gear

Other names:

None.

STATUS: Recent invader with known populations in Grafham Water (Cambridgeshire), Norfolk Broads, Cardiff Bay and Eglwys Nunydd (near Port Talbot). Tolerates poor water quality and survives in damp conditions for some time. Could therefore be spread accidentally with equipment used in water. An additional non-native *Dikerogammarus* species, *D. haemobaphes*, was discovered in Britain in 2012 and is well established, particularly in the Midlands. Both species are very similar and expert assistance should be sought to distinguish them.

HABITAT: Still or flowing freshwater and brackish water, often among hard surfaces, gravel or vegetation. Requires good oxygen levels and therefore rarely found at depth. Often associated with Zebra Mussel, another invasive species from the Ponto-Caspian region.

IMPACT: Voracious predator, taking a wide range of other invertebrates as well as fish fry and eggs. Likely to displace some native species and disrupt nutrient processing.

Range in size of the Killer Shrimp

Killer Shrimp with 20p coin for scale.

Key differences between similar species

D. villosus is most likely to be confused with the native *Gammarus pulex* and particularly *G. tigrinus* because of its striped appearance. It is less easy to confuse with *Crangonyx pseudogracilis* (page 258).

The key distinguishing feature of *D. villosus* is the two cone-shaped protrusions on the urosome ❶, which are absent in *Gammarus* species and *C. pseudogracilis* (page 258), although *Gammarus* species may have clusters of hair or spines.

D. villosus

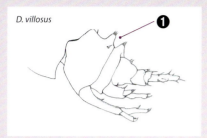

Gammarus species

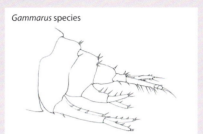

Crangonyx pseudogracilis

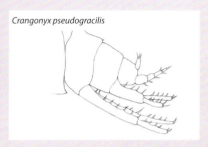

Gammarus species showing position of the urosome

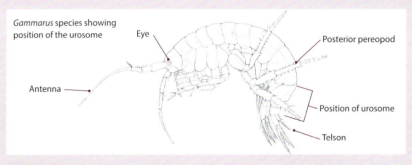

Eye

Antenna

Posterior pereopod

Position of urosome

Telson

Gammarus pulex

Native. Very common. Usually smaller, around 11 (20)mm long. May be striped or uniform colour. *Lacks cone shaped protrusions on tail*, though may have small clusters of hairs or spines.

Gammarus tigrinus

Non-native. Uncommon. Usually smaller, 10–15mm long. May have dark markings, but not usually stripes of Killer Shrimp. *Lacks cone-shaped protrusions on tail*, though may have small clusters of hairs or spines.

Northern River Crangonyctid

Crangonyx pseudogracilis

J F M A M J J A S O N D

Native range:

Eastern North America

Introduced:

Mid 1930s, probably via imported pond plants

Spread:

As a contaminant of aquatic plants, boats and on the plumage of birds

Other names:

None.

DESCRIPTION: Freshwater shrimp, 4–7 (up to 10)mm long. *Well-developed dark eyes*. Bluish-white colour when alive. Telson with a 'V'-shaped depression, but clearly a single structure ❶. Each of the last three pereopods has a serrated posterior edge ❷. *Urosome usually smooth dorsally* ❸, if present setae are small and fine.

BEHAVIOUR: *Characteristically walks upright*, unlike other shrimp species in GB which swim on their sides.

STATUS: Well established in England, Scotland and Wales.
HABITAT: Utilises a wide variety of flowing and still fresh and brackish waters. Often found in polluted, eutrophic waters and waters with low levels of oxygen where native species are unable to thrive.
IMPACT: Not known to have severe impacts, though may compete with some native species and could affect trophic systems either through feeding behaviour or as a prey item.

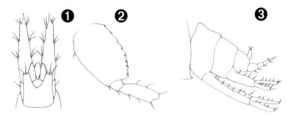

❶ ❷ ❸

Key differences between similar species

Gammarus pulex

Native, except in parts of Scotland, common and widespread. Up to *20mm long. Swims on side*. Telson divided by a long split, giving the impression of a paired structure Ⓐ. Less pronounced serrations on posterior edge of last three pereopods Ⓑ. Urosome with dorsal scales present on all three segments Ⓒ.

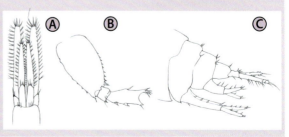

Ⓐ Ⓑ Ⓒ

Bloody-red Mysid

Hemimysis anomala

J F M A M J J A S O N D

Native range:

Ponto-Caspian region (lower reaches of rivers that flow into the Black Sea, Azov Sea and eastern Caspian Sea)

Introduced:

2004, probably introduced by shipping or recreational boating

Spread:

Probably on boats, fishing gear or by birds

Other names:

None.

DESCRIPTION: 6–13mm long freshwater shrimp. *Colourful*, ranging from deep red to ivory-yellow or translucent. Commonly *red-spotted*. Colour changes in response to light and temperature, with deeper red usually in shaded areas. Curved body, long antennae and *large bulbous eyes*. Distinguished from other freshwater mysids by the *truncated telson* with long spikes at both corners ❶.

BEHAVIOUR: Generally hides in crevices and under stones during daylight, more active at night. May be seen in evening in swarms just below water surface, creating reddish-tinged clouds of thousands of individuals. Breeds April–October.

STATUS: Established in England around the Midlands. Not present in Wales or Scotland. Has recently spread rapidly across Europe. Often found in ports and harbours.

HABITAT: Flowing and still, fresh and brackish waters. Avoids waters with strong current. Found among stones, rocks and crevices on river banks, lakes and other water bodies.

IMPACT: Impacts unclear, may compete with native species.

Position of the telson in mysids (this is *M. relicta*).

Key differences between similar species

There are only two other mysid crustaceans that enter British freshwater.

Mysis relicta

Native. Extremely uncommon in GB, possibly present in the Lake District (Ennerdale Water), but may have gone extinct. Truly freshwater. Telson is inverted V-shape without long spikes Ⓐ.

Neomysis integer

Native. Relatively common brackish water species, able to survive for some time in freshwater. May be encountered in freshwaters near the sea. Telson triangular, reaching a point Ⓑ.

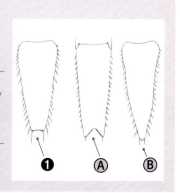

Terrestrial invertebrates

There are over 300 established non-native terrestrial invertebrates in Britain, over 100 of which have negative impacts. They have been imported most commonly as accidental contaminants of goods, such as imported food, plant products and soil.

The majority of terrestrial invertebrates that have a negative impact are insects feeding on, or otherwise damaging, crops, horticultural plants, forestry and food. Only a small proportion are known to cause wider environmental impacts; however these impacts can be devastating, for example Emerald Ash Borer and Citrus Longhorn Beetle are expected to cause severe damage to native trees and woodlands if they establish in Britain.

Only a few species of agricultural and garden pests are covered in this section. Instead, we focus on species which cause wider environmental and human health impacts.

Harlequin Ladybird larva preying on moth eggs. Harlequin Ladybirds eat a wide range of prey from aphids to butterflies and have been linked to the decline of many native ladybird species..

Identification tips

The range of different types of terrestrial invertebrates is considerable, from flatworms and termites to beetles and wasps. It is useful to have a basic understanding of how to distinguish between insects and other invertebrates and also identification of insect orders.

Field signs are particularly important for terrestrial invertebrates. In many cases these will be noticed long before individuals of the species are noticed. For example, the mines in Horse Chestnut leaves caused by the Horse Chestnut Leaf Miner and the distinctive tree holes created by Emerald Ash Borer.

Terrestrial invertebrates are often easiest to identify at a particular stage in their life cycle. For example, Oak Processionary Moth is most likely to be identified during the juvenile (larval) stage because of the nests the larvae form in the branches and trunk of trees.

Identification to species level of some terrestrial invertebrates can be very difficult, for example some of the non-native ants appear very similar to native species. A hand lens will be useful to help investigate specific features. If in doubt it may be necessary to seek expert assistance to confirm identification.

Land flatworms

| J | F | M | A | M | J | J | A | S | O | N | D |

● New Zealand
● Australian

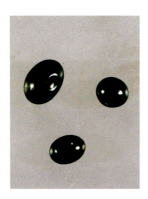

Native range:

Australia and/or New Zealand

Introduced:

See table on page 262

Spread:

In soil associated with plant movements

Other names:

Terrestrial flatworms

DESCRIPTION: Flattened and ribbon-like (larger species), small species are circular or oval in cross-section . Narrows towards the head end which is either blunt, tapers to a fine point, or, in *Bipalium kewense*, hammer-shaped. *2–4 times as long when crawling* as when resting, the head is often raised off the ground, searching from side to side. Smooth and slimy. Leaves a thin trail of slime similar to that of slugs. Eyes are tiny and black, often difficult to see due to the dark pigmentation. Most non-native species have *many eyes* down both sides of the body right to the back end (use a hand lens). All native species have a single pair of small or large eyes near the head end. **Juvenile:** Miniature lighter-coloured version of adult. **Egg capsules:** Shiny ovals laid in soil. 1–2mm long in small species, up to 5mm long in larger species. Initially red or brown turning black within hours.

STATUS: Normally found in the wetter, cooler, north and north-west of Britain, some records in the south-west. Expected to increase in distribution. Most likely spread as adults, juveniles or eggs in soil or plant material, often associated with the horticulture trade, for example in plant pots.

HABITAT: Parks, moorland, wasteland, pasture and arable land as well as gardens, nurseries, garden centres, under objects such as logs and stones, lying on soil in damp, shaded locations.

IMPACT: Non-native flatworms may prey upon and pose a threat to earthworm populations, indirectly having a negative impact on soil structure.

Key differences between similar species

Flatworms could be confused with earthworms, leeches and slugs, all found on or in the soil or under logs and stones.

	Terrestrial flatworms (native and non-native)	Earthworms (native)	Leeches (native, aquatic)	Slugs (native)
Slime or mucus trail	Yes	No. Rarely travels on the surface of the ground	No. Travels looping from sucker to sucker	Yes
Eyes	Tiny black dots - can be hard to see because of dark colour of body*	No	Present as tiny black dots at head end*	Dark 'eye' spots at tips of two pairs of head tentacles, upper pair being longer, tentacles may appear clubbed
Annulation (body segmented by rings along its length)	No	More than 20 rings or annulations along length of body	More than 20 rings or annulations along length of body*	No
Length	Body is longer in motion than when at rest	Body same length in motion as when at rest	Body is longer in motion than when at rest	Body may be longer in motion than when at rest
Saddle (clitellum)	No	Yes	No	No. Textured oval patch (mantle) on upper surfaced towards head end
Suckers	No	No	Suckers present at both head and end of body	No

* = use hand lens

Distinguishing between flatworm species

Key features of the most likely non-native species to be encountered and similar native species are presented in the table below.

	Australian Flatworm *Australoplana sanguinea***	*Kontikia ventrolineata* ***	*Kontikia andersoni***	New Zealand Flatworm *Arthurdendyus triangulatus***	*Microplana terrestris* **	*Microplana scharffi***
Date of first occurrence in the wild	1980s (non-native)	1840 (non-native)	Unknown (non-native)	1970s (non-native)	*(native)*	*(native)*
Population trend	Increasing rapidly	Increasing slowly	Increasing slowly	Increasing slowly		
Status	Widespread in south west England, less common in other parts of England and Wales	A few widely scattered sites in England	A few widely scattered sites in England	Widespread in Scotland and parts of north England	Widespread	Widespread
Size	At rest: 2cm; moving: 4 (8)cm; 3–8mm wide	1–2cm long; 1–2mm wide	1–2.5cm long, 1mm wide	At rest: *6cm long; moving: 15 (20)cm*; 1cm wide	Up to 2cm long; 1–2mm wide	2–5cm long; 1–2mm wide
Cross-section	*Flattened to oval*	*Oval or cylindrical*	*Oval or cylindrical*	*Ribbon-like, flat*	*Cylindrical and plump*	*Slightly flattened*
Body	Smooth. Pointed at both ends. Does not form coils when at rest	Smooth. Pointed at both ends. Does not form coils when at rest	Smooth. Pointed at both ends. Does not form coils when at rest	Narrowly pointed at both ends. Rests in a flat coil covered in slime. Leaves a slime trail	Blunt at head end	Smooth when extended, creased when contracted
Colour	*Pinky or peachy orange* with pink head. Underside pale yellow	*Almost black*	Upper *surface pale brown*	Upper surface dark, purplish-brown with *narrow pale buff edge*. Underside pale yellow	Upper surface *uniform dark grey-black or brown*. Underside pale	*Pinky-yellow or grey-yellow*. Head end whitish and translucent
Markings	Two narrow *pale grey lines* running along length of body close to mid-line	*Four dark lines* running length of underside. Upper surface with two narrow pale lines close to mid-line	Three *rows of dark brown spots* with middle row narrower than side rows	Sometimes with a darker stripe up middle of body	No longitudinal lines running down length of body	No longitudinal lines running down length of body
Eyes	Numerous tiny eyes present as a row along pale margin being dense and close together at head end, sparse and well separated towards tail end*	Many eyes along edge of upper surface but difficult to see because of dark body colour*	Relatively large eyes along edge of upper surface in a single row*	Numerous tiny eyes on pale margins at head end*	*2 tiny eyes near to head end**	*2 tiny eyes near to head end**

* = use hand lens ** = family Rhynchodemidae *** = family Geoplanidae

262

Australian Flatworm
Australoplana sanguinea

Kontikia ventrolineata

Kontikia andersoni

New Zealand Flatworm
Arthurdendyus triangulatus

Microplana terrestris (native)

Microplana scharffi (native)

Oak Processionary moth

Thaumetopoea processionea

J F M A M J J A S O N D

Native range:

Central and southern Europe

Introduced:

2006 , contaminant of imported plants and trees

Spread:

Could spread rapidly by natural flight, may also be spread on contaminated trees and plants

DESCRIPTION: Adult flies July to September (one generation per year). Well camouflaged against bark of oak trees so can be difficult to spot. Wingspan 30–40mm. Mottled grey wings with comma-shaped marking on centre of forewing. **Nest:** *Distinctive white webs* positioned on the underside of branches or on the trunk in which larvae congregate and complete their development. Small nests are typically tennis ball-sized, but can be much larger. **Caterpillar:** Seen from April to July. *Long white hairs* protrude from *reddish-brown warts along length of body*. Older caterpillars have dark stripe along middle of back and whitish line along each side. Gregarious and *found in large groups*. When moving between feeding sites or nests caterpillars will typically follow each other head to tail in a long line (hence processionary). **Eggs:** Laid in July to early September, overwintering before hatching in April. Hundreds are laid in rows on small branches in the canopy of oak trees and covered with a fine layer of grey scales.

STATUS: Established in northern France and some other parts of Europe. Males occasionally appear as vagrants on the south coast of England; females are weak fliers and do not naturally cross the Channel. Following the accidental introduction of larvae, breeding populations have established in west and south west London. Outside of London, an infestation was found in Berkshire in 2010. Also reported from Sheffield and Leeds but no longer thought to be present here.

HABITAT: Found in association with oak trees but also Hornbeam, Hazel, Common Beech, Sweet Chestnut and birches.

IMPACT: Caterpillars are major defoliators of oaks in continental Europe. Covered in hairs that *can cause skin irritation and allergic reactions.*

Key differences between similar species

The caterpillars of Oak Processionary moth are highly distinctive because of the long white hairs and reddish-brown warts and unlikely to be confused with other species. Adults of some native species may be more difficult to separate.

Pale Eggar *Trichiura crataegi*

Native, widespread but uncommon. Lacks comma-shaped marking in the centre of the forewing.

Pine Processionary Moth *Thaumetopoea pityocampa*

Non-native, rare migrant in adult form only. Host plant is key difference, closely associated with Corsican and Maritime Pines. Has smaller and weaker comma-shaped marking centrally in forewing.

Brown-tail Moth *Euproctis chrysorrhoea*

Native, relatively common on south and east coasts of England. Caterpillar has irritant hairs. Does not form processions. Usually found amongst coastal scrub and feeds on Bramble, hawthorns and Blackthorn, but sometimes other species. Spins similar tough white nests out of webbing, usually formed in food plant rather than trunks of trees. Adult distinctly different with bright white wings. Caterpillar quickly distinguished by blackish colour with **brown hairs** and a pair or **red-orange spots towards the rear of the body**.

Horse Chestnut Leaf-miner

Cameraria ohridella

Native range:

Unknown, possibly south-eastern Europe

Introduced:

2002, probably with imported plants

Spread:

Mainly spreading naturally in GB

Other names:

None.

SYMPTOMS: Most likely to be identified from June onwards by *distinctive blotchy brown markings (mines)* on Horse Chestnut leaves. Mines start off white or pale green, usually with a brown spot, often turning browner later in the year. They are usually translucent and the pupa may be visible. Mines are usually created between leaf veins, rarely crossing them, although many mines may merge together forming large patches. *Entire trees can appear autumnal* as early as August and are rapidly defoliated.

DESCRIPTION: Small orange-brown moth, body 5mm long, wingspan 7–9.5mm. *Orange tufted head*, antennae almost as long as forewing, legs with equal white and black bands or spots. Forewings metallic chestnut brown with *four silvery-white transverse stripes* edged in black. Hindwings dark grey or greyish-brown with *long fringes*. **Pupa:** Develops in a silken cocoon in the mine from about 2 weeks to up to 6 months; overwintering pupae survive among fallen leaves. **Caterpillar:** Small, up to 5.5mm long. Legs all short. **Eggs:** Laid along lateral veins on upper side of leaflet; each female lays 20–40 eggs (200–300 eggs per leaflet). May to August.

STATUS: First recorded in Europe near Macedonia in 1985. Spreading rapidly since first record in London in 2002, now common in south and midlands of England, spreading to north of England and Wales.
HABITAT: Only found on Horse Chestnut trees and other species in the genus *Aesculus*.
IMPACT: Trees severely disfigured but no evidence yet that long-term tree health is affected.

Trees appear unseasonally autumnal.

Translucent mines with dark spots follow the veins of the leaf.

Key differences between similar species

Cameraria ohridella is the only moth in GB to mine *Aesculus* trees. No other insects cause similar blotchy brown mines in the leaves of Horse Chestnut trees. Adults closely resemble some species of *Phyllonorycter* moths (native) and identification should not be made on adults alone. Larvae can be readily distinguished by legs which are shorter (both thoracic and abdominal pairs of legs) in Horse Chestnut Leaf-miner.

Horse Chestnut Leaf Blotch fungus, *Guignardia aesculi*, can cause damage that is similar to that of *C. ohridella* but the fungus causes blotches that are usually *large, red-brown patches*, starting at the tip of the leaf, with a *yellow margin*. They are *not translucent* and *do not follow the veins* of the leaf. Severely affected leaflets roll upwards lengthways and, as with Horse Chestnut Leaf-miner, leaves may fall prematurely. This leaf blotch is widespread and common in the southern half of England, becoming less frequent northwards.

Leaf damage caused by Horse Chestnut Leaf-miner.

Leaf damage caused by Horse Chestnut Leaf Blotch fungus.

Longhorn beetles

Anoplophora species (*A. glabripennis,* Asian Longhorn Beetle, and *A. chinensis,* Citrus Longhorn Beetle)

Native range:

Asia

Introduced:

Asian Longhorn Beetle 2012, probably in wood packaging; subsequently eradicated. No other records from the wild of either species

Spread:

Contaminated wood and trees

Other names:

None.

SYMPTOMS: *Bleeding sap* and *T-shaped slit* in bark can indicate oviposition sites. Pupal chambers under bark can create bulges in trunk. Sawdust or frass on trunk and at the base of the tree could indicate larval tunnels.

DESCRIPTION: *Large*, 25–40mm long with characteristically *long and striped (blue-white bands) antennae* and white markings on black body. The white markings are highly variable, consisting of white scales which may rub off. **Larvae:** Tunnel in trees for 2 to 4 years (depending on temperature) and unlikely to be observed. *Holes in trees* from which adult has emerged are usually first evidence of infestation. Most likely to be seen as adults emerging from host trees July–August.

STATUS: An outbreak of Asian Longhorn Beetle was recorded in the Paddock Wood area of Kent in 2012, but was subsequently eradicated. No other populations known in the wild in GB. These are regulated pest species, any sightings must be reported to the appropriate plant health authority.

HABITAT: Uses a range of host tree species including citrus, Apple, Cherry, poplars, willows, elms, maples, European Ash and Horse Chestnut.

IMPACT: Both species are a serious threat to a range of important deciduous tree species in Great Britain. Tunnels created by larvae render trees vulnerable to disease and wind damage. Adults feed on foliage and young bark, but cause less damage.

Oviposition site Ⓐ and larval hole exit Ⓑ.

Frass on bark of tree from larval tunnel.

A. chinensis

Larval tunnel.

Key differences between similar species

Asian and Citrus Longhorn Beetles are distinguished from each other by small protuberances at the base of the wing cases of the latter; expert assistance is required.

There are about 60 native or naturalised longhorn beetles in Britain; a high proportion are nationally threatened or scarce. None are easily confused with Asian or Citrus Longhorn Beetles. Some have striped antennae, but they are generally *smaller* and with *less prominent body markings*.

Colorado Beetle

Leptinotarsa decemlineata

J F M A M J J A S O N D

NP

Native range:
Mexico

Introduced:
Not yet present, could be imported with fresh goods

Other names:
None.

DESCRIPTION: 10–12mm long with oval body. Very distinctive *shiny yellow-orange* beetle with *10 black-stripes on back* (5 on each wing case). Head and thorax orangey-red with irregular black spots. Antennae not clubbed. Moves slowly across ground or on plants, but can fly.
Larvae: Up to 15mm long, can be much smaller. *Pink, red or orange* with *black spots along sides* and plain orange-red on top. Abdomen distinctly *swollen*. Head and legs black and distinct from rest of body. Active. **Eggs:** Small yellow-orange oblongs, usually deposited on underside of host plant leaf in groups of 10–40.

SYMPTOMS: Both adults and larvae are voracious grazers and will quickly defoliate food plants.

STATUS: Not established in Great Britain, though occasionally intercepted. Warming climate may increase risk of establishment. Hitchhikes on a wide variety of produce.
HABITAT: Plants from the potato family (*Solonaceae*) including potato, tomato, aubergine and pepper.
IMPACT: A major pest of potato and other crops.

Larvae

Key differences between similar species

Quite distinct, though has been confused with some species.

Cockchafer Beetle
Melolontha melolontha

Native, common. *Distinctly different*. Most likely to be seen on a spring evening. *Much larger*, 2–3 times size of Colorado Beetle. *Dull brown colour*, not shiny or strongly patterned. *Clubbed antennae*.

Harlequin Ladybird
Harmonia axyridis

Non-native (see page 276). *Adult distinctly different*. Pupae orange or red with rows of black spots and could be confused with Colorado Beetle larvae. However, the Harlequin Ladybird pupae are *immobile* and so easily distinguished from the mobile Colorado Beetle larvae.

Comparison between Colorado Beetle larva (left) and Harlequin Ladybird pupa (right).

Size difference between Colorado Beetle, Cockchafer Beetle and Harlequin Ladybird

Emerald Ash-borer

Agrilus planipennis

Not recorded in GB

NP

SYMPTOMS: Often first detected by symptoms of trees. Initial symptoms include *yellowing and thinning of foliage, dying branches* and *crown dieback*. Trees die 2–3 years after infestation. Vertical splits in bark 5–10cm long may be present. *Sinuous frass-filled galleries* created by larvae may be visible under bark. Emerging adults create *D-shaped exit hole* approximately 3mm across.

DESCRIPTION: Highly distinctive metallic green jewel beetle (family Buprestidae). Elongate 7–15mm long, 3–3.5mm wide. *Wedge-shaped*. Eyes kidney-shaped, bronze-coloured. **Larvae:** Creamy-white, 10–14mm long. Forms sinous galleries in ash trees that can extend to 30cm.

Native range:

China, Japan, Taiwan, Korea, Mongolia and Russian far east

Introduced:

Not yet present. Could be imported with wood or trees.

Other names:

None.

STATUS: Not yet recorded in GB, but a significant potential threat. Invasive in North America, where it has been highly damaging. Discovered in the Moscow region in 2005, from where it could spread to the rest of Europe. Adult beetles fly several kilometres in search of ash trees, but human activity likely to be the main cause of extensive spread particularly through movement of infested trees.

HABITAT: Ash trees (*Fraxinus* species). Has been recorded on North American species (*F. americana*, *F. nigra*, *F. pennsylanica*) and some species in native range, but not Mountain Ash (*Sorbus aucuparia*). Not yet known on European species (*F. excelsior* and *F. angustifolia*), but considered likely to attack them.

IMPACT: Causes serious decline and death of ash trees, which make up nearly 15% of broadleaved woodland in GB and are a valuable timber crop.

'D'-shaped exit hole.

Sinuous gallery in tree trunk.

Larva

Long, vertical split in bark

Defoliation of an Ash tree.

Key differences between similar species

Adults are distinctive and unlikely to be confused with other species. There are no European species of *Agrilus* known from ash and so the occurrence of galleries typical of this genus in ash trees should be regarded as suspicious.

Harlequin Ladybird

Harmonia axyridis

Native range:

Central and eastern Asia

Introduced:

First recorded in GB in 2004, having spread from an introduced population in mainland Europe

Spread:

Has naturally spread rapidly across GB

Other names:

Multicoloured Asian Ladybird, Halloween Ladybird

DESCRIPTION: Distinctive ladybird, 5–8mm long, *larger* than most native species. *Highly variable*, although there are three main forms present in Britain which are *distinguished by colour* '*succinea*' yellow/orange/red, 0–21 black spots; '*spectabilis*' black with 4 red/orange spots/patches; '*conspicua*' black with 2 red/orange spots/patches. *Pronotum white or cream* with up to 5 spots, or fused spots forming an M-shaped mark or solid trapezoid. Legs brown. Many have slight keel along posterior margin of dorsal surface. **Fourth-instar larva (immature stage):** Black, with thick spines, each branching at top into three prongs. Bright orange upside-down L-shaped marking apparent on flanks. Two pairs of orange dots on dorsal surface. **Pupa:** Orange with remains of shed spiky larval skin visible at base.

Fourth-instar larva

Pupa

STATUS: Rapidly spread across Europe following deliberate release in the 1980s as a biological control agent of pest insects. It was never released in GB, but was first recorded in Essex in 2004. Spread rapidly, becoming widespread and abundant by 2010. Local in Scotland, but likely to invade further.

HABITAT: Common in many habitats particularly deciduous trees, but moves into buildings during winter.

IMPACT: Voracious, generalist predator threatening native invertebrates. Nuisance to humans during winter because hundreds can occupy one house.

Key differences between similar species

For further guidance on identification refer to Roy *et al.* 2011.

10-spot Ladybird *Adalia decempunctata*

Native, commonly found on deciduous trees. Similar to '*succinea*' form but much smaller (3.5–4.5mm). Only has one shoulder spot (Harlequin has two).

● Harlequin Ladybird

Pine Ladybird *Exochomus quadripustulatus*

Native, commonly found on deciduous and coniferous trees. Similar to '*spectabilis*' colour form but smaller (3–4.5mm). More distinct rim around edge and no white markings.

● 10-spot Ladybird

● Pine Ladybird

Asian Hornet

Vespa velutina

Not recorded in Britain

NP

Native range:

Asia

Introduced:

Not yet present, could arrive through natural flight from continental Europe or imported plants or commodities

Other names:

Asian Predatory Wasp

DESCRIPTION: Slightly *smaller* than native European Hornet: Queens to 30mm long, workers 25mm. Thoracic region *almost entirely velvety black or dark brown* with a fine yellow band at the borders. Abdominal segments dark, except *fourth segment which is almost entirely yellow-orange*. Legs brown with *characteristic yellow tips*. Head black but with yellow-orange 'face'. **Nest:** Very *large*. Papery. Usually in tall trees in suburban areas. Possible in garages, sheds or under decking.

BEHAVIOUR: Adults day-flying (unlike European Hornet it stops flying at dusk). Queens overwinter and found new colonies from February onwards. Only one colony formed per year but adults active until late autumn, or even into winter.

STATUS: First record for Europe was south-west France in 2004, imported as a hitchhiker on clay pots from Asia. Has spread rapidly through France and into neighbouring countries. Not yet present in GB, but may be able to cross English Channel naturally from France, or arrive through imported goods. Most likely to arrive on the south coast of England or around major ports.

HABITAT: *Most likely to be found in areas where bees are kept*. Usually associated with Honey Bees, which it hunts, but also feeds on other insects, fruit and flowers. Nests usually high in trees and man-made structures, sometimes closer to the ground.

IMPACT: Predator of native pollinators and a significant risk to Honey Bee populations. Potential health risk from stings.

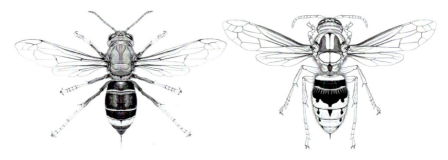

Asian Hornet   European Hornet

Asian Hornet nests are very large. The one pictured is of medium size.

Asian Hornet preying on honey bees by 'hawking' outside a hive.

Key differences between similar species

European Hornet *Vespa crabro*

Native, quite common mainly in Midlands and south of England and Wales. May be active at night, unlike Asian Hornet. Larger. *Extensive orange-yellow on abdomen*, not limited to fourth segment. *Legs dark without distinctive yellow tips*. Thorax not entirely dark.

Median Wasp *Dolichovespula media*

Non-native, recently arrived in GB from Europe. Quite common in southern England. Only queen is likely to be confused. *Smaller* than Asian Hornet. Has *yellow parts to thorax. Extensive yellow on abdomen. Legs dark without distinctive yellow tips*.

Non-native ants

Non-native ant species of concern in GB include:

- Argentine Ant *Linepithema humile* (occasionally found indoors)
- Asian Super Ant *Lasius neglectus* (one established super colony in Gloucestershire)
- Pharaoh Ant *Monomorium pharaonis* (established indoors, does not survive outside over winter)
- Red Imported Fire Ant *Solonopsis invicta* (potential invader, would not survive outside over winter)
- Ghost Ant *Tapinoma melanocephalum* (occasionally found indoors, does not survive outside over winter)

Argentine Ant and Asian Super Ant are the greatest threats. Pharaoh Ant is a nuisance in buildings but not found outdoors. Red Imported Fire Ant is not established in Europe but considered one of the most invasive ants globally. It is not likely to become a problem in GB. Ghost Ant is also considered a human nuisance but only recorded in one locality in GB. All ants are extremely difficult to identify. Basic descriptions are given here, but specialist advice should be sought.

Argentine Ant

Linepithema humile

DESCRIPTION: Small (2–3mm), medium to dark brown, smooth and hairless. No soldier caste. **Trails:** Found ascending from flowering trees and shrubs. **Nest:** Often under wood or stones or in plant pots. Forms large *supercolonies* (many individual colonies interconnected by trails) covering a large area. **Identification throughout the year:** Most likely to be seen in the summer months in large numbers on potted plants.

STATUS: One of the most invasive ants globally. Present in buildings in GB but not established outside, does not survive winter. Could possibly become established with climate change. Easily moved on potted plants which they regularly colonise.

HABITAT: Gardens, on potted plants.

IMPACT: Human nuisance. Dominant and aggressive competitor, displaces native ants, disrupting critical natural processes such as pollination and seed dispersal.

Other names: *Iridomyrmex humilis*

Native range:

South America

Introduced:

1927, probably as a contaminant of potted plants or other goods

Spread:

Most likely in potted plants

Key differences between similar species
- See Asian Super Ant, *Lasius neglectus* opposite.

Asian Super Ant

Lasius neglectus

Native range:

East Asia

Introduced:

2009, probably as a contaminant of potted plants or other goods

Spread:

Most likely in potted plants

Other names:

None.

DESCRIPTION: Small, 2.5–3.5mm long. *Body brown*, head sometimes darker. Hind legs paler. Antennae darkening towards tip. Can form *supercolonies* (many individual colonies interconnected by trails) covering a large area. **Nest:** Often in plant pots.

STATUS: Small population established in Gloucestershire country house. Nest resilient and easily transported in plant pots or other horticultural material.

HABITAT: Most likely to be seen in large numbers on potted plants during summer months.

IMPACT: Like Argentine Ant, displaces native ant species. May interfere with electrical outlets causing fire hazard.

Key differences between similar species

- **Black Garden Ant** *Lasius niger*. Native, common. Very difficult to distinguish. The Argentine Ant and Asian Super Ant are slightly smaller.

Asian Tiger Mosquito

Aedes albopictus

J F M A M J J A S O N D

Not recorded in Britain

NP

Native range:

South-east Asia

Introduced:

Not yet present, could be imported with goods, for example used tyres

Other names:

None.

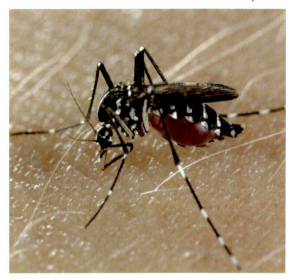

DESCRIPTION: *Small*, usually about 3mm but can be longer (10mm). Body slender, black with characteristic *white bands* on legs and body and a long *silvery-white stripe* running along the middle of the head and down the thorax. Long feeding mouth-part (proboscis). **Larvae:** Aquatic. Often found in old tyres and plant containers.

BEHAVIOUR: Females active and blood-feeding by day March–November. 5–17 generations per year. Overwinters as eggs. Will *feed on humans* unlike most native species.

STATUS: Not yet present in GB, but a significant risk particularly with warming climate. Present in many European countries, including France. **HABITAT:** Prefers urban and suburban habitats. Breeds usually in artificial but also natural aquatic habitats such as wood holes, tyres, barrels, vases and drinking troughs. Trade in used tyres has facilitated spread.
IMPACT: The most invasive mosquito globally, out-competing resident mosquito species. Significant biting nuisance with potential to become serious health threat. Transmits disease, notably chikungunya and dengue virus but also other arboviruses.

Key differences between similar species

There are more than 30 mosquito species present in Britain. All adult mosquitoes have a similar slender body, measuring 4–10mm in length with characteristic scale-covered wings and long mouth-part (proboscis). Most likely to be confused with *Culiseta annulata*, because this species also has black and white ringed legs.
● *Culiseta annulata.* Native. Common and widespread in Great Britain. Considerably *larger*. Has *beige and grey stripes* rather than black and white. Wings have noticeable veins and four dark, indistinct spots. *Lacks white or silver line from the middle of the head and down the thorax.*

Mediterranean Termite

Reticulitermes grassei

J F M A M J J A S O N D

Native range:

Southern Europe

Introduced:

1994, probably with imported plants or timber

Spread:

Most likely in potted plants

Other names:

None.

DESCRIPTION: Often called 'white ants' but not closely related to ants. Social insects living in colonies with a caste system comprising reproductive, worker and soldier castes. Workers and nymphs forage actively. **Workers and soldiers:** Approximately 4–6mm long, wingless and pale-bodied, often hidden in wood or below ground. **Kings and queens:** 12mm long, winged and black or brown in colour. **Field signs:** *Subterranean* and does not build mounds. Found all year under patio slabs, skirting board and other structures. Mud tubes or tunnels may be visible linking subterranean nest to food (timber). *Wood may look crushed* at load-bearing points. Damaged wood makes a hollow sound when tapped with a hammer.

STATUS: Possibly transported in a plant pot from the Canary Islands, Mediterranean Termites in GB are localised to a single site amongst private homes in Devon. The original population was well established and anecdotal evidence suggested it had been present for at least 25 years before being reported. An eradication and containment programme commenced in 1998 with extensive subsequent monitoring of the site. Despite no records of termites from the area for many years, a small population was found in 2009 which is believed to be a remnant of the original.

HABITAT: Subterranean. A species of temperate areas. In Europe notably present along railway lines and canals.

IMPACT: Causes significant damage to timber in properties.

Key differences between similar species

- Flying winged ants can resemble swarming winged termites but termite wings are about twice as long as the body and all four wings are the same size, whereas the hindwings of ants are smaller than the forewings. Termites also have a broader waist than ants.
- Identification of termites to species level is very difficult and requires specialist assistance.

Glossary

Terms printed in **bold** type within an explanation are also explained in the glossary.

abdomen: the posterior part of the body of an **arthropod** such as an insect, crustacean or spider

achene: a type of simple dry fruit produced by many species of flowering plants

acuminate: narrowing gradually to a point

acute: sharply pointed

adventive: a **non-native** plant growing unaided by direct human intervention but not yet permanently established (see **casual**)

allelopathy: inhibition of one species of plant by chemicals produced by another species of plant

anadromous: a fish that annually migrates from salt to freshwater

annual: a plant that completes its life cycle from germination as a seed to production of seed followed by death within one year

anther: the part of a stamen that produces and releases the pollen

arboviruses: diseases transmitted by **arthropods**, including insects

archaeophyte: a plant species which is **non-native** to a geographical region, but which was introduced in 'ancient' times, usually taken to be before 1500AD

arcuate: curved like a bow

arthropod: an invertebrate animal having an **exoskeleton**, a segmented body, and jointed appendages. Arthropods form the **phylum** Arthropoda, and include the insects, arachnids, and crustaceans

arum: a plant of the Araceae **family**, for example Sweet-flag, Slender Sweet-flag and Lords-and-ladies (Cuckoo-pint)

axil: the angle where a leaf or leaf stalk joins the stem

ballast water: water taken on board a ship as ballast to provide stability

barbel: a whisker-like projection from the jaw of some fish

benthic: an animal that lives at the bottom of a lake or sea

berry: a fleshy **fruit** with the seed or seeds surrounded by pulp, remaining closed when mature

biofouling: the accumulation of microorganisms, plants such as algae, or animals, on wetted surfaces such as boat hulls, cables, pipes and other equipment

biosecurity: has many different meanings, in the case of this guide it generally refers to action to slow the spread of **non-native** species and diseases

bole: the stem or trunk of a tree

brackish: between fresh and marine water, with a salinity of 0.5 to 30 parts per thousand total dissolved solids

bract: a leaf, often modified, that bears a flower in its **axil**

brownfield: land previously used for industrial purposes or some commercial uses

byssal groove: the groove in the shell of a mollusc where the **byssal thread** is attached

byssal (or byssus) threads: the threads used by some bivalve molluscs to anchor to hard surfaces

calyx: the sepals collectively forming the protective layer of a flower in bud

carapace: the hard, protective upper **exoskeleton** of some invertebrates as well as the 'shell' of some vertebrates such as terrapins

carpel: one of the structural units of a **pistil**, representing a modified, **ovule**-bearing leaf

casual: casual non-natives reproduce occasionally outside cultivation, do not form self-sustaining populations and rely on repeated introductions for their persistence (see also **adventive**)

catkin: a long tassel-like spike of small flowers especially in the oaks, Hazel and willows

caudal (rump) patch: the usually white-coloured patch on the rump of some deer species

clump: a dense cluster of plants, especially trees, shrubs, grasses and sedges, typically of a single species

crenate: of a leaf having a notched or scalloped edge

crepuscular: active at dusk and dawn

corm: a bulblike organ that provides the energy for the plant to grow

crown: the visible part of the rhizome or root of a plant from which buds or shoots erupt

cultivar: a cultivated plant variety produced by selective breeding

cuneate: wedge-shaped with straight sides converging at the base of a leaf

cyprinid: a large **family** of fish species, which includes carp

cypsela: a dry single-seeded **fruit** formed from a double **ovary** of which only one develops into a seed, characteristic of plants in the Compositae (daisy **family**)

deciduous: without leaves for part of each year

decurrent: having the base extended down the axis as in leaves where the blade continues down the petiole or stem as a wing

dioecious: of a plant or animal with male and female reproductive organs in different individuals

diurnal: active only during the day

dorsal-lateral fold: a fold of skin, visible as raised ridges, often running in pairs along the back of some frogs

drupe: any fleshy or pulpy fruit enclosing a stone containing one or a few seeds

ecosystem engineer: any species that creates, significantly modifies, maintains or destroys a habitat

ellipsoid: a three-dimensional body, elliptical in side view; as in elliptical

elliptical: a flat shape widest in the middle, tapering roughly equally at both ends

endemic: a species of plant or animal confined to a particular country, region or island and having originated there

entire: (of leaves) not toothed or lobed

established: a species with a self-sustaining, reproducing population in the wild

eutrophic: a water body rich in plant nutrients; artificial eutrophication of a water body can result in significant ecological change

evergreen: retaining leaves for more than one year

exoskeleton: the external skeleton that supports and protects an animal's body

extra-floral nectaries: nectar-secreting plant glands that develop outside of flowers and are not involved in pollination

family: a group in the classification of living organisms consisting of related genera (singular: **genus**). For plants the family name usually ends in – aceae and for animals –idae

fecund: prolific or fertile

foetid (fetid): stinking

follicle: a small secretory cavity, sac or gland

forewing: either of the two front wings of a four-winged insect

frass: debris or excrement produced by, usually wood-boring, insects

fruit: the ripened **ovary** of a seed plant containing the seed or seeds. Dry fruits are called **achene**, capsule and nut. Fleshy fruits are called **aril**, **berry** or drupe

glaucous: covered with a bluish or whitish layer

hepatic spine: in crayfish, a spine on the hepatic region of the carapace (see page 252).

hitchhiker: a species introduced or spread as a stowaway on a vehicle, commodity or other imported or moved good

horizon-scanning species: a **non-native** species that is not yet present or **invasive** within a given geographic region but could soon become so

hybrid swarm: a population of hybrids that has survived beyond the initial hybrid generation, with interbreeding between hybrid individuals and backcrossing with the parent types

inflorescence: the whole flowering part of a plant, combining the stems, **peduncles** (stalks) and **bracts** as well as the actual flowers

instar: the development stage of some arthropods between moults

internode: segment of stem, culm, branch, or rhizome between nodes

introgression or **introgressive hybridisation**: the diffusion of genes from one species into another through interbreeding and hybridisation

invasive non-native species: a **non-native** species that has a negative environmental, economic or social impact

keel: narrow ridge, for example on the scales of a reptile or fish

lateral line: a line of pores running along each side of a fish, part of a sensory system

lenticel: rounded or elliptical pore in bark, usually raised

leptomorphic: of bamboo, temperate, running bamboo rhizomes, usually thinner than the culms they support, the **internodes** are long and hollow

ligule: a small strap-like piece of tissue at the base of a leaf, especially in grasses (gently pull the leaf away from the stem to see if a ligule is present and if so its shape, etc.)

metatarsal tubercle: a tubercle on the foot of some frogs and toads that can be useful for identification

midventral line: the line between the two halves of a bivalve mollusc

midrib: central leaf-vein

micropyle: small opening in the surface of an **ovule** through which pollen passes

mycorrhizal: of mycorrrhiza, an association between a fungus with the roots of a higher plant, for example a tree

mysid: a group of small shrimp-like crustaceans found in salt, brackish and freshwaters

nacre: mother-of-pearl

naturalised: introduced by humans and growing as if naturally wild in a specific area, reproducing consistently without direct human intervention

nocturnal: active only at night

non-native species: a species (or subspecies) introduced by human action outside its natural past or present distribution

obovoid: a three-dimensional body, egg-shaped attached at the narrower end

omnivorous: an animal that eats both plants and animals

operculum: of a snail (gastropod mollusk), horny plate which closes the mouth of the shell when snail is retracted

opposite: leaves which are placed along a stem in pairs, one on each side

ovary: of a plant, the hollow base of the carpel of a flower containing one or more **ovules**

ovule: of a plant, the part of the **ovary** of seed plants that contains the unfertilised seed (germ cell)

palmate: divided like the fingers of a hand, palm-like

palmate antler: an antler with broad flattened areas between the tines, as in Fallow Deer

papillose: covered with small blunt protuberances (papillae)

parthogenetic reproduction: females bearing young without fertilisation by a male

pedicles: in deer, the part of the skull that attaches to the antlers

peduncle: the common stalk of a cluster of flowers

pereopods: the walking legs of crustaceans, the most posterior of which can be useful for the identification of some of the non-native shrimps

perennial: a plant that continues its growth from year to year

Phylum: a taxonomic rank below Kingdom (for example animals and plants) and above Class (for example insects and crustaceans). Traditionally, in botany the term Division is used instead of Phylum

pinnate: of a compound leaf, with the leaflets arranged in opposite pairs on either side of the **midrib**

piscivorous: feeds on fish

pistil: the female organs of a flower comprising **stigma**, **style** and **ovary**

plankton: small, often microscopic, plants and animals occurring in the water column.

Ponto-Caspian: the Black Sea and Caspian Sea region of eastern Europe and south-west Russia

pronotum: a prominent plate-like structure that covers all or part of the **thorax** of some insects

pseudofaeces: excreted by filter-feeding molluscs as a way of passing particles that are not suitable for food and do not go through the digestive system

pupa: a life stage in some insects that undergo complete metamorphosis, occurring between the larva (or caterpillar) stage and the adult (or imago) stage

rhizome: horizontal underground stem bearing both roots and shoots

robinine: an alkaloid found in flowers and seeds of False Acacia (see page 19) which is toxic to humans and can cause gastroenteritis

rostrum: in crayfish, a pointed, beak like prolongation of the head, the shape of which can be useful for identification

rut: the annual period of sexual activity in deer, when males will often fight and defend territory

scrub: land dominated by low shrubs and bushes with no trees more than 8m

serrated: saw-toothed

sessile: without a stalk

seta (plural: setae): hairs or bristles

spadix: sterile axis on which the flowers of an arum inflorescence are packed

spathe: a **bract** enclosing an inflorescence of some monocotyledons, for example arums

stand: a group of growing plants usually relatively tall and of one or a few species

stele: core of vascular tissue in centre of roots and stems

sepal: each of the divisions or leaves of the **calyx**

stigma: the part of a **pistil** that receives the pollen in pollination

stipule: one of a pair of appendages at the base of a leaf or its stalk

stolon (or runner): a creeping stem above ground that roots at the tip or nodes to form a new plant that may eventually become independent of its parent

striae (singular: stria): linear marks or furrows on a surface

striated: marked with **striae**

style: the narrow extension of the **ovary** supporting the **stigma**

sub-: almost (botanical)

subulate: awl shaped; long, narrow and gradually tapering to a fine point

succulent: fleshy and juicy or pulpy

sucker: a shoot which grows from underground sucker, in horticultural terms, is a sprout or shoot that grows from a bud at the base or roots of a tree

suture: the seam-like juncture of two parts

telson: the terminal segment of some **arthropods** (see page 257)

tepal: a term covering both petals and **sepals**, used where flowers do not have distinct petals and **sepals**

terete: round, not grooved, ridged or angled

ternate: arranged or divided into threes

thicket: dense scrub

thoracic: of the **thorax**

thorax: in invertebrates, the part of the body between the head and the abdomen

triquetrous: three-angled, the angles being **acute**

trophic level: the position an organism occupies in a food chain

tubercles: small, rounded protuberances

turbid (turbidity): cloudiness in a water body caused by suspended materials

tussock: a **clump** of plants, typically grasses and of a single species

twig: ultimate branch of a woody stem

umbel: an umbrella-shaped compound flower head in which all the flowers are borne on stalks arising like the stalks of an umbrella from a single point or common stalk

umbilicus: of snails (gastropod molluscs), hollow cone-shaped space within the **whorls** of the shell

urosome: useful for the identification of **non-native** shrimps, the structure that comprises the rear segments of the **abdomen**

vector: an organism that acts as a host for a disease and transmits it to a susceptible host

veliger: the mobile larvae of some molluscs

vocal sac: the sac inflated by male frogs and toads to help amplify their call

whorl (botanical): a ring of leaves or flowers around a stem arising at the same level

whorl (zoological): a single, complete 360° turn in the spiral growth of a mollusc shell

zooplankton: the animal component of **plankton**

References

General

Booy, O., Wade, M. and White, W. 2008. *Invasive Species Management for Infrastructure Managers and the Construction Industry*. CIRIA, London.

Daisie 2009. *Handbook of Alien Species in Europe*. Springer Science and Business Media B. V.

Defra 2008. *The Invasive Non-native Species Framework Strategy*. Defra, London.

Genovesi, P. and Scalera, R. 2007. *Assessment of existing lists of invasive alien species for Europe, with particular focus on species entering Europe through trade and proposed responses*. Draft report for the Council of Europe.

Great Britain Non-native Species Information Portal. Available at: www.nonnativespecies.org (accessed 2013–2014).

Great Britain Non-native Species Risk Assessments. Available at: www.nonnativespecies.org (accessed 2012–2014).

Great Britain Non-native Species Secretariat Identification Sheets. Available at: www.nonnativespecies.org (accessed 2012–2014).

Hill, M.O., Baker, R., Broad, G., Chandler, P.J., Copp, G.H., Ellis, J., Jones, D., Hoyland, C., Laing, I., Longshaw, M., Moore, N., Parrott, D., Pearman, D., Preston, C., Smith, R.M., Waters, R. 2005. *Audit of Non-native Species in England. English Nature Research Reports*. English Nature, Peterborough. Available at: http://www.english-nature.org.uk/pubs/publication/PDF/662.pdf (accessed 2005).

Hill, M.O., Beckmann, B.C., Bishop, J.D.D., Fletcher, M.R., Lear, D.B., Marchant, J.H., Maskell, L.C., Noble, D.G., Rehfisch, M.M., Roy, H.E., Roy, S., Sewell, J. 2009. *Developing an Indicator of the Abundance, Extent and Impact of Invasive Non-native Species*. Defra, London.

Keller, R. P., zu Emergassen, P. S. E., Aldridge, D. C. 2009. 'Vectors and timing of freshwater invasions in Great Britain.' *Conservation Biology*, 23, 1343–1671.

Lowe, S., Browne, M., Boudjelas, S., de Poorter, M. 2000. *100 of the World's Worst Invasive Alien Species A selection from the Global Invasive Species Database*. Published by The Invasive Species Specialist Group (ISSG) a specialist group of the Species Survival Commission (SSC) of the World Conservation Union (IUCN). 12pp.

Parrott, D., Roy, S., Baker, R., Cannon, R., Eyre, D., Hill, M., Wagner, M., Preston, C., Roy, H., Beckmann, B., Copp, G. H., Edmonds, N., Ellis, J., Laing, I., Britton, J. R., Gozlan, R. E. and Mumford, J. 2009. *Horizon scanning for new invasive non-native species in England. Natural England Contract No. SAE03-02-189*, Natural England Commissioned Report NECR009, 111pp. Natural England, Sheffield.

Roy, H.E., Bacon, J., Beckmann, B., Harrower, C. A., Hill, M. O., Isaac, N. J., Preston, C. D., Rathod, B., Rorke, S. L., Marchant, J. H., Musgrove, A., Noble, D., Sewell, J., Seeley, B., Sweet, N., Adams, L., Bishop, J., Jukes, A. R., Walker K. J. and Pearman, D. 2012. *Non-native species in Great Britain: establishment, detection and reporting to inform effective decision-making*. Defra, London.

Roy, H.E, Preston, C.D., Harrower, C., Rorke, S., Noble, D., Sewell, J., Walker, K., Marchant, J., Seeley, B., Bishop, J., Jukes, A.R. Musgrove, A., Pearman, D. and Booy, O. 2014. GB Non-native Species Information Portal: documenting the arrival of non-native species in Britain. Biological Invasions Online, Digital identifier: 10.1007/s10530-014-0687-0, 1–11.

UK Technical Advisory Group on the Water Framework Directive 2013. *Guidance on the assessment of alien species pressures*. Available at: http://www.wfduk.org/

Welch, D., Carss, D.N., Gornall, J., Manchester, S.J., Marquiss, M., Preston, CD., Telfer, M.G., Arnold, H.R. and Holbrook, J. 2001. *An audit of alien species in Scotland*. Review No. 139. Scottish Natural Heritage, Perth.

Wittenberg, R. and Kenis, M. 2005. *An inventory of alien species and their threat to biodiversity and economy in Switzerland*. CABI Bioscience Switzerland Centre report to the Swiss Agency for Environment, Forests and Landscape: 417.

Plants

Atherton, I., Bosanquet, S. and Lawley, M. (editors) 2010. *Mosses and Liverworts of Britain and Ireland. A Field Guide*. British Bryological Society.

Blamey, M. and Grey-Wilson, C. 2003. *Cassell's Wild Flowers of Britain and Northern Europe*. Cassell, London.

Blamey, M., Fitter, R. and Fitter, A. 2003. *Wild Flowers of Britain and Ireland*. A & C Black, London.

Booy, O and Wade, P M 2007 *Giant Hogweed (*Heracleum mantegazzianum*) Management in the United Kingdom*. RPS Group plc, St Ives, Cambridgeshire.

Child, L.E. and Wade, P.M. 2000. *The Japanese Knotweed Manual. The management and control of an invasive weed*. Packard Publishing, Chichester.

Clay, D.V. and Drinkall, M.J. 2001 'The occurrence, ecology and control of *Buddleja davidii* in the UK.' *British Crop Protection Council Weeds*, 1, 155–160.

Clements, E.J., Smith, D.P.J. and Thirlwell, I.R. 2005. *Illustrations of Alien Plants of the British Isles*. Botanical Society of the British Isles, London. Line drawings including many of the species in this field guide (annotated CS&T).

Cullen, J. 2005. *Hardy Rhododendron Species. A guide to identification*, Timber Press, London.

Ellis, R.G. 1993. 'Aliens in the British flora.' *British Plant Life* No. 2. National Museum of Wales, Cardiff.

Fryer, J. and Hylmő, B. 2009. Cotoneasters. *A Comprehensive Guide to Shrubs for Flowers, Fruit and Foliage*, Timber Press, London.

Graham, G.G. and Primavesi, A.L. 1993 (2005 reprint). *Roses of Great Britain and Ireland*. Botanical Society of the British Isles, London.

Grey-Wilson, C. and Marjorie Blamey, M. 2003. *Cassell's Wild Flowers of Britain and Northern Europe*. Cassell, London.

Hill, M.O., Preston, C.D. and Roy, D.B. 2004. *PLANTATT – Attributes of British and Irish plants: status, size, life history, geography and habitats*. Centre for Ecology and Hydrology, Huntingdon.

Lang, D.C. 1987. *The Complete Book of British Berries*. Threshold Books, London.

Lansdown, R.V. 2009. *A Field Guide to the Riverine Plants of Britain and Ireland*. Summerfield Books.

Lousley, J.E. and Kent, D.H. 1981. *Docks and Knotweeds of the British Isles. Botanical Society of the British Isles*, London. 'Identification of the Asiatic knotweeds (*Fallopia japonica* and *F. sachalinensis*).'

McQuire, J.F. and Robinson, M.L.A. 2009. *Pocket Guide to Rhododendron Species based on the descriptions by H.H. Davidian*. Royal Botanic Gardens, Kew, London.

Meredith, T.J. 2009. *Timber Press Pocket Guide to Bamboos*. Timber Press, Oregon.

Pearman, D.A. and Preston, C.D. 2003. *First Records of Alien Plants in the Wild in Britain and Ireland*. Botanical Society of the British Isles.

Poland, J. and Clement, E. 2009. *The Vegetative Key to the British Flora*. Botanical Society of the British Isles, London.

Preston, C.D., Pearman, D.A. and Dines, T.D. (editors) 2002. *New Atlas of the British and Irish flora. An atlas of the vascular plants of Britain, Ireland, the Isle of Man and the Channel Islands*. Oxford University Press, Oxford.

Rich, T. and Jermy, A.C. 1998 (2006 reprint). *Plant Crib*. Botanical Society of the British Isles, London.

Rutherford, A. and Stirling, A. McG. 1987. 'Variegated Archangels.' BSBI News, 46, 9–11.

Sell, P.D. and Murrell, G.A. 2009. *Flora of Great Britain and Ireland. Volume 3 Mimosaceae – Lentibulariaceae*. Cambridge University Press, Cambridge.

Sell, P.D. and Murrell, G.A. 1996 (2007 reprint). *Flora of Great Britain and Ireland. Volume 5 Butomaceae – Orchidaceae*. Cambridge University Press, Cambridge.

Smith, A.J.E. 2004 (2nd edition). *The Moss Flora of Britain and Ireland*. Cambridge University Press, Cambridge.

Stace, C. 2010 (3rd edition). *New Flora of the British Isles.* Cambridge University Press, Cambridge.

Streeter, D. 2009. *Collins Flower Guide*. Harper Collins, London.

Stuart, D. 2006. *Buddlejas*. Timber Press, Oregon.

Tutin, T.G. 1980. *Umbellifers of the British Isles*. Botanical Society of the British Isles, London.

Animals

Ahern, D., England, J. and Ellis, A. 2008. 'The virile crayfish, *Orconectes virilis* (Hagen, 1870) (Crustacea: Decapoda: Cambaridae), identified in the UK.' *Aquatic Invasions*, 3, 102–104.

Araujo, R., Moreno, D. and Ramos, M. 1993. 'The Asiatic clam *Corbicula fluminea* (Müller, 1774) (Bivalvia: Corbiculidae) in Europe.' *American Malacological Bulletin*, 10, 39–49.

Arnold, N. and Ovenden, D. 2002. *Reptiles and Amphibians of Britain and Europe*. HarperCollins, London.

Aulagnier, S., Haffner, P., Mitchell-Jones, A.J., Moutou, F., and Zima, J. 2009. *Mammals of Europe, North Africa and the Middle East*. A&C Black, London.

Bącela, K., M. Grabowski and A. Konopacka 2008. '*Dikerogammarus villosus* (Sowinsky, 1894) (Crustacea, Amphipoda) enters Vistula – the biggest river in the Baltic basin.' *Aquatic Invasions*, 3, 95–98.

Baker, S. 2006. 'The eradication of coypus (*Myocastor coypus*) from Britain: the elements required for a successful campaign.' *Assessment and Control of Biological Invasion Risks*. Shoukadoh Book Sellers, Kyoto, Japan and IUCN, Gland, Switzerland: 142–147.

Bang, P. and Dahlstrom, P. 1972. *Animal Tracks and Signs*. Collins, London.

Bartoszewicz, M. 2006: *NOBANIS – Invasive Alien Species Fact Sheet – Procyon lotor* – From: Online Database of the North European and Baltic Network on Invasive Alien Species – NOBANIS. Available at: www.nobanis.org (accessed 2012).

Beyer, K. 2008. 'Ecological implications of introducing *Leucaspius delineatus* (Heckel, 1843) and *Pseudorasbora parva* (Temminck and Schlegel, 1842) into inland waters in England.' PhD Thesis, University of Hull.

Boiteau, G. and Le Blanc, J-P.R. 1992. *Colorado Potato Beetle, Life Stages*. Ministry of Supply and Services Canada, catalogue number A43–1878/1992E.

Brede, E., Thorpe, R., Arntzen, J. and Langton, T. 2000. 'A morphometric study of a hybrid newt population (*Triturus cristatus/T. carnifex*): Beam Brook Nurseries, Surrey, UK.' *Biological Journal of the Linnean Society*, 70, 685–695.

Brown, R., Lawrence, M. and Pope, J. 2004. *Animals Tracks, Trails and Signs*. Octopus Publishing Group. London.

BTO *Birdfacts*. Available at: www.bto.org/index.htm (accessed 2010–2014).

Buczacki, S. and K. Harris 2014 (4th edition). *Pests, Diseases and Disorders of Garden Plants*. HarperCollins, London.

Burton, M. 1976. *Guide to the Mammals of Britain and Europe*. Elsevier International Projects Ltd., Oxford.

Buszko, J. 2006: *NOBANIS – Invasive Alien Species Fact Sheet – Cameraria ohridella.* – From: Online Database of the North European and Baltic Network on Invasive Alien Species – NOBANIS. Available at: www.nobanis.org (accessed 2012).

Caffrey, J. M., Evers, S., Millane, M. and Moran, H. 2011. 'Current status of Ireland's newest invasive species– the Asian clam *Corbicula fluminea* (Mueller, 1774).' *Aquatic Invasions*, 6, 291–299.

Carmona-Catot, G., Benito, J. and García-Berthou, E. 2011. 'Comparing latitudinal and upstream–downstream gradients: life history traits of invasive mosquitofish.' *Diversity and Distributions*, 17, 214–224.

Chandra, S. and Gerhardt, A. 2008. 'Recent establishment of the invasive Ponto-Caspian mysid (*Hemimysis anomala* GO Sars, 1907) in the Hungarian part of the Danube River.' *Aquatic Invasions*, 3, 99–101.

Davies, C. E., Shelley, J., Harding, P. T., McLean, I. F. G., Gardiner, R. and Peirson, G. 2004. *Freshwater Fishes in Britain – the species and their distribution*. Harley Book, Colchester.

Dobson, M. 2012. *Identifying Invasive Freshwater Shrimps and Isopods*. Freshwater Biological Association, Cumbria.

Dumont, S. 2006. 'Notes and news: a new invasive species in the north-east of France, *Hemimysis anomala*.' *Crustaceana*, 79, 1269–1274.

Dunstone, N. 1993. *The Mink*. T. & A. D. Poyser Natural History, London.

Elliott, P. and zu Ermgassen, P. S. 2008. 'The Asian Clam (*Corbicula fluminea*) in the River Thames, London, England.' *Aquatic Invasions*, 3, 54–60.

Espadaler, X. and Bernal, V. 2005. *Lasius neglectus*: a polygynous, sometimes invasive, ant. Universitat Autònoma de Barcelona, Spain.

Feldhamer, G. A., Thompson, B. C., Chapman, J. A. 1982. *Wild Mammals of North America: biology, management, and conservation*. The Johns Hopkins University Press.

Fishbase. Available at: www.fishbase.org (accessed 2006–2013).

Garland, E. 1980. 'The colonization of Windermere by *Crangonyx pseudogracilis* (Crustacea, Amphipoda) 1961 to 1964.' Occasional Publication No. 12, 13 pp, Freshwater Biological Association, Cumbria.

Gozlan, R. E., Britton, J. Cowx, I. and Copp, G. 2010. 'Current knowledge on non-native freshwater fish introductions.' *Journal of Fish Biology*, 76, 751–786.

Harris, S. and Yalden, D. (editors) 2008 (4th edition). *Mammals of the British Isles: Handbook*. Mammal Society, Southampton. ISBN 9780906282656.

Holdich, D. 2002. 'Distribution of crayfish in Europe and some adjoining countries.' *Bulletin Français de la Pêche et de la Pisciculture*, (367), 611–650.

Holdich, D. M. 2009. 'A bibliography of studies relevant to crayfish conservation and management in the British Isles in the 2000s.' *Crayfish Conservation in the British Isles*, 16, 165.

Holdich, D. and Black, J. 2007. 'The spiny-cheek crayfish, *Orconectes limosus* (Rafinesque, 1817) [Crustacea: Decapoda: Cambaridae], digs into the UK.' *Aquatic Invasions*, 2, 1–15.

Holdich, D., Gallagher, S., Rippon, L. Harding, P. and Stubbington, R. 2006. 'The invasive Ponto-Caspian mysid, *Hemimysis anomala*, reaches the UK.' *Aquatic Invasions*, 1, 4–6.

Holling, M. and the Rare Breeding Birds Panel 2007. 'Non-native breeding birds in the United Kingdom in 2003, 2004 and 2005.' *British Birds* 100, 638–649.

Hulme, R. 2009. *RSPB Complete Birds of Britain and Europe*. DK, London.

Inns, H. 2009. *Britain's Reptiles and Amphibians*. Wildguides Ltd. Hampshire.

Kowalczyk, R. 2006: *NOBANIS – Invasive Alien Species Fact Sheet – Nyctereutes procyonoides*. – From: Online Database of the North European and Baltic Network on Invasive Alien Species – NOBANIS. Available at: www.nobanis.org (accessed 2012).

Lainé, L. 2002. The invasion of the termites? Research report, Plymouth University.

Lever, C. 2005. *Naturalised Birds of the World*. A&C Black, London.

Lever, C. 2009. *The Naturalised Animals of Britain and Ireland*. New Holland, London.

Ludwig, A. 2008. 'Identification of *Acipenseriformes* species in trade.' *Journal of Applied Ichthyology* 24, 2–19.

Maitland, P. S. 2004. 'Keys to the freshwater fish of Britain and Ireland with notes on their distribution and ecology.' Scientific Publication No. 62, 248 pp, Freshwater Biological Association, Cumbria.

Martin, P., N. J. Dorn, T. Kawai, C. van der Heiden and Scholtz, G. 2010. 'The enigmatic Marmorkrebs (marbled crayfish) is the parthenogenetic form of *Procambarus fallax* (Hagen, 1870).' *Contributions to Zoology*, 79, 107–118.

Miller, P.J. and Loates, M. J. 1997. *Collins Pocket Guide: Fish of Britain and Europe*. HarperCollins, London.

Mitchell-Jones, T., Amoria, G., Bogdanowicz, W., Krystufek, B., Reijnders, P., Spitzenberger, F., Stubbe, M., Thissen, J., Vohralik, V., and Zima, J. 1999. *The Atlas of European Mammals*. T.& A.D. Poyser, London.

Mullarney, K., Swensson, L., Zetterstrom, D. and Grant, P. J. 1999. *Collins Bird Guide*. HarperCollins, London.

Nyári, A., Ryall, C. and Townsend Peterson, A. 2006. 'Global invasive potential of the house crow *Corvus splendens* based on ecological niche modelling.' *Journal of Avian Biology*, 37, 306–311.

Oscoz, J., R. Miranda and Leunda, P. M. 2008. 'Additional records of eastern mosquitofish *Gambusia holbrooki* (Girard, 1859) for the River Ebro Basin (Spain).' *Aquatic Invasions*, 3, 108–112.

Parks, R. and L. House, L. 2011. 'Tree inspection and control of infestations of Oak Processionary Moth *Thaumetopoea processionea* (Linnaeus) (Lepidoptera: Thaumetopoeidae) in London in 2011.' Forestry Commission Report.

Parrott, D., Roy, S. and Fletcher, M. 2007. *Assessing scarce established non-native birds and mammals in England*. Central Science Laboratory, York.

Pérez-Bote, J. L. and Fernández, J. 2008. 'First record of the Asian clam *Corbicula fluminea* (Müller, 1774) in the Guadiana River Basin (southwestern Iberian Peninsula).' *Aquatic Invasions*, 3, 87–90.

Pöckl, M., Holdich, D. and Pennerstorfer, J. 2006. *Identifying native and alien crayfish species in Europe*. European project CRAYNET.

Pyke, G. H. 2005. 'A review of the biology of *Gambusia affinis* and *G. holbrooki*.' Reviews in *Fish Biology and Fisheries*, 15, 339–365.

Pyke, G. H. 2008. 'Plague minnow or mosquito fish? A review of the biology and impacts of introduced *Gambusia* species.' *Annual Review of Ecology, Evolution, and Systematics*, 39, 171–191.

Reptiles and Amphibians of the UK. Available at: www.herpatofauna.co.uk (accessed 2005–2013).

Roy, H.E., Beckmann, B.C., Comont, R.F., Hails, R.S., Harrington, R., Medlock, J., Purse, B., Shortall, C.R. 2009. 'An Investigation into the Potential for New and Existing Species of Insect with the Potential to Cause Statutory Nuisance to Occur in the UK as a Result of Current and Predicted Climate Change.' Defra, London.

Roy, H. E., de Clercq, L.-J., Handley, J., Poland, R.L., Sloggett, J.J. and Wajnberg, E. 2011. 'Alien arthropod predators and parasitoids: an ecological approach.' *BioControl*, 56, 375–382.

Sapota, M.R. 2006: *NOBANIS – Invasive Alien Species Fact Sheet – Neogobius melanostomus*. – From: Online Database of the North European and Baltic Network on Invasive Alien Species – NOBANIS. Available at: www.nobanis.org (accessed 2012).

Sibley, P., Brickland, J. and Bywater, J. 2002. 'Monitoring the distribution of crayfish in England and Wales.' *Bulletin Français de la Pêche et de la Pisciculture* (367), 833–844.

Sousa, R., Antunes, C. and Guilhermino, L. 2008. 'Ecology of the invasive Asian clam *Corbicula fluminea* (Muller, 1774) in aquatic ecosystems: an overview.' *Annales de Limnologie*, Cambridge University Press.

Sterry, P. 2005. *Complete British Animals*. HarperCollins, London.

Strachan, R. and Moorhouse, T. 2006 (2nd edition). *Water Vole Conservation Handbook*. The Wildlife Conservation Research Unit.

Suleiman, A. S. and Taleb, N. 2010. 'Eradication of the House Crow *Corvus splendens* on Socotra, Yemen.' *Sandgrouse* 32, 136–140.

Sutcliffe, D. W. 1991. 'British Freshwater Malacostracan.' *Freshwater Forum*, 1, 225–237.

Townsend, M. 2008. Report on survey and control of Oak Processionary Moth *Thaumetopoea processionea* (Linnaeus) (Lepidoptera: Thaumetopoeidae) in London in 2008. Available at: www.forestry.gov.uk/pdf/fcopmsurvey07.pdf (accessed 2011).

Verkerk, R.H.J. and Bravery, A.F. 2004. 'A case study from the UK of possible successful eradication of *Reticulitermes grassei*.' Final Workshop COST Action E22 'Environmental Optimisation of Wood Protection' Lisbon.

Verkerk, R.H.J. and Bravery, A.F. 2010. 'Termite eradication programme, Information Leaflet – Update No.19.' Department for Communities and Local Government.

Walker, P., Fraser, D. and Clark, P. 2010. 'Status, distribution and impacts of mitten crab in the Nene Washes and Ouse Washes: Stage 1 Report for Natural England.' *APEM Scientific Report 411010*: 1–51.

Weidema, I. 2006: *NOBANIS – Invasive Alien Species Fact Sheet – Arthurdendyus triangulatus* – From: Online Database of the North European and Baltic Network on Invasive Alien Species – NOBANIS. Available at: www.nobanis.org (accessed 2012).

Wetterer, J. K., Wild, A.L., Suarez, A.V., Roura-Pascual, N. and Espadaler, X. 2009. 'Worldwide Spread of the Argentine Ant, *Linepithema humile* (Hymenoptera: Formicidae).' *Myrmecological News*, 12, 187–194.

Wheeler, A. 1978. *Key to the fishes of Northern Europe*. Frederick Warne Ltd, London.

Wild, A. L. 2004. 'Taxonomy and distribution of the Argentine ant, *Linepithema humile* (Hymenoptera: Formicidae).' *Annals of the Entomological Society of America*, 97, 1204–1215.

Witkowski, A. 2011: *NOBANIS – Invasive Alien Species Fact Sheet – Pseudorasbora parva*. – From: Online Database of the European Network on Invasive Alien Species – NOBANIS. Available at www.nobanis.org (accessed 2012).

Index

A

Acacia, False 19, 21
Acaena anserinifolia 105
Acaena inermis 105
Acaena novae-zelandiae 104–105
Acaena ovalifolia 105
Acaena, Two-spined 105
Acipenser baerii 236
Acipenser ruthenus 236
Acipenser sturio 236
Acorus calamus 146
Acorus gramineus 146
Adalia decempunctata 275
Adder 218
Aedes albopictus 280
Agapornis roseicollis 186
Agrilus planipennis 270–271
Agrimonia eupatoria 105
Agrimony 105
Ailanthus altissima 18, 20–21
Aix galericulata 194
Aix sponsa 194
Alburnus alburnus 221
Alder 23
    Grey 23
    Italian 22–23
    Red 23
    Speckled 22
Alexanders
    Biennial Perfoliate 93
    Perfoliate 93
    Yellow 93
Alisma plantagoaquatica 148
Allium carinatum 73
Allium paradoxum 73
Allium roseum 73
Allium triquetrum 72–73
Allium ursinum 73
Allium vineale 73
Alnus cordata 22–23
Alnus glutinosa 23
Alnus incana 23
Alnus rubra 23
Alopochen aegyptiacus 190–191
Alytes obstetricans 205, 210–211
Ambrosia artemisiifolia 90
Ambrosia psilostachya 90
Ambrosia trifida 90
Ameiurus melas 230–231
Ameiurus nebulosus 231
Angels Trumpets 111

Anguis fragilis 218
Anoplophora chinensis 268–269
Anoplophora glabripennis 268–269
Ant
    Argentine 278
    Asian Super 278, 279
    Ghost 278
    Pharaoh 278
    Red Imported Fire 278
Apodemus flavicollis 155
Apodemus sylvaticus 155
Aponogeton distachyos 142–143
Aratinga acuticaudata 186
Archangel
    Aluminium 112
    Variegated Yellow 112
    Yellow 112
Arctostaphylos uva-ursi 47
Arrowhead 148, 150
    Canadian 150
    Chinese 150
    Grass-leaved 150
    Narrow-leaved 150
Arthurdendymus triangulatus 262–263
Arundo donax 115
Arvicola terrestris 157
Ash, European 21
Astacus astacus, 246, 247, 248, 249
Astacus leptodactylus 246, 247, 250
Aunt Eliza 71
Australoplana sanguinea 262–263
Austropotamobius pallipes 246, 248, 249
Avocet 197
Azalea pontica 53
Azalea, Yellow 51, 53, 54
Azolla filiculoides 8, 134, 137–138

B

Balsam
    Himalayan 7, 95, 96
    Indian 95, 96
    Kashmir 95
    Orange 95
    Small 95, 97
    Touch-me-not 95
Bamboo 116–117
    Arrow (Metake) 117
    Broad-leaved 117
    Chinese Fountain 117
    Dwarf 117
    Hairy 117
    Indian Fountain 117

N

O

P

299

Acknowledgements

We warmly acknowledge all of those that have supported this work. Niall Moore, Huw Thomas and Angela Robinson were vital in getting this project off the ground and guiding us throughout. Paul Stebbing, Gareth Davies, Nigel Hewlett and Vicky Ames generously contributed to the text, while many others provided support, helped with research and commented on drafts including James Armitage, Simon Baker, Julie Bishop, Sam Bishop, Joe Caffrey, Arnold Cooke, Jo Denyer, Kevin Doidge, Mike Heylin, Alice Hiley, Steve Hunter, Jim Foster, Chris Malumphy, Mark Owen, Dave Parrott, Trevor Renals, Sugoto Roy, Sophie Thomas, Robin Stevenson, Robin Ward, Danial Winchester and Philine zu Ermgassen. We are very grateful to Graham French, with support from Mandy Henshall, who generated the majority of the maps.

Data for many of the maps in this guide are courtesy of the NBN Gateway with thanks to all the data contributors. While we are unable to list all of the contributors individually, they are shown alongside each map online. The full list of data providers to the NBN Gateway can also be found here https://data.nbn.org.uk/Organisations. We owe particular thanks to the Botanical Society of Britain and Ireland who provided most of the data for the plant distribution maps. The NBN and its data contributors bear no responsibility for the further analysis or interpretation of this material, data and/or information. See more at: http://www.nbn.org.uk/use-data/using-maps-or-data/using-and-referencing-data-from-the-gateway.aspx#sthash.gAMzmpqP.dpuf. Maps were prepared with the DMAP software written by Dr. A. J. Morton. In the case of mammals, most maps have been based on those in the Handbook of British Mammals (Harris and Yalden, 2008). None of these maps could have been produced without the dedication and expertise of the many volunteers who record and share their records. We are grateful to Michael Dobson/FBA for permission to use his illustrations and to Marc Dando for drawing the remaining illustrations.

We are very grateful to Defra and the Scottish Government for sponsorship. We are also very grateful to the many people that have helped provide images for this guide, specific acknowledgements for which are given below.

Photo credits

The author and publishers are grateful to the following for permission to use their illustrations. While every effort has been made to contact copyright holders, if any have been inadvertently left out we will endeavour to rectify this at the earliest opportunity.

Plants

We are grateful to the following for the use of their photographs. All other photographs are by Max Wade, Crown Copyright © Non-native Species Secretariat and Shutterstock.

8 t John W Anderson, m Anne Halpin, b Corrie Bruemme, 9 t Catherine Chatters, 10 Jean Haxaire, 23 tl, bl Marcus Webb/FLPA, 24 t David Hosking/FLPA, 25 cl Keith Rushforth/FLPA, t Bob Gibbons/FLPA, cr Martin B Withers/FLPA, bl Martin B Withers/FLPA, br Bernd Brinkmann/Imagebroker/FLPA, 26 t Ian Rose/FLPA, 27 t David Fenwick, 31 tcr Mike J Thomas/FLPA, bcr Krystyna Szulecka/FLPA, br ImageBroker/Imagebroker/FLPA, 42 tl Phil Smith, tcl T. Fanger, 46 Simon Harrap, 57 tl John Grimshaw, tcr Chew Valley Trees, cl David Fenwick, ccr David Fenwick, cr David Fenwick, 59 t Brian Davis/FLPA, b ImageBroker/Imagebroker/FLPA, 65 bl Wyevale Garden Centres, 67 tl Jan Wesenberg, bl Ernst Horak, 69 tc Graham Day, bc Simon Harrap, 74 c, b David Fenwick, 75 l Simon Harrap, 76 t Bernd Brinkmann/Imagebroker/FLPA, 80 t Wikipedia Commons/Edal Anton Lefterov, 89 tr, b Simon Harrap, 90 David Fenwick, 92 t Ron Stevens, 93 t, b NPL/Wild Wonders of Europe / Della Ferrera, 98 David Fenwick, 99 b Roger Wilmshurst/FLPA, 103 tl Wikipedia Commons/Kaldari, tc Wikipedia Commons/Kristian Peters, bl, br Wikipedia Commons/Fornax, 106 David Fenwick, 107 David Fenwick, 111 b David Fenwick, 113 NPL/Jean E Roche, 118 Jo Denyer, 119 Jo Denyer, 120 Wikipedia Commons/James K Lindsey, 129 tl Josef Hlasek, tc David Fenwick, bl Richard V Lansdown, bc David Fenwick, 132 t Wikipedia Commons/Christian Fischer, 133 t David Fenwick, 138 cr www.mossmania.ru, 139 t David Fenwick, 141 t Mike McCabe, 142 t David Fenwick , 144 Alain Dutartre, 145 l Jurgen & Christine Sohns/FLPA, 145 r Alain Dutartre, 148 bl Wikipedia Commons, 149 t Creative Commons.

Animals